TWILIGHT ZONES

Susan Bordo

UNIVERSITY OF CALIFORNIA PRESS

TWILIGHT

ZONES

The Hidden Life of Cultural Images from Plato to O.J.

BERKELEY   LOS ANGELES   LONDON

University of California Press

Berkeley and Los Angeles, California

University of California Press, Ltd.

London, England

© 1997 by

The Regents of the University of California

Library of Congress Cataloging-in-Publication Data

Bordo, Susan, 1947-

   Twilight zones: the hidden life of cultural images

   from Plato to O.J. / Susan Bordo.

      p.   cm.

     Includes bibliographical references (p.) and index.

     ISBN 0-520-21101-4 (cloth : alk. paper)

      1. Popular culture—United States—Psychological

aspects. 2. Consumers—United States—Attitudes. 3.

Body image—United States. I. Title.

E169.04.B665 1997

306—dc21   97-2223

                              CIP

Printed in the United States of America

9 8 7 6 5 4 3 2 1

The paper used in this publication meets the mini-

mum requirements of American National Standard

for Information Sciences—Permanence of Paper for

Printed Library Materials, ANSI Z39.48-1984.

For Binnie and Mickey

CONTENTS

Acknowledgments ix

Introduction 1

Braveheart, Babe, and the Contemporary Body 27

P.C., O.J., and Truth 66

Never Just Pictures 107

Can a Woman Harass a Man? 139

Bringing Body to Theory 173

The Feminist as Other 192

Missing Kitchens with Binnie Klein and Marilyn K. Silverman 214

Notes 243

Index 257

I owe thanks to many people for many different kinds of help on this collection. My deepest gratitude goes to Binnie Klein and Edward Lee, who read the entire manuscript and whose intellectual insights and keen editorial suggestions are reflected throughout. The members of my writing group—Virginia Blum, Dana Nelson, and Suzanne Pucci—provided extensive and extremely helpful comments on early drafts of "Can a Woman Harass a Man?" and "Bringing Body to Theory," as did Paul Taylor for "Bringing Body to Theory" and "P.C., O.J., and Truth," Leslie Heywood for "Never Just Pictures" and "The Feminist as Other," Scott Shapleigh and Virginia Blum for "*Braveheart, Babe,* and the Body," Lynne Arnault for "The Feminist as Other," Ted Schatzki for "Bringing Body to Theory," Dana Nelson for "Never Just Pictures," and Eugene Gendlin for "P.C., O.J., and Truth." Often these comments helped me turn crucial corners in formulating and clarifying what I was trying to say. In addition, I owe a large but difficult to specify debt to the many people who heard versions of these pieces as talks and provided informal criticisms and suggestions and to those friends and colleagues who may not have commented on specific essays but who are a part of my intellectual community and have played an important role in the development of my ideas. I would also like to thank Lynn Chancer, who read this collection for the press, and who made me aware that my arguments about the Simpson trial in "P.C., O.J., and Truth" were not working the way I intended. Revisions I made on the basis of her reader's comments have made this, I believe, a much stronger piece. Thanks also to Amanda Frost for her careful copyediting, which has made this a clearer and more readable book, and to Marilyn Schwartz, who skillfully shepherded the manuscript through production. My editor at U.C. Press, Naomi Schneider, has provided enthusiasm, support, perspective, and insight from the first day I discussed with her the possibility of this collection. My research assistant at LeMoyne College, Rachel Hertel, helped me compile scholarly resources for "The Feminist as Other." My current research assistant at the University of Kentucky, Jill Norton, did the same for several pieces in this collection, prepared the index, and helped in myriad ways with many other tasks involved in the preparation of the manuscript. My staff assistant, Linda Wheeler, has been involved in so many aspects of this project that I hardly know how to enumerate her contributions or adequately express my appreciation; her knowledge and skills continually smooth the road for me. Thanks also to all the other members of the staff, both at LeMoyne College and the University of Kentucky, who provided services that helped bring this collection to fruition. I thank the University of Kentucky for my generous research endowment, which covered the expense of preparing this book, and a teaching reduction in Spring 1996, which enabled me to write and present several talks on which essays in this book are based.

My family is small but infinitely precious to me. To Estelle Klein I give my thanks for the renewed life you gave my father and for being such a loving second mother to me. My sisters Binnie Klein and Marilyn Silverman, to whom this collection is dedicated, are not only coauthors of "Missing Kitchens" but my best friends and cherished colleagues. With Edward Lee, they are my home in this world, and all three make everything that I accomplish possible.

The essays in this book have grown out of a personal love/hate struggle: my rebellious but often dazzled, beguiled but skeptical, always intimate relationship with cultural images. I come to my criticisms of these images from deep inside this house of mirrors, not from the position of detached spectator, wielding high-powered theory to cut like a scythe through my "ordinary" responses, but with respect for those responses ("incorrect" as they sometimes are, and angry and embarrassed as they sometimes make me). They keep me honest and they teach me about this culture. I do not think that one can do responsible criticism in any other way.

In *The Republic* Plato presents a parable well known to students in introductory philosophy classes. He asks us to imagine our usual condition as knowers as comparable to life in a dark cave, where we have been confined since childhood, cut off from the world outside. In that cave we are chained by the leg and neck in such a way that we are unable to see in any position but straight ahead, at a wall in front of us, on which is projected a procession of shadow figures cast by artificial puppets manipulated by hidden puppeteers. In such a condition, Plato asks us, would not these shadow images, these illusions, seem to be "reality" to us? They would be the only world we knew; we would not even be aware that they were artificially created by other human beings. If suddenly forced outside the cave, we would surely be confused and even scornful of anyone who tried to tell us that this, not the cave, was the real world, that we had been living inside an illusion, deceived into believing that artificial images were the real thing. But our enlightenment would require this recognition.

Never has Plato's allegory about the seductiveness of appearances been more apt than today, but note the contemporary twist. For Plato, the artificial images cast on the wall of the cave are a metaphor for the world of sense perception. The illusion of the cave is in mistaking that world—what we see, hear, taste, feel—for the Reality of enduring ideas, which can only be "seen" with the mind's eye. For us, bedazzlement by created images is no metaphor; it is the actual condition of our lives. If we do not wish to remain prisoners of these images, we must recognize that they are not reality. But instead of moving closer to this recognition, we seem to be moving farther away from it, going deeper and deeper into the cave of illusion. Many of the essays in this book are about the seductiveness of those illusions, the deceptive "virtual realities" they create and the actual human realities they obscure and mystify, and the consequences of this deception on some of the most intimate (bodily, sexual, emotional, and also "political") aspects of our lives.

That we live in an image-saturated culture has come to seem normal, routine, to us. But our great-grandparents would probably have their brain circuits blown if they were plunked down in our culture. Massive and dramatic cultural and technological changes have taken place in an extraordinarily brief period of historical time—and so recently that we have barely begun to chart their effects on our perception, cognition, and most basic experience of the relation between reality and appearance. The images are much more ubiquitous in our lives today than they were just a decade ago. The technology for producing them is far more sophisticated, and those who produce the images seem to have no compunction about using that technology in the service of a deceptive verisimilitude. The glamorized images of movie stars of the past—Ingrid Bergman, Greta Garbo, Merle Oberon—were always presented to us bathed in visual cues (soft focus, dramatic lighting) that signified illusion, the magic of the medium. Today our created images boldly attempt to "pass" as reality. Cut and spliced music

CDs present themselves as continuous performances. Body doubles are used routinely in movies to make the less-than-ideal bodies of stars into the icons that young girls then emulate (hating themselves because they are not as "perfect"); moreover, 85 percent of those body doubles, according to Shelley Michelle (who stood in for Julia Roberts in *Pretty Woman*), have had breast implants. The Dior ad (figure 1), which claims to show a real human body, was almost certainly generated by a computer!

Even less radically reconstructed images are usually massively retouched before they get to us. A few years ago *Harper's* magazine tried to make a point of this by printing the invoice *Esquire* had received for photo retouching of a cover picture of Michelle Pfeiffer, a picture that was accompanied by copy that read "What Michelle Pfeiffer needs . . . is absolutely nothing." But what Pfeiffer's picture alone needed to appear on that cover was actually $1,525 worth of chin trimming, complexion cleansing, neck softening, line removal, and other assorted touches. *Harper's* editor Lewis Lapham said he had published the invoice to "remind the reader in an amusing way that there's a difference between life and art." Such a distinction, however, is fast fading in an era when the constructed image has become, as Stewart Ewen puts it, "the conclusive expression of reality." So Pfeiffer's *Esquire* photo was retouched. Who cares? She's gorgeous in the picture, and we want to date her or be her. Who cares that the body depicted in the Dior ad is not "real"? We want to look like it anyway.

With created images setting the standard, we are becoming habituated to the glossy and gleaming, the smooth and shining, the ageless and sagless and wrinkleless. We are learning to expect "perfection" and to find any "defect" repellent, unacceptable. We expect live performances to sound like CDs, politicians to say nothing messy or disturbing, real breasts to be as round and firm as implants. Even our idolatry of the competitive athlete—strikingly exhibited in our celebration of the 1996 Olympic contenders—has become aestheticized into a visual iconography of the perfected body. A few weeks before the opening of the games, major photoessays appeared in *Vanity Fair,* the *New York Times Magazine,* and *Life.* Replete

FIGURE 1

Computer-generated "reality"

with gorgeous photographs of chiseled muscles and firmly set jaws, coolly and dramatically glamorized à la Robert Mapplethorpe (in the *Life* feature, the athletes were all naked), these stories focused to an unprecedented degree in sports coverage on the rock-hard beauty of the athletic body. (Why am I reminded of Leni Riefenstahl here?) In the *Life* article blurbs accompanying the photos praised the low body fat of the athletes as though the lean physique was as significant an accomplishment as athletic skill and dedication.

But even our habituation to perfection is masked by illusion. Lately I've been reading a lot about a new "inclusiveness" in ideas about beauty, "anti-fashion" fashion, and the like.[1] In a 1996 editorial for the trendy magazine *Interview,* Ingrid Sischy celebrates the end of "the old limited ideas of beauty." We now live in a culture, she says, where beauty has had "its chains taken off." Now, I am not opposed to beauty. I love looking at beautiful faces and bodies, and I enjoy "beautifying" myself. I don't consider our powerful responses to physical beauty as base or superficial either. Far from it. The beauty of the human body, as Plato describes it in the *Symposium,* is the presence of the Divine on earth. Such beauty not only draws us to each other but awakens the soul to the beautiful and good beyond the particular body to which we are attracted, inspiring spiritual aspiration, artistic creativity, philosophical speculation, the desire to better the self. Put more simply, beauty lights up the world for us.

But just what culture is Sischy writing about? A world in which beauty was "unchained" to release all its diverse and unexpected forms would truly be wonderful. But ours is a culture in which personal want ads list rigid specifications for weight, body tone, youthfulness! Racial diversity? Calvin Klein's CK One ad campaign—an exemplar of Sischy's "revolution" in beauty—seems to be making the visual point that whether you are male or female, young or old, gay or straight, black or white, you are required to have the same toned, adolescent-looking body (figure 2). The female cast of NBC's Thursday night comedy lineup, beginning with the

FIGURE 2

Commercial diversity?

fabulously successful *Friends,* has got to be the tidiest, tiniest—and whitest—collection of bodies ever assembled in one place. Don't show me avant-garde photographs. Look at *Newsweek*'s October 1996 cover story on JFK's bride, Carolyn, which touts her "clean, classic" patrician good looks as the "perfect image of the American girl" and provides step-by-step instructions for looking just like her (be blond, pluck your eyebrows, and—above all else—lose weight); then check out the statistics on eating disorders, plastic surgery, and the diaries of nine-year-olds convinced that they must be physically "perfect" in order to be loved.

We've always had icons of high fashion, a style nobility. But few people today regard our contemporary icons as belonging to some out-of-reach world of (extremely expensive) glamour and artifice. No, we're encouraged to believe that we can have at least the bodies, if not the lifestyles, of the rich and famous. My undergraduate students, whatever their genetic predisposition or cultural heritage, want to look like the women on *Friends,* hair straight and swinging, buns tight, breasts perky. And why not? The technology exists and it's becoming cheaper all the time. Your hair doesn't swing like Jennifer Aniston's? No problem—a good "relaxer" will do the trick. Buns need work? If the StairMaster doesn't carve them into steel, liposuction will vacuum out your unsightly excess. Breasts too small or saggy? Cosmetic "augmentation" will ensure that they stand at attention. If you can't afford to perfect yourself, your flawed body becomes a physical announcement that you are not among the success stories, the beautiful people, those who are able to get their act together and "Just Do It!" in this land of limitless opportunity. Poverty has always been visible on the human body, but with money now able to buy perfection, the beauty gap between rich and poor is widening into a chasm.

And those of us who are years beyond perkiness? The current cultural hype is that fifty, even sixty and seventy, can still be sexy. As if! The reality is that the movie stars and models are establishing new norms—achievable only through continual surgery—which make those of us who actually look older at fifty than we did at thirty seem like crones! Over the past five years my diagnosis of the emergence of a culture of infinitely malleable "plastic" bodies, which I first detailed in my *Unbearable Weight* in 1993, has been borne out dramatically.[2] There's barely a movie or television star whose upper lip has not recently become magically fuller—and thus "younger" and sexier, according to our current aesthetic codes. (African and Semitic lips are now "in style"; our noses have yet to make the grade.) Even Heather Locklear, platonic form of the WASP princess, has suddenly acquired a plump upper lip. And has anyone noticed how these actresses are all beginning to look alike? During the heyday of the *Twilight Zone,* there was an episode about a futuristic culture in which everyone, at a certain age, would choose one of two or three available models of face and body. They'd then go into some sort of apparatus and a few moments later would emerge, transformed into an identical copy of the model they had chosen. Cher and Faye Dunaway, it appears from recent photos (figures 3 and 4), have found the inventor of that apparatus. Or the same plastic surgeon. But this is not the twilight zone; this is the culture we live in.

Not all the illusions of our image-bedazzled culture have to do with glamorized visual images and fantasies of bodily transformation and perfection. It is virtually a truism that politics today is almost purely about images, spin doctoring, how various policies "play," and so forth. In the Menendez, King, and Simpson trials we've seen how effective skillful manipulation on the part of image-conscious lawyers can prove; in each of these trials the defense—aided and abetted by the sympathies and susceptibilities of jurors—was able to construct an alternative reality to replace the evidence of the case. Rush Limbaugh and other self-proclaimed conservative guardians of truth continually fudge the line between entertainment and information, but so too does left-leaning filmmaker Oliver Stone. His fictional documentaries of the Kennedy assassination and the Watergate scandal are such an inseparable stew of fact and fantasy that one

FIGURES 3 AND 4

Different hairstyles, converg-
ing faces

shudders to think of the next generation learning its history lessons from them—as it undoubtedly will, despite Stone's disclaimers at the start of the films.

Ours is an "infomercial" culture in which the desire to sell products and stories continually tries to pass itself off as "helping" and "informing" the public, satisfying their "right to know." We get our deepest philosophies of life from jingles and slogans. The fantasy-governed, pumped-up individualist rhetoric of commercial advertisements—like "Just Do It!" or "Know No Boundaries," or "I'm Worth It!"—has become the ethics, political ideology, and existential philosophy of our time, constituting what is probably the only set of communally shared ideas we have, providing people with the one coherent (if reprehensible) set of standards they draw on in justifying their own behavior. The ethical code of Nike and Revlon! Talk about puppeteers being in charge of reality!

We are not helped to see through these illusions by contemporary beliefs about the "relative" nature of truth—beliefs that one doesn't need to be fully aware of or have had a college education in order to hold. Talk shows convey the message that everyone has his or her own version of things; some teachers, unfortunately, reinforce that message with theory about the infinite interpretability of texts and the perspectival nature of all knowledge. I have used such arguments myself and still believe that they have validity. But they are not absolutes, and they are no longer as useful or illuminating as they once were in the days when fixed and dogmatic conceptions of reality seemed to be the chief enemies of human communication and understanding. In some quarters, of course, the old enemies remain. (Give me a postmodernist over John Silber any day!) But arch-conservative Silber aside, today most people behave less like deluded philosopher-kings than like captives in the cave of the image masters. In a world in which appearances can be so skillfully manipulated, the notion that everything is "open to interpretation" is no longer an entirely edifying one. Without toppling into absolutist conceptions of truth, we need to rehabilitate the notion that not all versions of reality are equally trustworthy, equally deserving of our assent.

Adults of the baby-boom generation or older sometimes scorn or dismiss the notion that cultural images have such power over our lives. I think that they are out of touch with their students, their children, the culture, and possibly themselves. Recently I gave a talk to a group of academics and health professionals. My topic was the cultural consequences of the images of physical perfection that now surround us. I used examples from my own life as well as other material, most of which appears in various essays in this book. At one point someone in the audience—a therapist—called out derisively: "Well, why don't you just turn off the television!" Another cavalierly dismissed the idea that young women's problems with eating and body image had grown any worse over the last thirty years. A third said he thought my perceptions were skewed by my "emotional overinvolvement" with the material. He himself did not think these body issues were all that important. Barely a moment later he was expressing his concern that his still-growing daughter add some inches to her height.

Such responses are culturally uninformed. ("Just turn off the television!" Right. Tell that to your adolescent patients. Try doing it yourself, doctor.) These reactions also betray a lack of critical consciousness of the individual's participation in culture. Just where does therapist number three think his anxiety over his daughter's height comes from? Does he not remember when he was growing up in the fifties and 5'4" was the tallest a girl could get before being considered a giantess? As to emotional involvement with the material, I consider that an asset, not a liability. Unless one recognizes one's own enmeshment in culture, one is in no position to theorize about that culture or its effects on others. But unless one strives to develop critical distance on that enmeshment, one is apt to simply embody and perpetuate the illusions and mystifications of the culture (for example, communicating anxiety about body weight and height to one's children). So, for me, the work of cultural criticism is not exactly like that of Plato's philosopher, whose enlightenment requires that he transcend his experience of *this* world and ascend to another, purer realm. (Actually, I'm not so sure Plato believed that, either, but it is certainly the way his ideas have been dominantly interpreted.) Cultural criticism does not so much ask that we leave the cave as turn a light on *in* it.

Cultural criticism clears a space in which we can stand back and survey a scene that we are normally engaged in living in, not thinking about. In that space, we can function not merely as consumers of cultural pleasures and rewards but also as phenomenologists and diagnosticians of those pleasures and rewards. As a consumer, I get mild enjoyment from *Friends,* relaxed by its affable predictability and tempted to cut my own hair like Jennifer Aniston's. (But I know my own, which I used to iron in the sixties, wouldn't swing right.) As a cultural critic, my responses to *Friends* become material for concerned reflection on the current fantasies of our culture; I think, for example, about how all these women remind me of Mary Tyler Moore in her early TV shows, and I wonder what this says about cultural nostalgia for that model of femininity. As a forty-nine-year-old whose face has quite suddenly, it seems, decided to make me over on its own terms, I buy alpha-hydroxy face creams with calming and exotic French names like "Primordiale" and "Bienfait Total." As a cultural critic, I think about how we are rapidly creating a world in which a Martian, leafing through a magazine or catalog from earth, would come to the conclusion that human men and women are two different species, one of which ages and the other of which doesn't. As a consumer and a Simpson case junkie, I rush out to buy the latest in the seemingly never-ending effluence of books about the case and devour it like candy. As a cultural critic, I think about the long-term consequences of all these competing versions of "history" being manufactured out of the machinery of consumerism. What may be a tasty treat for the consumer can appear a poison to the cultural critic.

It is essential that we cultivate the practice of turning a critical light on popular culture, particularly among our children and students, who were born into this world of created images and are an important target of its seductions. The consequences of remaining in the dark, intoxicated by the illusions cast on the wall, are beginning to become apparent: the collapse of any intelligent political discourse (we prefer soothing images, heart-warming anecdotes, euphemistic rhetoric), the inability to sustain love relationships (we expect them to be like the movies, where "love" is visually coded by playful romps on the beach, photogenic sex, dinners in chic restaurants, and where all human beings have great clothes and live in terrific apartments), a perilous detachment from the realities of environmental damage, and of course the distractions and dangers of trying to *become* the bodies in the technologically fabricated images that surround us. That pursuit not only drains and diverts us from more communal, socially directed projects of change but is treacherous to physical health and psychological well-being. Disordered patterns of bingeing, purging, exercising, and dieting are virtually the norm among high school and college women. And any "real" woman who tries to keep up with the movie stars in the "unreal" (airbrushed, filtered, surgically altered, technologically cut-and-pasted) state in which they come to us has a hard if not impossible task ahead of her. Not to mention trying to look like a computer-generated image!!

Some of the paths our culture is following today are at the edges of a Brave New World that we ought to think twice about entering—as individuals and as contributors to the shaping of our culture. For we all are culture makers as well as culture consumers, and these transformations don't happen without our participation. In promoting their products, advertisers frequently invoke the stirring rhetoric of freedom, choice, and individualism; academics, on their part, have lately become infatuated with "agency" and "resistance." But both commercial and scholarly rhetoric and arguments often boil down to a celebration of how "creative" we *already* are as individual consumers of this culture. I don't deny that this culture provides many opportunities—if one has the money—for personal enhancement and creativity. And I don't disdain those choices. I do not feel at all superior, for example, to the woman who has a face-lift in order to feel young and attractive for just a little while longer before she becomes culturally invisible; believe me, I understand where she's coming from. But I prefer to reserve my congratulations for those choices that are undertaken in full consciousness that they are not only about "creating" our own individual lives but constructing the landscape of our culture. Each of us shapes the culture we live in every moment of our lives, not only in our more public activities but also in our most intimate gestures and personal relationships, for example, in the way we model attitudes toward beauty, aging, perfection, and so on for our children, friends, students, lovers, colleagues.

In reminding people of these public responsibilities, am I being judgmental about their personal choices? Some might see it this way, and perhaps in some sense they would be right. But because I experience myself as so completely "inside" the dilemma of finding my way in this culture, I think of my criticisms—of cosmetic surgery, for example—less as a judgment of others than as an argument with myself, a way to shore up my own consciousness and resolve, which is continually being worn down. Cultural criticism, for me, isn't about lacking sympathy for people's personal choices (or my own—and they often require that I let myself "off the hook"); it's about preserving consciousness of the larger context in which our personal choices occur, so that we will be better informed about their potential consequences, for ourselves as well as for others. But this requires vigilance. The more a cultural practice is engaged in, by greater and more diverse numbers of people, the more "normal" it seems and the less likely we are to point the beam of evaluative or critical consciousness in its direction. In this way, even the most bizarre cultural practice can become part of the taken-for-granted environment of our lives, as unremarkable, as invisible, as water to goldfish in a bowl. Thus, before we can figure out what to do, we first have to learn to *see* with something other than bedazzled eyes. I think Plato was dead right about that.

Where I think Plato is less useful to us is in the notion that lying beyond illusion are timeless ideals or norms, true always and for all occasions. Perhaps there are such truths. But if there are, I can't imagine how any finite, *human* being could ever lay hands on them. In continuing to pine after them and to make them a condition for a "shared" or "common" culture, we only encourage more cynicism and nihilism among our children and students, who know quite well these are the worn (and often dangerous) fantasies of another time. Yet if all we give them is a more sophisticated version of "You've got your truth and I've got mine," how can we expect them to question the dangers of their *own* fantasies, their own time?

Similarly, I don't think there is a stripped-down, basic-model body to contrast with the cultural forms I criticize in my work. All human bodies are culturally worked on, adorned, shaped, evaluated. But that doesn't mean that I am ready, along with some postmodernists, to embrace the wholly artificial, ideological nature of "the body" and celebrate the spectacle of its cultural self-fashionings and reconfigurations. Postmodern performance artist Orlan has undergone dozens of cosmetic surgeries—exhibiting pieces of her own excised flesh as part of the presentation—in order to make such points graphically, using her own body as a "text." Orlan's face is now a composite of the most highly valued parts of different historical models of female beauty (Mona Lisa's forehead, Botticelli's Venus's chin), which have been "cut and pasted" to demonstrate the artifice of our historical conceptions of the ideal woman.

While I am in some agreement with the "theory" behind Orlan's performances,[3] I find such art more symptomatic of the pathologies of our culture than exposing of them. While it may not be possible (or perhaps desirable) to designate a "natural" body or biological norm, it is still possible (and necessary) to critically assess the *cultural* forms and practices our bodies are engaged in. I don't need to have a vision of some natural order of things in order to worry about the effects that new technologies may have on human beings, any more than dystopian novels need to present a prior utopia in order to issue their warnings about where we are heading. Postmodernists may talk in theoretical terms about "mutating selves" and nomadic identities. I am more concerned about what happens when *practices* of self-deconstruction and "self-improvement" have become a way of life. These consequences are not so easy to determine, and we have little guidance. (Plastic surgeons certainly aren't talking about them, and neither is the media, except in the most shallow terms.) But we have to try nonetheless.

We can try to plug up a decaying dam. We can give up and swim in the flood. But there are other choices than pining for Reality with a capital *R* or tripping on plurality(s) with a postmodern *(s)*. Right now, it is not so much the instability of particular *versions* of reality that concerns me (as it does, for example, those who complain about challenges to the canon) but the undermining of *any* habits of distinguishing between appearance and reality. If truth is a fiction, as Nietzsche said, he also emphasized that it is a life-enhancing fiction, one we try to do without at our peril. I think we've been discovering just how right he was on this point. But in this particular historical context, instead of looking backward nostalgically to a mythical, unchanging *realm* of Truth with a capital *T,* I think we need to encourage *practices* of truth-*seeking,* practices that aim not so much at gazing at Timeless Forms as at "seeing through" our temporal forms, our cultural appearances, to expose the hype, the bad faith, the mystification.

Too frequently, academics imagine themselves as "outside" this cave of cultural mystification. Because we deal with concepts, methodologies, theoretical entities, we fancy ourselves occupying a loftier perch, scrutinizing the proceedings below. Conversing only with each other helps keep this fantasy intact. I once heard a speaker at an elite university sharply criticize the hierarchical, "binary" thinking of the (then) Republican administration, its good guys/bad guys, we-are-the-saviors-of-the-Western-world mentality. Without missing a beat, the speaker went on to congratulate the assembled audience for "of course" being "beyond such hierarchical, dualistic thinking." Pardon me, but I *think* the notion that there are those who are unimpeachably "beyond" and those that are hopelessly stuck in the muck is just a *bit* "binary." (Note, too, the presumption that one can tell the good guys from the bad guys on the basis of neighborhood.)

I do not mean to suggest, however, that it is only postmodern academics who are blind to the foibles of their own intellectual constructions. My example is only one variation on an age-old theme. Ever since Aristophanes sent Socrates up in a balloon, it has been well known that scholars have a tendency to become lost in the clouds of their own hubris. My impulse has always been to prick that balloon, not so much to cut would-be philosopher-kings down to size as to bring us all down to earth. Academic theories do not descend from someplace outside time and space, and they are as appropriate—and necessary—to culturally scrutinize as presidential elections and consumer trends. Theoretical pronouncements and arguments, in their own nonpictorial way, may circulate images (for example, of what feminists are up to) that are as caricatured and ideological as political cartoons. Intellectual fashions (for example, the view that reality is a "text" with an infinite number of interpretations) may unwittingly collaborate with styles of thinking encouraged by talk shows and sound bites. Often, academic and popular trends, although speaking a different language, mirror each other and participate in the same stereotypings and self-deceptions.

My desire in this book is that we see our culture not merely as "diverse" (which it assuredly is), but with overlapping and continuities between its various realms. Throughout my work, in *Unbearable Weight* as well as in this book, I insist that academic cultures be seen as part of the fabric of culture in general. The ideas of those who work for Calvin Klein and those who work for Oxford University Press (or University of California Press) are in conversation with each other, no doubt about it. The question that remains is whether we are content to allow that conversation to remain covert and unanalyzed. I am not; I find the interplay between the academic and popular domains fascinating and revealing. So, in this collection the reader will find analyses of academic discourse and Nike ads sitting side by side. I have also included two pieces that focus specifically on the world of academic scholarship. Initially, I questioned the inclusion of these pieces in a book about cultural images. The more I thought about it, the more I realized that to not include these pieces would be false to my view of culture and to my own experience. It is not only jeans commercials that have a "hidden life" of images and messages that are being communicated and disseminated. It is not just when we turn on the television that we are invited into a cultural twilight zone populated by bizarre entities and regulated by surreal social conventions. I have felt just as dazed and confused at academic conferences—and been made just as furious at the posturing, obfuscation, and name calling—as I have watching commentary on the O.J. trial.

The reader of this book will undoubtedly note that whether I am discussing academic or popular culture, I suffer chronically from what Nietzsche described (not entirely admiringly) as the Socratic impulse to tear the covers off things. This impulse is not merely an intellectual habit, it's a strategy of self-preservation. Not a day goes by when I don't feel angered and saddened, personally compromised and made a bit crazy, by the falseness and vapidity of the images and smooth-talking "discourses" of the cultures I live in, both popular and academic. Most frequently, I find myself gravitating toward a particular subject to write about because of my frustration with a certain veil of illusion or entranced captivation that hangs over that subject. The captivation may be the result of bedazzlement (as with media images and other elements of consumer culture) or it may be the result of professional or political attachments or investments (as with certain forms of academic discourse or political ideology) or it may be the result of deeply entrenched stereotypes or historically ingrained ideas. But the captivation, whatever its source, seems to be keeping us mystified and "stuck" in certain ways—in impossible and destructive fantasies, in unquestioned dogmas, in self-deceptions, in falsely polarizing antagonisms. Often I sense that others share my frustration, and in my interactions with them start to discern ideas (and feelings) as yet not fully articulated, simmering just under the surface, building up steam. Then my Socratic impulse to start taking the covers off kicks in and I begin excavating, collecting cultural paraphernalia, looking deeper down the well. In a culture of illusion this philosopher's disease doesn't seem like such a bad model for truth-seeking—and sanity-preservation.

The first essay in this book, "*Braveheart, Babe,* and the Body," tries to take the cover off the "Just Do It!" version of personal empowerment by showing how extensively and variously deployed it is throughout our culture, from movies like *Braveheart* to the coverage of the Olympics, to (of course) commercials, and even to academic theory. In my work I frequently look to the body and bodily practices as a concrete arena where cultural fantasies and anxieties are played out, and this piece—the middle section of which examines the mystique and the reality of "empowerment" through cosmetic surgery—is in this genre. What is masked by the rhetoric ("taking control of one's life" through surgery), I argue, is a consumer culture that depends on the continual creation and proliferation of "defect," that is always making us feel bad about ourselves at the same time as it pumps us up with excitement over our own "agency": take charge, "Just Do It!" etc. In the last part of this essay I look at the alternative image of empowerment presented in the movie *Babe,* a film that moved me (and many other people) enormously and whose appeal I attempt to explore.

It's been just a few years since Alan Bloom, in *The Closing of the American Mind,* took aim against feminism, relativism, and rock and roll for destroying higher education in this country, thus firing the first shot in what has since come to be known as the "culture wars." From the start, it's been a battle of slogans and stereotypes. On one side of the barricades: Dead White Males, "the Canon," enduring values, and Truth. On the other side: Feminazis, "minorities," cultural diversity, and "political correctness."

Most reasonable people know there is something wrong with this picture, but too frequently they only see the defects in the portrayal of their own "side." In "P.C., O.J., and Truth," I explore some of the caricatures that have been prominent in the public face of the "culture wars" and attempt to allocate responsibility for the polarized, stereotyped nature of those wars. Strongly motivating this essay is my belief that we need to rehabilitate the concept of "truth" for our time, avoiding the extremes of both "right" and "left" and focusing on helping the next generation learn to critically see through the illusions and mystifications of the image-dominated culture they have grown up in. In this connection I discuss the O. J. Simpson trial as exemplary of our times and describe a class that I taught in which we studied the truths that were obscured in the media representations of the trial.

"Never Just Pictures," was developed from talks I have been giving in response to invitations to elaborate and update themes first presented in my *Unbearable Weight: Feminism, Western Culture, and the Body* (1993). That book was undertaken to present a multidimensional cultural understanding not only of eating disorders but also of our horror of fat and our veneration of the thin body. Since the book appeared, that veneration shows no sign of abating; indeed, it is arguably more entrenched than ever before. Just last week the current Miss Universe was commanded to lose twenty-seven pounds *in two weeks* or have her crown taken away. (She is, by the way, 5'10" and when crowned had weighed just 110 pounds—the weight she is now ordered to reattain.) But as awareness of the role of cultural images in eating disorders has increased, a heated controversy has developed. Since my book appeared, there have been two flurries of controversy involving attempts to censor images of hyperthin models (the first in connection with the reemergence of the "waif look"; the second in connection with British *Vogue*'s use of emaciated models—models who make the waif look well fed!), with responses from the fashion industry and the therapeutic community on the connection between these images and eating disorders. In "Never Just Pictures" I take up the positions that have emerged in such controversies and I argue that they *all* rest on a mistake about the nature of cultural images, namely, that they are "just" pictures. Looking closely at images of slenderness, I explore the deeper cultural meanings contained in them.

Among those meanings are covert racial codes. In *Unbearable Weight* I argued against the clinical mythology that held that nonwhite racial groups, because they have their own, more flesh-admiring ideals of beauty, are less vulnerable to the power of dominant cultural images and so (as the old clichés had it) are "protected" against developing eating problems. Some academic critics accused me of submerging cultural "difference"; my point, however, was that it is our *culture* that submerges difference, in its racialized preferences for certain styles of beauty over others. In "Never Just Pictures" I look at those styles in closer detail, confronting feelings about my own "Jewish" body and exploring notions about femininity, race, and the body which have generally been overlooked in the literature on eating disorders.

"Can a Woman Harass a Man?" began as a presentation for a more philosophical audience but evolved into a general talk. This article grew out of my frustration with popular images of the sexual harasser (*Disclosure,* media representations of Bob Packwood) as either a salivating sex fiend or a scheming, power-mad female executive. These images, I argue, mystify and obscure the realities of power involved in harassment as well as perpetuating a puritanical, hyperliteral attitude toward sexuality and the body. My discussion of harassment, like my arguments about the culture wars, attempts to stake out a position that avoids dogma and evades easy caricature. In both cases I want to freshen up discussions that have grown stale and encrusted with stereotypes, getting in the way of open and intelligent conversation between the different "sides" of debates. This piece also was one of the first in which I began the study of masculinity and the male body, which is the focus of my current work in progress.[4]

It's clear how a movie like *Disclosure* circulates stereotypes and reductive images; academics do it more subtly but no less vigorously. Academics sometimes use the accessories of theory (for example, specialized forms of jargon, predictable critical moves, references to certain authors) less in the interests of understanding the world than to proclaim themselves members of an elite club. In the process they create caricatures of themselves and of those who don't belong, peopling the scholarly world with typecast players and carving out narrow theoretical niches within which all ideas and authors are force-fit. Certain theoretical preferences, moreover, run throughout disciplines like incurable diseases, often carrying invisible racial and gender stereotypes and biases along with them. Such stereotypes and biases overlap with, support, and help to perpetuate more visible and obvious images on the popular scene.

"Bringing Body to Theory" and "The Feminist as Other" explore the "hidden life" of some of the academic biases that I have encountered in my experience as a philosopher and a feminist. The first, "Bringing Body to Theory," is part academic autobiography and part philosophical reflection on my ongoing struggle with the Socrates-in-the-balloon phenomenon, within philosophy and other disciplines that pride themselves on being "theoretical." In this piece, originally written for Donn Welton's *Body and Flesh* (forthcoming from Blackwell) at his invitation to explicate the differences between my theoretical alliances and those of other contemporary philosophers who write about the body, I reflect on why I think it is so important that we bring theory down to earth where it belongs. In this effort I was aided by a wonderful essay by Susan Hekman ("Material Bodies," also in *Body and Flesh*) in which she compares and contrasts my perspective with that of Judith Butler. Not infrequently, Butler and I have been positioned at diametrically opposed ends of the spectrum, a characterization that Hekman challenges and that I hope "Bringing Body to Theory" will challenge as well. The essay, I should forewarn readers, is more located within academic conversations than other pieces in this book. I hope, however, that even those who are unfamiliar with Butler's work or who couldn't care less about whether I am an "essentialist" will find in this piece an interesting glimpse into the "hidden life" of academic theorizing.[5]

"The Feminist as Other" explores how academic scholarship—including the scholarship of some feminists—has covertly (and often unconsciously) misread and misrepresented the contribution of feminism to twentieth-century thought. When we think of negative cultural images of feminism, nineteenth-century caricatures of sexless bluestockings and Rush Limbaugh's humorless, male-bashing feminazis may come to mind. Subtler prejudices, which may have far more extensive cultural consequences, go unnoticed. Let me provide an example from my own life. Ten years ago, while teaching my first graduate course on the history of feminist thought, I was stunned and embarrassed to recognize that until then my map of the intellectual world had located feminist writers outside the borders of all major continents. For example, I had been teaching Enlightenment thought for years, yet I had never thought to include Mary Wollstonecraft, whose work is a crystalline illustration of certain key Enlightenment ideas. Why not? I realized that I had categorized Wollstonecraft solely within "the history of women" and as such I did not expect her to have anything to say of a more "general," cultural nature.

Several years later I was asked by philosopher Janet Kourany to contribute a piece to her collection *Philosophy in a Feminist Voice* (forthcoming, Princeton University Press). Janet asked me to survey the contribution of feminist philosophy to contemporary reconstructions of the "self." As I worked on that assignment, I realized that the Wollstonecraft phenomenon was far more extensive than I had imagined and hardly limited to historical figures. Feminists had contributed to the contemporary concept of the self in myriad and profound ways, yet no one except other feminists —and sometimes not even they—seemed to realize this! So instead of writing about how feminists had critiqued conceptions of the self, I wound up writing about the continuing portrayal of feminist thought as the narrow, gendered "Other" to the broader, "general interests" of nonfeminist writers. This ghettoization has often taken extremely subtle forms, hence the need for the cultural "exposé" which I undertake in "The Feminist as Other."

The final essay in this book, "Missing Kitchens," may stand out for the reader as perhaps not fitting with the rest. It's not a critique of cultural images or ideas (although these figure occasionally in the piece) but a collective memoir, written jointly by my sisters, Binnie Klein and Marilyn Silverman, and me. It is, however, an exploration of a "hidden life" beneath the surface of appearances. In the case of this essay the archeological work is more personal. Originally commissioned by Heidi Nast and Steve Pile for their planned collection, *Places through the Body* (Routledge, forthcoming), our piece is a family topoanalysis (as Bachelard might have called it), an exploration of our lives and that of our parents from the vantage points of our different birth order in the family and in cultural time, focusing on how our bodies were imprinted with the important "places" and spatial dramas of that history. This description may make the piece seem philosophical and abstract; actually, it is the most personal and autobiographical in this volume. Looking back at *Unbearable Weight,* I find it remarkable that I wrote about agoraphobia without a whisper of my own long bout with that disorder, which I explore in the last piece in this collection. I still do not care for confessional writing when it is done for the sake of personal disclosure or narcissistic pleasure. But I have found that my "expertise" in my own history, the concreteness and intimacy of the details that are available to me, and the practice at honesty with myself that it affords me are all tremendous resources for me as a writer and a critic. Writing this piece with my sisters was an intense, enlightening, and moving experience for us as a family. I thank them for their amazing insight, intelligence, and creativity and for participating with me in the adventure of this collaboration. I dedicate this book of essays to them.

BRAVEHEART, BABE, AND THE CONTEMPORARY BODY

BRAVEHEART AND "JUST DO IT"

I was stunned when Mel Gibson's *Braveheart* won the Oscar for best picture of the year. I know Hollywood loves a "sweeping" epic, and I liked the innovative use of mud and the absence of hairbrushes for the men (a commitment to material realism not matched in the commercial-perfect shots of the movie's heroines). But as interesting as it was to see Mel in unkempt cornrows, I didn't think it would add up to an Academy Award. Usually we require at least the semblance of an idea from our award-winning epics. *Braveheart* is a one-liner (actually a one-worder)—and an overworked one. "Your heart is free. Have the courage to follow 'er," the young William Wallace is told by his father's ghost at the start of the film. And he does, leading an animal-house army of howling Scotsmen against the yoke of cruel and effete British tyrants. "Freedom!" he screams, as he is disemboweled in the concluding scene, refusing to declare allegiance to British rule. Between these two scenes, "free," "freedom," and "freemen" were intoned reverently or shrieked passionately. And that was about it for "content."

"Live free or die." That slogan does have historical and ideological resonance for Americans. But it's clearly not the collective fight against political tyranny that counts in the movie; it's the courage to *act* and the triumph of the undauntable, unconquerable action hero. Yes, Gibson makes William Wallace a fluent linguist, educated in Latin, well traveled, a man who uses his brain to plot battle strategy. But this is just a ploy to create the appearance of masculine stereotype busting. It's *doing,* not thinking, that reveals a man's worth in the film, whose notion of heroics is as tough-guy as they come. In the last scene Wallace endures public stretching, racking, and evisceration so that Scotland will know he died without submitting, and Gibson (who directed the film as well as starred in it) makes the torture go on for a long, painful time. Wallace's resistance is really the point of the film. Braveheart has his eyes on a prize, and his will is so strong, so powerful, that he is able to endure anything to achieve it. The man has the right stuff.

This macho model of moral fortitude has a lot of living currency today—and for the first time, we now see it as applying to women as well as men. Undiluted testosterone drives *Braveheart.* Its band of Scottish rebels is described in a voice-over as fighting "like warrior-poets," an unmistakable nod to the mythopoetic men's movement to reclaim masculinity. King Longshank's son is a homosexual, and this is clearly coded in the film as signifying that he lacks the equipment to rule. But the movie's women, within the limits of their social roles, are as rebellious and brave-hearted as the men and enjoy watching a good fight too. (In an early scene Wallace's girl's eyes light up as he and a fellow Scot have sport throwing bricks at each other's heads.) I think this is Gibson's idea of feminism—that one doesn't have to be male in order to be a real man—and it is an idea that is widely shared today, with "power" and "muscle" feminism the culturally approved way of advancing the cause of women.

That women have just as much guts, willpower, and *balls* as men, that they can put their bodies through as much wear and tear, endure as much pain, and remain undaunted, was a major theme of the coverage of the 1996 Summer Olympics. As I observed in the introduction, not since Leni Riefenstahl's *Olympiad* of 1936 has there been such a focus on the aesthetics of athletic perfection. But *this* version of beauty, like Riefenstahl's and like those stressed in the numerous photo-articles celebrating the

Olympic body, has little to do with looking pretty. It's about strength, yes, and skill, but even more deeply it's about true grit. "Determined, defiant, dominating," the bold caption in the *New York Times Magazine* describes Gwen Torrence. (The same words, applied to rebellious wives or feminist politicos, have not been said so admiringly.) As in *Braveheart,* the ability to rise above the trials of the body is associated with the highest form of courage and commitment. Mary Ellen Clark's bouts of vertigo. Gail Devers's Graves' disease. Gwen Torrence's difficult childbirth. Amy Van Dyken's asthma. *Life* magazine describes these as personal tests of mettle sent by God to weed out the losers from the winners. And when gymnast Kerri Strug performed her second vault on torn tendons, bringing her team to victory in the face of what must have been excruciating pain, she became the unquestionable hero of the games (and set herself up with ten million dollars in endorsement contracts).

It's not the courage of these athletes I'm sniping at here; I admire them enormously. What bothers me is the message that is dramatized by the way we tell the tales of their success, a message communicated to us mortals too in commercials and ads. Nike has proven to be the master manipulator and metaphor maker in this game. Don't moan over life's problems or blame society for holding you back, Nike instructs us. Don't waste your time berating the "system." Get down to the gym, pick up those free weights, and turn things around. If it hurts, all the better. No pain, no gain. "Right after Bob Kempainen qualified for the marathon, he crossed the finish line and puked all over his Nike running shoes," Nike tells us in a recent advertisement. "We can't tell you how proud we were." A Nike commercial, shown during the games: "If you don't lose consciousness at the end, you could have run faster." Am I the only one who finds this recommendation horrifying in its implications? But consciousness apparently doesn't figure very much in our contemporary notions of heroism. What counts, as in *Braveheart,* is action. *Just Do It.* This is, of course, also what Nike wants us to do when we approach the cash register. (The call to *act* sends a disturbing political message as well. Movies like *Braveheart*, as a friend of mine remarked after we'd seen the film, seem designed to provide inspiration for the militia movement.)

The notion that all that is required to succeed in this culture is to stop whining, lace up your sneakers, and forge ahead, blasting your way through social limitations, personal tribulations, and even the laws of nature, is all around us (see figure 5). Commercials and advertisements egg us on: "Go for It!" "Know No Boundaries!" "Take Control!" Pump yourself up with our product—a car, a diet program, hair-coloring, sneakers—and take your destiny into your own hands. The world will open up for you like an oyster. Like the Sector watch advertisement, AT&T urges us to "Imagine a world without limits" in a series of commercials shown during the 1996 Summer Olympics; one graphic depicts a young athlete pole-vaulting over the World Trade Center, another diving down an endless waterfall. And, indeed, in the world of these images, there are no impediments—no genetic disorders, no body-altering accidents, not even any fat—to slow down our progress to the top of the mountain. All that's needed is the power to *buy*.

The worst thing, in the *Braveheart*/Nike universe of values, is to be bossed around, told what to do. This creates a dilemma for advertisers, who somehow must convince hundreds of thousands of people to purchase the same product while assuring them that they are bold and innovative individualists in doing so. The dilemma is compounded because many of these products perform what Foucault and feminist theorists have called "normalization." That is, they function to screen out diversity and perpetuate social norms, often connected to race and gender. This happens not necessarily because advertisers are consciously trying to promote racism or sexism but because in order to sell products they have to either exploit or create a perception of personal *lack* in the consumer (who buys the product in the hope of filling that lack). An effective way to make the consumer feel inadequate is to take advantage of values that are already in

FIGURE 5

No limits

place in the culture. For example, in a society where there is a dominant (and racialized) preference for blue-eyed blondes, there is a ready market for blue contact lenses and blonde hair-coloring. The catch is that ad campaigns promoting such products also reglamorize the beauty ideals themselves. Thus, they perpetuate racialized norms.

But people don't like to think that they are pawns of astute advertisers or even that they are responding to social norms. Women who have had or are contemplating cosmetic surgery consistently deny the influence of media images.[1] "I'm doing it for me," they insist. But it's hard to account for most of their choices (breast enlargement and liposuction being the most frequently performed operations) outside the context of current cultural norms. Surgeons help to encourage these mystifications. Plastic surgeon Barbara Hayden claims that breast augmentation today is "as individual as the patient herself"; a moment later in the same article another surgeon adds that the "huge 1980s look is out" and that many stars are trading their old gigantibreasts for the currently stylish smaller models![2]

I'm doing it for me. This has become the mantra of the television talk show, and I would gladly accept it if "for me" meant "in order to feel better about myself in this culture that has made me feel inadequate as I am." But people rarely mean this. Most often on these shows, the "for me" answer is produced in defiant refutation of some cultural "argument" (talk-show style, of course) on topics such as "Are Our Beauty Ideals Racist?" or "Are We Obsessed with Youth?" "No, I'm not having my nose (straightened)(narrowed) in order to look less ethnic. I'm doing it *for me.*" "No, I haven't had my breasts enlarged to a 38D in order to be more attractive to men. I did it *for me.*" In these constructions "me" is imagined as a pure and precious inner space, an "authentic" and personal reference point untouched by external values and demands. A place where we live free and won't be pushed around. It's the *Braveheart* place.

But we want to both imagine ourselves as bold, rebellious Bravehearts *and* conform, become what our culture values. Advertisers help us enormously in this self-deception by performing their own sleight-of-hand tricks with rhetoric and image, often invoking, as *Braveheart* does, the metaphor and hype of "political" resistance: "Now it's every woman's right to look good!" declares Pond's (for "age-defying" makeup). "What makes a woman revolutionary?" asks Revlon. "Not wearing makeup for a day!" answers a perfectly made-up Claudia Schiffer (quickly adding, "Just kidding, Revlon!"). A recent Gap ad: "The most defiant act is to be distinguished, singled out, marked. Put our jeans on." The absurdity of suggesting that everyone's donning the same (rather ordinary-looking) jeans can be a "defiant" and individualistic act is visually accompanied by two photos of female models with indistinguishable bodies.

POWER AS AGENCY: MASKING REALITY

From evisceration at the hands of tyrants to defiance through dungarees may seem like a large leap. And in real terms, of course, it is. But we live in a world of commercial rhetoric that brooks no such distinctions. And not only commercial rhetoric. "Just Do It" is an ideology for our time, an idea that bridges the gulf between right and left, grunge and yuppie, chauvinist and feminist. The left wing didn't like "Just Say No," perhaps because it came from Nancy Reagan, perhaps because it was aimed at habits they didn't want to give up themselves. It isn't that easy, they insisted. The neighborhoods, the culture, social despair. . . . But the mind-over-matter message of "Just Do It," with its "neutral" origins (the brain of an ad woman) and associations with jogging, nice bodies, and muscle-lib for women, has roused no protests.

In a recent interview rock star Courtney Love urged "liberals" to "breed" in order to outpopulate the Rush Limbaughs of the world. "It's not that hard," she said. "It's nine months. You know, just do it."[3] But right-wing ideologues like Limbaugh, who celebrate bootstrapping and Horatio Alger and scorn (what they view as) the liberal's creation of a culture of "victims," also advocate "just doing it."[4] And so too do celebrities like Oprah when they present themselves as proof that "anyone can make it if they want it badly enough and try hard enough." The implication here—which Oprah, I like to believe, would blanch at if she faced it squarely—is that if you *don't* succeed, it's proof that you *didn't* want it badly enough or try hard enough. Racism and sexism? Just so many hurdles to be jumped, personal challenges to be overcome. And what about the fact that in a competitive society someone *always has to lose?* We won't think about that, it's too much of a downer. Actually, in the coverage of the 1996 Olympics, everything short of "getting the gold" was constructed as losing. The men's 4 × 100 relay team, which won the silver medal, was interviewed by NBC after, as the commentator put it, their "defeat"! How can everyone be a winner if "winning" is reserved only for those who make it to the absolute pinnacle?

As far as women's issues go, "power feminists" are telling us that we're past all those tiresome harangues about "the beauty system" and "objectification" and "starving girls." What's so bad about makeup, anyway? Isn't it my right to go for it? Do what I want with my body? Be all that I can be? Just a few years back "third-wave" feminist Naomi Wolf wrote a bestselling book, *The Beauty Myth* (1991), which spoke powerfully and engagingly to young women about a culture that teaches them they are nothing if they are not beautiful. But in a wink of the cultural zeitgeist, she declares in her latest, *Fire with Fire* (1993), that all that bitching and moaning has seen its day. Now, according to the rehabilitated Wolf, we're supposed to stop complaining and—you guessed it—"Just Do It." Wolf, in fact, offers Nike's commercial slogan as her symbol for the new feminism, which as she describes it is about "competition . . . victory . . . self-reliance . . . the desire to win."[5] Wolf is hardly alone in her celebratory mood. Betty Friedan has also said she is "sick of women wallowing in the victim state. We have empowered ourselves." A 1993 *Newsweek* article—most of its authors women—sniffs derisively at an installation of artist Sue Williams, who put a huge piece of plastic vomit on the floor of the Whitney Museum to protest the role of aesthetic ideals in encouraging the development of eating disorders. That kind of action once would have been seen as guerrilla theater. In 1993, *Newsweek* writers sneered: "Tell [the bulimics] to get some therapy and cut it out."[6]

Getting one's body in shape, of course, has become the exemplary practice, symbol, and means of empowerment in this culture. "You don't just shape your body," as Bally Fitness tells us. "You shape your life." As a manufacturer of athletic shoes, Nike—like Reebok and Bally—is dedicated to preserving the connection between having the right stuff and strenuous, physical activity. "It's about time," they declare disingenuously in a recent ad, "that the fitness craze that turned into the fashion craze that turned into the marketing craze turned back into the fitness craze." But despite Nike's emphasis on fitness, in contemporary commercial culture the rhetoric of taking charge of one's life has been yoked to everything from car purchases to hair-coloring, with physical effort and discipline often dropping out as a requirement. Even plastic surgery is continually described today—by patients, surgeons, and even by some feminist theorists —as *an act* of "taking control," "taking one's life into one's own hands" (a somewhat odd metaphor, under the circumstances).

These are the metaphors that dominate, for example, in sociologist Kathy Davis's arguments about cosmetic surgery and female "agency" in her *Reshaping the Female Body.* Among some academic feminists, an insistence on the efficacy of female "agency" is the more moderate, sober, scholarly sister of "power feminism." "Agency feminists" are not about to sing odes of praise to Nike, Reebok, or competition. They acknowledge that our choices are made within social and cultural contexts that are not all cause for celebration. But they do offer themselves as an alternative to what they caricature as the grim, petrified, politically dogmatic feminism of the past, now viewed as out of touch with the lives of real women. Those bad "old" feminists (I am one of these retrograde kvetchers, in some accounts) have a demeaning view of women as passive victims, tyrannized and suffocated by social norms, helpless pawns of social forces "beyond their control or comprehension." In contrast, the good, "new" feminism respects and honors the individual's choices as a locus of personal power, creativity, self-definition. So, for example, Davis argues that when a woman claims to have had her breasts enlarged "for herself," it's degrading and unsisterly not to accept this construction at face value. To deconstruct it—who is this "self"? where does it reside? in outer space? and where did it get the idea that it needed implants?—is to view the woman as a kind of helpless child who doesn't know her own mind and is not in charge of her own life. Contrasting herself to those feminists who view the industries in feminine self-improvement as "totalizing and pernicious" agents of women's oppression, Davis insists that these industries in fact play an important role in empowering women.

In a moment I will look more closely at Davis's arguments, which seem to me typical of a certain contemporary preference for the rhetoric of "agency" over close analysis of social context and cultural reality, a preference that mirrors—in more scholarly style, of course—the more popular images of empowerment I have been discussing. I will then talk about what aspects of reality these models of empowerment obscure. But first I'd like to note that arguments such as Davis's are often presented in the way she presents them—as an antidote against an imagined feminist position that holds that women are utterly passive and unconscious sponges, as subservient to cultural images as a browbeaten wife is to her abusive husband. Phrases like "cultural dope"—which are used to describe how the bad feminists allegedly view women—help vivify a nasty picture of condescending politicos who push women around with their theory as disdainfully as they claim the images do. Once such a picture is created, of course, the audience nods in agreement and approval, for the "new" feminism is sure to follow. But portraits of "victim feminists" are almost always caricatures. Davis, for example, accuses me of viewing women as "cultural dopes." But in fact where the power of cultural images is concerned, Davis and I actually have very little quarrel with each other. We both see cultural images as central elements in women's lives and we see them as contributing to a pedagogy of defect, in which women learn that various parts of their bodies are faulty, unacceptable. Neither of us views women as passive sponges in this process but (as I put it in *Unbearable Weight*) as engaged "in a process of making meaning, of 'labor on the body.'" We both recognize that there is ambiguity and contradiction, multiple meanings and consequences, in human motivations and choices.

While I object to Davis's placing the blame on feminists, I do have sympathy with Davis's desire to correct a *general* cultural tradition that has equated women with passivity rather than activity—the done to, not the doers, the acted upon, not the actors. But like many other attempts at "correcting" the mistakes of the past, Davis goes too far in the opposite direction. In this reaction we see a clear similarity between current academic obsessions with "agency" and the more popular versions of "power feminism," like Katie Roiphe's. Roiphe insists that most of what passes for "date rape" is actually an after-the-fact attempt on the part of young women to avoid responsibility for their own actions, like getting drunk on a date, for example. Roiphe, like academic "agency feminists," wants us to stop casting women as passive "victims," and she connects that perspective to the passé feminism of the past. But what Roiphe and Davis both seem to forget is that the main point of what is disparagingly (and misleadingly, I believe) called "victim feminism" was not to establish women's passivity or purity but to draw attention to the social and political context of personal behavior. Remember "The personal is the political"? Let's not forget that it wasn't so long ago that it was common coin to believe that women who get raped "ask for it" and that as far as beauty is concerned we are "our own worst enemies."

Where agency feminists and I most differ is over that magic word "agency." I don't see the word as adding very much beyond rhetorical cheerleading concerning how *we,* not the images, are "in charge" (the theory equivalent of "I did it for me"). More important, I believe that the cheers of "agency" create a diversionary din that drowns out the *real* orchestra that is playing in the background, the consumer culture we live in and need to take responsibility for. To make this point clear, I need to look a bit more closely at Davis's arguments. Advertisements, fashion photos, cosmetic instructions, she points out (drawing on the work of eminent sociologist Dorothy Smith), all require "specialized knowledge" and "complex and skilled interpretive activities on the part of the female agent," who must "plan a course of action, making a series of on-the-spot calculations about whether the rigorous discipline required by the techniques of body improvement will actually improve her appearance given the specifics of her particular body." By showing her how to correct various defects in her appearance ("Lose those unsightly bags under your eyes," "Turn your flabby rear-end into buns of steel," "Have a firm, sexy bosom for the first time in your life!" "Get a sexy stomach—fast!" [figure 6]) the ads and instructions transform the woman into an agent of her own destiny, providing concrete objectives, goals, strategies, a plan of action. Davis quotes Smith here: "The text instructs her [the woman] that her breasts are too small/too big; she reads of a remedy; her too small breasts become remediable. She enters into the discursive organization of desire; now she has an objective where before she had only a defect."[7] So the "sexy stomach" article (just one example of the scores of fitness features that appear regularly in women's magazines) (see figure 6) addresses a consumer whose stomach, the text implies, is not *yet* sexy; at the same time, the lean body of the model offers visual "proof" to all but the fittest readers that they are indeed in less than ideal shape "for bikini weather." But it's not too late, we are reassured; those abs can still be whipped into shape with the right exercises. This prescription for improvement, as Davis would interpret it, allows the woman to take control of her own body in a way that was unavailable to her before she read the article.

Now, just so you know that I'm not really some sour old "victim feminist," let me say at once that makeup and fashion can be creative fun, and I enjoy exchanging beauty tips with my friends. But Davis is claiming more—that it is precisely our instruction in learning to see ourselves as defective and lacking, needful of improvement and remedy (too fat, too flat-chested, too dark-skinned, too wrinkled), that mobilizes us, puts us in charge of our lives! Is this argument not strained, if not downright perverse? I know that Davis views what she is doing as correcting the sins of other feminists, who, as she describes them, are so focused on the "tyranny" of the big bad beauty system that they don't notice the female *subjects* who are participating in it. But her critique goes beyond regarding women as subjects to equating the self-scrutinizing subjectivity these ads encourage with a state of liberation. In the quote from Smith, just when is the woman in question supposed to have been in her disempowered "before" state, when she "only had a defect" without an objective? Before she read the liberating "text" that tells her how to remedy her too small breasts or insufficiently flat stomach? In telling her how to remedy this "defect" is the text not simply providing a cure (at a price, of course—they are *selling* something here, let's not forget) for the very poison it has administered?

To see this point more concretely, consider this ad (I have chosen one from another cultural period, situated within notions of femininity that emphasize delicacy and fragility, in order to encourage a bit of distance): "Conspicuous Nose Pores: How to Reduce Them" (figure 7). The formula here is exactly as Davis describes it. First we are warned that "complexions otherwise flawless are often ruined by conspicuous nose pores." The ad then goes on to describe with great specificity and detail the beauty regime that will correct those conspicuous nose pores. As Davis would theorize this ad, the specification of such a regime makes the "female agent the *sine qua non* of the feminine beauty system." By telling women what they need to *do* in order to bring their bodies up to par (defined here, I

get a sexy stomach—fast!

Whip your abs into shape in time for bikini weather with these exercises from trainer Glenn Philipson of Crunch Fitness in New York City:

It's a cinch: ultraflat abs

FIGURE 6

Be an agent. Whip those abs!

want to note, as "flawless"—a goal that will keep female agents busy till they topple into the grave, perfectly embalmed), they inspire women to no longer suffer their dissatisfaction passively, impotently, but as "an active process." "Rather than immobilizing women, bodily imperfections provide the opportunity for action."

But what made the woman with the conspicuous nose pores dissatisfied to begin with? What gave her the idea that they were "ruinous" to her beauty? Probably not this ad alone. But certainly this ad, among other

You will find the proper treatment for oily skin and shiny nose in the booklet around every cake of Woodbury's Facial Soap

Conspicuous Nose Pores

How to reduce them

COMPLEXIONS otherwise flawless are often ruined by conspicuous nose pores. In such cases the small muscular fibres of the nose have become weakened and do not keep the pores closed as they should be. Instead, these pores collect dirt, clog up and become enlarged.

To reduce enlarged nose pores: wring a cloth from very hot water, lather it with Woodbury's Facial Soap, then hold it to your face. When heat has expanded the pores, rub in very gently a fresh lather of Woodbury's. Repeat this hot water and lather application several times, *stopping at once if your nose feels sensitive*. Then finish by rubbing the nose for thirty seconds with a lump of ice.

Do not expect to change in a week, however, a condition resulting from years of neglect. Use this treatment *persistently*. It will gradually reduce the enlarged pores until they are inconspicuous.

You will find a 25c cake of Woodbury's Facial Soap sufficient for a month or six weeks of this treatment, and for general use for this time. Get a cake today. For sale everywhere throughout the United States and Canada.

Send for sample cake of soap with booklet of famous treatments and samples of Woodbury's Facial Cream and Facial Powder

Send 5 cents for a trial size cake (enough for a week or ten days of any Woodbury's Facial Treatment) together with the booklet of treatments, "A Skin You Love to Touch." Or for 12 cents we will send you the treatment booklet and samples of Woodbury's Facial Soap, Facial Cream and Facial Powder. Address The Andrew Jergens Co., 8202 Spring Grove Avenue, Cincinnati, Ohio.

If you live in Canada, address The Andrew Jergens Co., Limited, 8202 Sherbrooke St., Perth, Ontario.

A-SKIN-YOU
LOVE-TO-TOUCH

JOHN H. WOODBURY'S FACIAL SOAP

Woodbury's Facial Soap

Woodbury's Facial Soap

FIGURE 7

Ruined by conspicuous nose pores

social factors, creates the very condition of perceived defect that it now tells women how to overcome. By this logic it would be a sorry day indeed if women were to become content with the way they look. Without all those defects to correct we would lose an important arena for the enactment of our creative agency! There doesn't seem to be much chance of that happening though. Instead, the sites of defect have multiplied for women, and men increasingly have been given more of these wonderful opportunities for agency, too, as magazines and products devoted to the enhancement and "correction" of their appearance have multiplied.

I have spent so much time on this point not to whip the agency feminist position to its knees but because what is obscured in Davis's discussion of ads and beauty features is exactly what must be kept at the forefront of any cultural analysis of practices of bodily improvement. There is a consumer system operating here that depends on our perceiving ourselves as defective and that will continually find new ways to do this. That system—and others connected to it, generating new technologies and areas of expertise organized around the diagnosis and correction of "defect"—is masked by the rhetoric of personal empowerment.

Take cosmetic surgery, which Davis describes as an empowering "solution" to an individual's problems with body image, a way for women to actively "take control" of their bodies and "take the reins" of their lives "in hand." (Ads for cosmetic surgery, by the way, use the exact same argument.) Davis supports her position by drawing on interviews with a handful of individual women, whose "defects" range from facial deformity to too small breasts and who all describe surgery as having helped them. I am disturbed, to begin with, by Davis's failure to draw distinctions between *kinds* of body alteration. Cosmetic surgery covers an enormous range of corrections, from the repair of major birth defects to Roseanne's cheek implants to Liz's liposuction. But for Davis all women's body-image problems are given the same weight, and they are represented by her in terms such as "terrible suffering" and "valiant struggle." I don't deny that many of us in this culture have deep wounds of shame about our bodies (I certainly do); I have written extensively about just this, I believe with empathy and understanding. But there are still distinctions to be drawn here, distinctions that are rapidly disappearing in our talk-show culture, where everyone's story is worth a show and is sensationalized on the air as dramatically as possible.

By treating breast augmentations and operations to correct facial deformities as the same by virtue of their "empowering" individuals, we lose the ability to critique the former from a cultural point of view. I don't have a problem with the notion that an individual's long and fruitless struggle to live with a particular "defect" may end happily when that defect is corrected. But assessing "the dilemma of cosmetic surgery" (as Davis calls it) requires more than taking these individual snapshots of satisfied customers (or dissatisfied ones, for that matter). We need a picture of the landscape too. For cosmetic surgery is more than an individual choice; it is a burgeoning industry and an increasingly normative cultural practice. As such, it is a significant contributory *cause* of women's suffering by continually upping the ante on what counts as an acceptable face and body. In focusing on narratives of individual "empowerment," Davis—like Oprah's guests who claim they did it "for themselves"—overlooks the fact that the norms that encouraged these individuals to see themselves as defective are enmeshed in the practice and institution of cosmetic surgery itself. And so is individual behavior.

I now want to sharpen my focus to discuss some of the cultural and institutional aspects of cosmetic surgery that are missing from Davis's stories of individual empowerment. Let me say, as a general introduction to this discussion, that we have barely begun to confront—and are not yet in a position to adequately assess—the potential cultural consequences of regarding the body as "cultural plastic,"[8] to be deconstructed and rearranged as we desire. For this reason alone, we need to keep track of cultural trends, not just personal narratives. Our relationship to our bodies clearly has become more and more an investment in them as "product" and image, requiring alteration as fashions change. Consider breast augmentation, now increasingly widespread, and its role in establishing new norms against which smaller or less firm breasts are seen as *defective.* Micromastia is the clinical term, among plastic surgeons, for "too small" breasts. Such "disorders" are, of course, entirely aesthetic and completely socially "constructed." Anyone who doubts this should recall the 1920s, when women were binding their breasts to look more boyish. Today, with artificial implants the norm among movie stars and models, an adolescent boy who has grown up learning what a woman's body looks like from movies, cable television, and magazines may wonder what's wrong when his girlfriend lies down and her breasts flop off to the side instead of standing straight up in the air. Will we soon see a clinical term for "too floppy" breasts?

As the augmented breast becomes the norm, the decision to have one's breasts surgically enhanced becomes what the psychiatrist Peter Kramer has called "free choice under pressure." We can choose not to have such surgery. No one is holding a gun to our heads. But those who don't— for example, those who cannot afford the surgery—are at an increasingly significant professional and personal disadvantage. The same is true of face-lifts and other surgeries to "correct" aging, which are also becoming more normative. More and more of my friends—these are teachers, therapists, writers, not movie stars and models—are contemplating or even planning surgery. We scan our faces every morning for signs of downward drift, and we measure our decline against the lifted and tightened norms of the images that surround us. For me, viewing the Academy Awards was something of an exercise in self-flagellation, as actresses my own age and older stepped up to the podium, each one looking younger and tighter around the eyes than she had ten years ago. At forty-nine I have come to feel each fresh capitulation to surgery on the part of these actresses as a personal affront; my own face, after all, will be judged by the standards that these actresses are establishing. As a teacher and writer, my status and success depend far less on my looks than they do for other women. If it all gets to me, imagine how women feel in the countless service and public relations positions for which youthful looks are a job prerequisite.

The fact is that the plastically reconstructed and preserved faces and bodies of the forty- and fifty-something actresses who came of age with us have made the ideal of aging beautifully and "gracefully" obsolete. Now we are supposed to "defy" our age, as Melanie Griffith (her own lips decidedly poutier than they were a few years ago) instructs us in her commercials for Revlon. In thinking about this "defiance" of age, I often wonder what existential traumas lie in store for those who have not been slowly acclimated to the decline of their bodies, learning to accept and accommodate the small changes that happen gradually over the years, but who have become habituated instead to seeing those changes as an occasion for immediate action. Although for now true "scalpel slaves" are generally found only among the fairly wealthy, first surgeries *are* becoming more and more common among people of all classes, races, and ages.[9] (We should know by now how such practices tend to "trickle down" in this culture.)[10] And first surgeries often lead to more. Some surgeons acknowledge that once you begin "correcting" for age, it's all too easy to start sliding down the slope of habituation. "Plastic surgery sharpens your eyesight," says one. "You get something done, suddenly you're looking in the mirror every five minutes—at imperfections nobody else can see."[11]

The pressure to have age-defying surgery is now creeping across the gender gap too. Men used to be relatively exempt from the requirement to look young; gray hair and wrinkles were (and still mostly are) a code for experience, maturity, and wisdom. But in a "Just Do It" culture that now equates youth and fitness with energy and competence—the "right stuff"—fortyish businessmen are feeling increasing pressure to dye their hair, get liposuction on their spare tires, and have face-lifts in order to compete with younger, fitter-looking men and women. In 1980 men accounted for only 10 percent of plastic surgery patients. In 1994 they were 26 percent.[12] These numbers will undoubtedly rise, as plastic surgeons develop specialized angles to attract men ("penile enhancement" is now advertised in the sports sections of major newspapers) and disinfect surgery of its associations with feminine vanity. Also thanks to the efforts of surgeons, who now argue that one should start "preventive" procedures while the skin is still elastic, younger and younger people are having surgery. Here is an advertisement I came across recently in the local (Lexington, Kentucky) paper:

> Picture this scenario. You're between the ages of thirty-five and fifty. You feel like you are just hitting your stride. But the face in the mirror is sending out a different message. Your morning facial puffiness hangs around all day. You're beginning to resemble your parents at a point when they began looking old to you. If you prefer a more harmonic relationship between your self-perception and outer image, you may prefer to tackle these concerns before they become too obvious. You may benefit from a face-lift performed at an earlier age. There is no carved-in-stone perfect time or age to undergo a face-lift. For those who place a high priority on maintaining a youthful appearance, any visual disharmony between body and soul can be tackled earlier when cosmetic surgical goals tend to be less aggressive and it is easier to obtain more natural-looking results. The reason is: Younger skin and tissues have more elasticity so smoothness can be achieved with surgery.

What this ad obscures is that the "disharmonies" between body and soul that thirty-five- and forty-year-old (!!) women may be experiencing are not "carved-in-stone" either but are in large part the product of our *cultural* horror of wrinkles and lines—a horror, of course, that surgeons are fueling. Why should a few lines around our eyes be experienced as "disharmonious" with the energy and vitality that we feel "inside," *unless* they are coded as a sign of decrepitude (looking like our parents—good heavens, what a fate!). That these lines can be coded otherwise is a theme of a Murad ad (see figure 8). But while Dr. Murad acknowledges that our various lines and wrinkles are markers of the accumulated experience and accomplishment of our lives, the ad recommends that we wipe our faces clean of them. This ad, like many others, attempts to have its commercial cake without having to "eat" criticism along with it, to value "character" (along with critics of the beauty system) while insisting that it doesn't have to show on our faces (just buy our product).

The woman in the ad is dazzling, of course; this only serves as a reminder of just how fragile beauty is, how important it is to start protecting it against age *before* time gets the upper hand. We are now being encouraged to view this aging process as a disaster for our sense of "who we really are" (our "self," our "soul," as the ad puts it) and as a slippery slope heading for the time when we will be utterly beyond saving, social detritus. (A fifty-nine-year-old face-lift patient describes the skin around her neck as "garbage—old, ugly, sagging . . . garbage.")[13] We are always holding our finger in that dam, getting in as much "life" as we can before the deluge— as though "life" ends when we are no longer young and firm. If we thought of the "real self" as evolving into new and unpredictable forms (perhaps with "harmonies" in store that are deeper and more satisfying than looking good), we might look on wrinkles and lines as an opportunity to engage in a learning process about the inevitability of change, the impermanence of all things. Yes, and about our own physical vulnerability, and mortality. Others around us are dying too. Focusing on unsightly wrinkles and disfiguring nose pores, we don't have to look at that.

Every "correction" of aging represents a lost opportunity to do this important psychological work. And if cosmetic surgery becomes the normalized, affordable alternative that it now seems to be becoming, how will generations used to "correcting" their bodies surgically according to

FIGURE 8

Erase your life from your face

perfected norms cope with the inevitable failure of such correction? For, you know, you just can't go on doing it forever. For those who try, the stretched and staring, often cadaverous mask of plastically preserved beauty becomes itself a marker of age and impending death. This is partly why I am not inclined to surgery. I would rather get used to aging gradually, to changes in the way I am seen by others, to the inevitability of frailty creeping into my presence and mode of being in the world, to my own mortality, so that I can be prepared and respond consciously and with dignity and, yes, in a way that I hope will actually enhance my physical appearance. I care about looks (I don't live on Uranus, after all). But I'd rather be a vibrant old woman than embalm myself in a mask of perpetual youth.

In assessing the consequences of our burgeoning surgical culture, there are ethical and social as well as existential issues to be confronted. As I noted in *Unbearable Weight,* the surgeries that people "choose" often assimilate ethnic and racial features to a more "white" norm. "Does anyone in this culture," I asked, "have his or her nose reshaped to look more 'African' or 'Jewish'?" The answer, of course, is no. Given our history of racism—a history in which bodies that look "too black" or obviously Jewish have been refused admittance to public places and even marked for death—how can we regard these choices as merely "individual preferences"? In Japan it has become increasingly common for job-seeking female college graduates to have their eyes surgically altered to appear more occidental. Such a "Western" appearance, it is widely acknowledged, gives a woman the edge in job interviews. But capitulating to this requirement—although it may be highly understandable from the point of view of the individual's economic survival and advancement—is to participate in a process of racial normalization and to make it harder for others to refuse to participate. The more established the new norm, the higher the costs of resisting—"free choice under pressure." The same points can be made about many of the operations that people have performed on them in this country. And while some might celebrate being able to "choose" one's features as part of a "melting pot" society, as eradicating racial differences that we don't need and that have only caused pain and suffering, we should face the fact that only certain ingredients in the pot are being encouraged to "melt" here.

Situating "personal" choices in social, cultural, and economic contexts such as these raises certain issues for the thoughtful individual, one being the interpretation of his or her own situation, which becomes harder to see as a "free," autonomous choice done "for oneself," another being his or her complicity in the perpetuation of racialized norms *and* in the suffering of other people. These issues of complicity may be most striking in the case of influential and highly visible culture makers such as Cher and Madonna—who never take any responsibility for the images they create, of course. But those of us who aren't celebrities also influence the lives we touch. Mothers (and fathers) set standards for their children, sisters and brothers for their siblings, teachers for their students, friends for their friends. Adult behavior reinforces cultural messages sent to teens and preteens about the importance of looking good, of fitting in—pressures young people then impose, often brutally, on one another. (One of my students wrote that the images of slenderness only began to "get to her" when she realized that her parents "believed in them" too.)

Not that many years ago parents who smoked never thought twice about the instructional effect this might be having on their children, in legitimating smoking, making it seem adult and empowering. A cultural perspective on augmentation, face-lifts, cosmetic "ethnic cleansing" of Jewish and black noses, Asian eyes, and so on similarly might make parents think twice about the messages they are sending their children, might make them less comfortable with viewing their decisions as purely "personal" or "individual" ones. And they *should* think twice. We are all culture makers as well as culture consumers, and if we wish to be considered "agents" in our lives—and have it mean more than just a titular honor—we need to take responsibility for that role.

To act consciously and responsibly means understanding the culture we live in, even if it requires acknowledging that we are not always "in charge." That we are not always in charge does not mean that we are "dopes." In fact, I think the *really* dopey thing is living with the illusion that we are "in control," just because some commercial (or ad for surgery) tells us so. In the culture we live in, individuals are caught between two contradictory injunctions. On the one hand, an ideology of triumphant individualism and mind-over-matter heroism urges us to "Just Do It" and tries to convince us that we *can* "just do it," whatever our sex, race, or circumstances. This is a mystification. We are not runners on a level field but on one that is pocked with historical inequities that make it much harder for some folks to lace up their Nikes and speed to the finish line—until the lane in which they are running has been made less rocky and the hidden mines excavated and removed. A few of us, if we are very, very lucky (circumstances still do count, willpower isn't everything, despite what the commercials tell us), do have our moments of triumph. But it is often after years of struggle in which we have drawn on many resources other than our own talent, resolve, and courage. We have been helped by our friends and our communities, by social movements, legal and political reform, and sheer good fortune. And many, of course, don't make it.

But on the other hand, while consumerism assures us that we can (and should) "just do it," it continually sends the contradictory message that we are defective, lacking, inadequate. This is the missing context of the stories of empowerment that Davis tells, rewriting the "old" feminist scripts. But what she leaves out just happens to be the very essence of advertising and the fuel of consumer capitalism, which cannot allow equilibrium or stasis in human desire. Thus, we are not permitted to feel satisfied with ourselves and we are "empowered" only and always through fantasies of what we *could* be.

This is not a plot; it's just the way the system works. Capitalism adores proliferation and excess; it abhors moderation. One moment the culture begins talking about greater health consciousness, which is surely a good thing that no one would deny. But the next moment we've got commercials on at every hour for every imaginable exercise and diet product, and people are spending huge quantities of their time trying to achieve a level of "fitness" that goes way beyond health and straight into obsession. Technological possibilities emerge that allow surgeons to make corrective repairs of serious facial conditions; before long our surgeons have become Pygmalions of total self-transformation, advertising the slightest deviation from the cultural "norm" as a problem needing to be solved, an impediment to happiness (as in this ad, figure 9). Drugs like Prozac are developed to treat serious clinical depressions; the next moment college clinics are dispensing these pills to help students with test anxiety.

The multiplication of human "defect" is aided by factors other than economic. Drug companies may be focused on profits, but those folks at the university clinic are genuinely concerned about students and want to make their lives easier. Cosmetic surgeons, while fabulously paid, are rarely in it for the money alone. Often, they are carried to excess not by dreams of yachts but by savior fantasies and by pure excitement about the technological possibilities. Nowadays, those can be pretty fantastic, as fat is suctioned from thighs and injected into lips, breast implants inserted through the bellybutton, penises enlarged through "phalloplasty," and nipples repositioned. Each of us, working in our own professional niche, is focused on the possibilities for our own "agency" and personal effectiveness working within that niche, so we rarely stand back to survey the big picture. That's precisely why we need cultural criticism.

Recently I had a personal experience that brought freshly home to me the central and complex role the multiplication of "defect" plays in our culture and the way this may be masked by a rhetoric of agency. With a very specific request, I went to a dentist specializing in cosmetic dentistry. Because of antibiotics I had been given in infancy, my front teeth were starting to darken and I wanted to have them capped. I described the problem to the dentist and he asked me to smile. No problem with

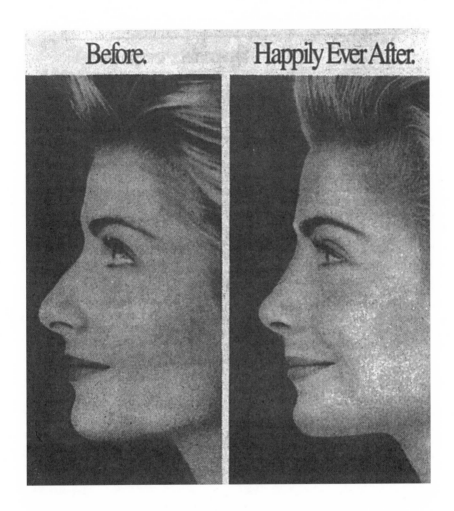

FIGURE 9

Normalizing noses

capping the teeth, he said. But wouldn't I also like a less gummy smile and a correction of my overbite? I told him that I thought I had a pretty nice smile as it was. He was stone silent. I was somewhat hurt, even shaken by his refusal to reassure me, and suddenly old childhood insecurities began to surface. At the age of eight I was convinced that I looked like Alfred E. Neuman, from *Mad* magazine. On better days I saw a small, freckled, overweight rabbit in the mirror. I had thought those days were long gone, but now I was looking again in the mirror for signs that "What, Me Worry?" Neuman or chubby Bugs really were still lurking there. Letty Cottin Pogrebin, in her new book on aging, describes a similar experience at her dermatologist:

> It started with a small cyst on my back and two bumps, each the size of a lemon pit, on my thigh. For no apparent reason, my skin occasionally produces these outcroppings—my friend Gale calls them the "barnacles of age"—and, given the gaping hole in the ozone layer and the idiosyncrasies of skin cancer, I've learned to take it seriously. Off I went to the dermatologist, who performed minor surgery on the lemon pits and, to my relief, pronounced the bumps benign. At the end of the checkup, the doctor glanced at my face, then at my chart, then again at my face. "You look pretty good for your age," he declared. "But you'd look a hundred percent better without those fat pouches under your eyes."[14]

Pogrebin then goes on to describe in fresh and honest detail her own ambivalence about the possibility of surgery (she decided against it). She does not, however, comment further on the role her doctor played, not just in normalizing surgery in her eyes but in suggesting that she was an appropriate candidate for it—when she had come in on an entirely different matter. When people claim to be having surgery "for themselves," they frequently mean that they are not being urged to do so by husbands or boyfriends. But husbands and boyfriends are not the only eyes that survey and evaluate women; the gaze of the doctor, especially with the tremendous authority that doctors have in this culture, may hold a lot of weight, may even be experienced as the discerning point of view of a generalized cultural observer, an "objective" assessor of defect. Writing for *New York* magazine, twenty-eight-year-old, 5'6" and 118-pound Lily Burana describes how a series of interviews with plastic surgeons—the majority of whom had recommended rhinoplasty, lip augmentation, implants, liposuction, and eyelid work—changed her perception of herself from "a hardy young sapling that could do with some pruning . . . to a gnarled thing that begs to be torn down to the root and rebuilt limb by limb."[15]

Under these cultural conditions the desire to be "normal" or "ordinary," which Kathy Davis claims is the motivation for most cosmetic surgeries, is much more slippery than she makes it out to be. Davis makes the point that none of her subjects describe their surgeries as having been done for the sake of "beauty" but insist they only wanted to feel "ordinary." But in a culture that proliferates defect and in which the surgically perfected body ("perfect" according to certain standards, of course) has become the model of the "normal," even the ordinary body becomes the defective body. This continual upping of the ante of physical acceptability is cloaked by ads and features that represent the cosmetic surgeon as a blessed savior, offering miraculous technology to end long-standing pain. The "Before/Happily Ever After" noted earlier ("She didn't like her nose. She felt it kept her from looking and feeling her best.") offers its advice to an imagined consumer who is *already* troubled and ashamed of her defect. An unhappy reader is also assumed in "Correcting a Gummy Smile" (figure 10): "Do you hold back when you smile so as not to reveal too much gum? If you've always hated your smile and tried to hide it, you'll learn how a simple plastic surgery procedure . . ."). But how many women who are basically satisfied with their appearance begin to question their self-image on the basis of images and advice presented in these features or—

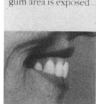

FIGURE 10

The shame of a gummy smile

even more authoritatively—dispensed to them by their doctors? The "gum-miness" of my own smile was of no concern to me when I first visited the dentist; under his care I began to wonder if a feature of my appearance that I had taken to be perfectly "ordinary" (even rather attractive) wasn't in actuality something I'd better hide . . . or "correct."

   This spell was broken, however, when a few days after my appointment I received a computer-generated set of recommendations from the dentist's office. The recommendations were phrased so as to make his prescribed course of cosmetic alteration seem precisely individualized and entirely a matter of his satisfying *my* stated desires. My name was plugged in, of course, and the recommendations chosen from a set list of options, ready to be inserted with a keystroke, each with its own little prefabricated paragraph. The pretense that this was all written specially for me didn't bother me *too* much (we are used to this nowadays), but I became enraged when I saw that he had inserted all the options that were *his* idea as though they represented *my* expressed dissatisfactions and desires. It went something like this: "Susan Bordo: You have taken an important step toward giving yourself a beautiful, youthful smile. You have told us that you are dissatisfied with the discoloration in your teeth, with the gumminess of your smile, that you would like a shorter, neater bite, and a brighter, younger look." The recommendations that followed would have cost me about $25,000 to implement.

I realized while going over this form that no patient was going to get away without at least one or two of those prefabricated keystrokes. "Gummy smile." "Shorter bite." And so forth. If you are trained to see defect, you will. I went for a second opinion, from a *family* dentist, and I was relieved to hear that she thought my smile was fine as it was and that there was no need to cut huge trenches in my gums in order to make me look more like Michelle Pfeiffer. I never called the first dentist back, but a few days later I received a message on my answering machine in which he wondered why I had not come back. He had wanted so much, he said, to give me the nice smile I wanted.

BABE: A REAL METAPHOR FOR OUR LIVES

Freedom. Choice. Autonomy. Self. Agency. These are powerful words in our culture, fighting words. But they are also words that are increasingly empty in many people's experience. Are we invoking the rhetoric with such desperation precisely because the felt reality is slipping away, running through our fingers? I think about the pain and self-doubt, the compulsions and disorders that often accompany our efforts at becoming what the culture rewards—particularly among my students, so many of whom have serious problems with food, weight, and body image. Then I listen to the rousing cries of "power feminism" in both its commercial and its academic formulations: "Just Do It!" "Take Control!" "Go for It!" There is a discordance there for me between the celebration of "agency" and empowerment and what I see going on in people's lives today.

Don't misunderstand me here. I think that there have been great gains in the status of women in this culture. And I love seeing women with muscles, particularly when they project strength and solidity—as they did on the bodies of some of the Olympic runners, swimmers, ball players— and not merely a tighter, toned, anorexic aesthetic. I'm thrilled to see women who don't feel they need to hold back on their skill and power in order to remain "feminine." But let us not be deceived into believing, along with the magazine articles and TV commentaries, that we are at the dawn of a new, "postfeminist" age for women.

Do we really think that the twelve-year-old who becomes obsessed with looking like Gabriel Reece is really in *such* an alternative universe to the one who wants to look like Kate Moss? Sure, rigorous weight training is probably less dangerous and makes you feel better than compulsive diet- ing (although my students seem perfectly capable of combining the two in a double-punishing daily regime). But isn't the real problem here the tyrannized relation in which young women stand to these images (what- ever they may be), their sense that they personally are of no use, no value, ugly, unacceptable, without a future, unless they can get their bodies into the prescribed shape? How can feature writer Holly Brubach of the *New York Times* look around her—at the eating disorders, the exercise com- pulsions, the self-scrutiny and self-flagellation of young women today— and honestly write that "women, as they have gradually come into their own, have at last begun to feel at home in their bodies"?[16] Call me a "vic- tim feminist," but I just don't see it.

The triumphs that we wrest from those arenas of bodily improvement in which we are all supposed to be able to "just do it" are especially tenuous, reflecting the more generally unstable and desperate quality of life today. Both literally and figuratively there is an on-the-treadmill quality to the lives of most women (and men) as we struggle to achieve some sort of homeostasis in a culture that doesn't really want that from us. The practices of dieting and exercise succinctly capture this treadmill quality. Dieting, it has now been fairly decisively established, is self-defeating and self-perpetuating, for physiological as well as psychological reasons. Our bodies, thinking we are starving, slow down their metabolism and make it harder for us to burn up the few calories we are eating. Feelings of deprivation (especially combined with the demoralization of working hard at a diet and not getting very far) lead to bingeing, which leads to a sense of failure and hopelessness, and so more bingeing. Even the "successful" diet that results in the desired weight loss is a tenuous achievement. While dieting, pumped up with excitement over the project of "taking control," imagining our gorgeous bodies-to-be, we may be able to live (in hope, if not contentment) on broccoli and fat-free cheese. But once we reach our goal, this regime is no longer part of a *project* with a clear beginning and end. It's a life sentence. The "Healthy Choice" dinners stare at us: "This is how it's gonna be from now on, baby. Get used to it!" Most of us, understandably, don't feel we can.

Nowadays they tell us that the way to beat the diet syndrome is to exercise. So, many of us exercise in *order* to be able to eat. I have friends who use the StairMaster like a purge; after a big meal, they hop on it. The oddness of this practice notwithstanding, exercise can of course be healthy, stress-relieving, and empowering. It can also become a compulsive daily ritual around which people organize and subordinate all other activities, and frankly I've found this compulsiveness to be more common than not. I have friends and students who become intensely anxious when they miss just one day at the gym, who view their daily routines not as maintaining *health* or fitness but as a kind of finger-in-the-dam against disaster. I don't see this as paranoia but as a recognition of the reality that something in them is always near rebellion against the struggle to simply maintain the status quo. That rebellious little imp—the imp that wants to "let go" instead of stay in control—can't be let out of the bottle, ever. He's too dangerous.

I have serious problems with any theory, rhetoric, or narrative that masks these realities in favor of the inspiring (but inevitably deceptive) "success story" that, like the commercials and ads, captures a moment of "empowerment" and makes it stand for the reality of things. And so I come to *Babe,* which did not win the Academy Award but which moved and haunted me for weeks after I saw it. For a long time I tried to put my finger on just why that was. As I've said, I generally bristle against the triumphant success story. And *Babe,* like *Braveheart* (and *Rocky*), is a success story, a tale of individual empowerment and personal triumph against enormous odds, of questing, self-transformation, and, you might even say, transcendence of the body. A little pig, seemingly destined to be dinner, dreams of becoming a sheepdog—and he succeeds! Crowds cheer and tears flow. And so did mine (dry at the end of *Braveheart* and *Rocky*).

When I tried to explain to a more cynical friend why I loved the film, I grasped impotently at the available takes on the film then circulating in magazines and among intellectuals. "Allegory of social prejudice," that sort of thing. But I knew that wasn't exactly what did it for me, and when my friend pressed on, amazed that I could be so taken by what she saw as a sentimental fantasy, I realized that sentimental—in the sense of wrenching emotion while falsifying reality—was precisely what I found *Babe* not to be and that this was a large part of the reason why it moved me so powerfully. *Braveheart,* apparently based on real events, seemed like a slick commercial to me from start to finish. But *Babe*—a fable with talking animals—was for me a moment of reality in a culture dominated by fantasy.

Babe, on the face of it, seems far removed from the land of StairMasters, liposuction, and face-lifts—and it is certainly nothing like a Nike commercial. Babe's personal triumph takes place in a world that—as the film never lets us forget—permits such moments only for a very few. On the farm most of the animals eke their joy humbly from the circumscribed routines and roles allotted to them—and they are the lucky ones, the safe ones. The others—those who are destined to be eaten—tremble on little islands of temporary peace, the vulnerability and perishability of their existence always hovering before them. Death for them will not be accompanied by the dignifying hoopla of the big battle or the knowledge that they have made a statement for history. They will have no control over when death comes, and they will be unable to make the "why" of it more meaningful than the fact that others are luckier and more powerful and more arrogant than they are. This is a world in which those who can "just do it" are a privileged few. A world in which "agency" is real but limited and "empowerment" possible but hardly an everyday affair. A world in which the notion that we are "in charge," "in control," "at the reins" is strictly an illusion. Existence is precarious for the animals on the farm, as it is materially for many people, and as it is existentially for all of us, whether we recognize it or not. We can try to avoid this recognition with illusions of "agency," fantasies of staying young forever, and the distractions of "self-improvement," but it only lies in wait for us.

It is very important to the emotional truth of the film that Babe himself learns about the fragility of his safety. When he decides to go on anyway, it is not as a hopeful hero-to-be, dreaming of glory, but out of the simple fact that despite "the way things are" in the awful world he has learned about, there is still the unanswerable, unbreakable bond between him and the Boss. The men in *Braveheart* are bonded too. But, as Gibson directs it, the relationship amounts to a fraternity handshake, a pledge of affiliation; they're all pumped up, looking out over the grandeur of the countryside, ready to take up arms together. The bond between Babe and the Boss is established in a very different sort of exchange, in which each, in a Kierkegaardian leap of faith, bravely lets down his defenses in a moment of simple caring for and trust in the other. The taciturn and reserved farmer, trying to get depressed Babe to eat and obeying some wild impulse of inspiration, leaps up and performs an unrestrained, goofy hornpipe for him. Babe watches and, although he has heard "the way things are" from Fly, his surrogate-mother (pigs get eaten, even by the Boss and his wife), cedes final authority to the reasons of the heart. He eats.

Babe's world is the one we live in; heroic moments are temporary and connections with others are finally what sustain us. This is a reality we may be inclined to forget as we try to create personal scenarios that will feel like Olympic triumphs and give us the power and "agency" over our bodies and lives that the commercials promise. But we still feel the emotional tug of abandoned dreams of connection and intimacy and relationships that will feed us in the open-hearted way that the Boss feeds little Babe and Babe's eating feeds *him*. My cynical friend disliked the movie for—as she saw it—idealizing parent-child relations through scenes such as this (and Babe's relationship with his surrogate mother, the Border collie Fly). But unlike the Gerber's commercials that feature mother and child ensconced in an immaculate nursery, cocooned together by the accoutrements of cozy furniture, perfectly tended plants, good hair and skin, *Babe*'s images of caring and intimacy do not work through sugarcoating but by keeping the darker realities always on the horizon. They are the reason we need to take care of one another.

Babe is, of course, a success story. But unlike *Rocky, Flashdance, Braveheart,* and the many other fantasies of empowerment in which socially underprivileged heroes and heroines rise above their circumstances and transform themselves through discipline, will, and dazzling physical prowess, *Babe* is a fable about the power of "difference," of nonassimilation. The polite little pig, who talks to the sheep rather than snap and bark, turns out to be a better herder than the bossy Border collies! And in a significant way he transforms the culture and the values of the world he lives in. (It is suggested both at the beginning and the end of the film that attitudes toward pigs were never the same after Babe won the competition.) The *Rocky* model of success, like the "power feminism" model, is one of "making it" in a world that remains unchanged while the hero or heroine's body transforms itself to meet—and perhaps even surpass—the requirements of that world. This is what we celebrate when female athletes demonstrate that they can develop the strength and power of men, when "special" Olympians cross the finish lines in their competitions, when those who have struggled to lose weight finally squeeze into those size eight Calvin Kleins; the "outsider" is included by showing that he or she can "do it" too—on the terms of the culture. When the media celebrates such successes (and I do not deny that they are cause for celebration, as dramas of individual will, courage, and dedication), it usually leaves those cultural terms unquestioned.

Babe illustrates a different kind of success, one in which the "it" (of "Just Do It," "making it," "going for it") is interrogated and challenged. Those collies own the world (their own little world, that is) by virtue of their physical prowess and aggression, which—until Babe comes along—are the dominant values of that world. No one could have imagined that sheepherding could be done in any other way. How many of us have found ourselves struggling to prove our worth in worlds which do not value us or our contributions? Often, the pressure to conform is overwhelming. Babe, unable to transform his waddly little body and unwilling to transform his empathic little soul into a mean, lean, fighting machine, represents the possibility of resisting that pressure—and transforming "the way things are." In a culture in which people are shamed for their "defects" and differences and seek safety in conformity, this may be a fantasy. But it is a precious one, one more worthy of our imaginations and ambitions— and our children's, surely—than "Just Do It!"

Babe is a fable and presents its message through the conventions of that genre, not through gritty realism. A glorious triumph is the reward for the "alternative" values that the little pig represents. Few of us experience such definitive or resounding validation of our efforts. But it is not necessary to win the big race in order to transform "the way things are." All of us, in myriad small ways, have the capacity to do this, because nothing that we do is a self-contained, disconnected, isolated event. Seemingly minor gestures of resistance to cultural norms can lay deep imprints on the lives of those around us. Unfortunately, gestures of capitulation do so as well. Consider the message sent by the mother who anxiously monitors her own weight and ships her daughter off to Jenny Craig at the first sign that her child's body is less than willowy, or the father who teases his wife (perhaps in front of their daughter) for being "out of shape." I don't mean to sound harsh; these responses may reflect personal insecurity, concern about the social acceptability of loved ones, panic over a child's future. But when we demonstrate seamless solidarity with our culture of images, we make its reign over the lives of those we love just a little bit stronger. And we unwittingly promote for them a life on the cultural treadmill.

I have learned a great deal about the extremes of that treadmill existence from my students' journals and from conversations with them in my office. Yes, my students know that as long as they keep up their daily hours at the gym, they can feel pumped up, look like Madonna, and burn enough calories so perhaps they will not have to throw up after dinner. But how, they wonder, can they possibly keep it up their entire lives? They know there is no equilibrium there, that the conditions of their feeling all right about themselves are *precarious.* Here is where *Babe* does speak to the situation of those who try to stop those breasts from sagging, thighs from spreading, wrinkles from forming. The parable not only makes visible more basic struggles that our obsession with appearance masks but also presents us with a metaphor for the *pathos* of that seemingly "superficial" obsession. The little pig performs in the final competition without any solid assurance of a happy ending. Even as he herds the sheep into the pen, he has not been told, in so many words, that he will be spared the carving knife. He wins the sheepherding trials, and, as is customary, the farmer utters the standard words "real" dogs hear at the end of their runs. "That'll do, Pig. That'll do." A formality usually—but in the context of Babe's long struggle, these words say more, both to Babe and to the viewer. They represent, I believe, an acknowledgment that so many of us fervently long for in our lives—and are so rarely given. So many of us feel like Babe, trying our hardest to become something valued and loved, uncertain about whether we will ever be granted the right to simply exist. "That'll do. That'll do." These are words to break the heart. Enough. You've worked hard enough. I accept you. You can rest.

P.C., O.J., AND TRUTH

Over the past ten years we have witnessed an increasing polarization in what has come to be known as the "culture wars." As these wars have progressed, my basic allegiances have remained clear, but I've become increasingly frustrated with the public theater of the conflict, as performed by both "right" and "left."

I am sick of hearing feminists and multiculturalists described as a brigade of P.C. fanatics out to purge all Dead White Males from the college curriculum (as a philosopher, I also have to laugh at this; if we purge our DWMs, there's not much left). But the left has drawn its caricatures too; I have colleagues who are all too quick to demonize as "essentialist," "ethnocentric," and even "racist" anyone who hints at belief in a shared human nature or even dares talk about a shared *cultural* context. I get furious when sophisticated critics of the myths of Western science are caricatured by physicists as denying the laws of gravity, as they frequently were by defenders of Alan Sokol, who hoaxed the cultural studies journal *Social Text* into publishing as a serious critique a jargon-clogged parody of postmodern views on objectivity. But I find postmodern dogma intellectually stifling and clubby, and I sometimes think I will scream if I see the terms "site," "negotiate," and "inscribed" stuffed together in the same sentence one more time. Having studied the historical evidence, I agree with critics of extreme Afrocentrism that Egypt is not the plundered source of every important doctrine in Greek philosophy. But I want those critics to acknowledge—much more emphatically than they seem willing to—that traditional philosophical histories have effaced the significant contributions of Egypt and Mesopotamia, that Afrocentrism is the mirror image of the equally skewed Eurocentrism that has shaped our narratives until now.

I have frequently wished (a fruitless wish, I know; I'm not naive) that each side in the "culture wars" would acknowledge the extremes of its own position and so move the conversation to something less cartoon-like. During the Sokol *affaire* I often wondered how the debate might have proceeded if the editors of *Social Text* had been able to acknowledge that there are indeed self-feeding and pretentious tendencies within post-modernism—as within virtually every other academic culture—and had given credit to Sokol for forcing them out of the clubhouse and into public view. Such a response, I believe, would have done more to bust Sokol's stereotypes than the pages of defensive explanation and "refutation" that issued from the editors and their supporters. But then, too, I would want Sokol and his supporters to admit that his parody sends up the excesses of postmodernism at the expense of creating a badly distorted picture of what the academic left looks like, thus contributing to the increasingly polarized and inflamed nature of the culture wars.[1]

I deeply believe that acknowledging a region of validity to an opposing point of view is often all that is required to turn a fight between self-perpetuating caricatures into a real conversation. Of course, the culture wars are not a heated "conversation" among disputing friends at a dinner table. There are deep differences, commitments, and social interests at stake, and I'm certainly not suggesting that a little open-mindedness would bring an end to the conflagration. But I do think it's useful to imagine what a depolarizing perspective might look like, one that begins with the premise that no party in the debate—in any debate—is pure. That's part of what I will try to do in this essay, focusing on what seems to be the heart of the right's critique of the left: that we have abandoned truth in favor of politics.

My argument in this essay is multifaceted. It also examines some controversial and highly charged contemporary issues and events—such as the O. J. Simpson trial—through a set of concerns and connections that are rather different from those that have recently dominated public conversation. I am trying to cut a different path through the forest, or perhaps better put, to landscape the terrain in a slightly different way, so that certain topographical features will stand out against the ones that are currently so prominent as to obscure all else. But I recognize too that this is a terrain on which many people stand with firmly planted flags, ready to "read" anyone who utters certain words or makes certain moves as an enemy. (In part, it is just these sorts of reactions that this piece tries to move beyond.) For all these reasons, the potential for misinterpretation and misunderstanding of this piece is high and the requirements for clarity and precision on my part are great. In the interests of such clarity, I'm going to begin in the hopefully not too ponderous mode of outlining in advance my plan for this piece.

In the first section, "Just Who Has Abandoned Truth Here?" I will briefly sketch some defining moments in the development of the right's position in the culture wars, from Bloom through D'Souza and the emergence of the inflammatory rhetoric of "P.C.," with a view to exposing the inaccuracy and even perversity of the right's claim to be the guardian of truth. Working with an illustration from Hegel, I will argue that those who complain that feminists and multiculturalists are trashing the classical canon and its eternal verities are actually themselves advocating a form of censorship of the classics. The defenders of Truth emerge, ironically, as concealers of the truth.

In "Beyond Diversity," however, I will explore what the left has contributed to the public perception that it has abandoned the search for truth in favor of the representation of sheer "diversity"—the multiplication and encouraging of equal respect for all cultures, all points of view, all interpretations of texts and events. I argue in this section that diversity rhetoric *has* tended to dominate in the left's public presentation of itself and that it has fed into existing caricatures. More important, the diversity model is inadequate for an understanding of the social, cultural, and political inequalities of the world we live in—and distressingly supportive of the kind of relativistic "you've got your truth, I've got mine" thinking that our students are already learning from television talk shows and even from media analysis and commentary on events like the Rodney King and O. J. Simpson trials.

In the following section, "Epistemology and O.J.," I will leave the culture wars per se to explore the notion I've just introduced, namely, that with the media as our prime instructors we have been developing some very problematic *cultural* norms and practices with regard to truth seeking. If everyone has his or her own "truth," how do we decide what to believe in any given circumstance? It is my contention that as a culture—all of us, whether we are black, white, male, female, young, old—are learning from our image-dominated culture to respond most powerfully and to give our ultimate assent to what seems to us to be the most compelling *story* or picture, the narrative plot or set of images that makes most sense to us, coheres with our picture of the world, or has simply been presented in the most convincing way by the most trusted or skillful storyteller. Once we have the story that "rings" true, that has the "feel" of reality, the sifting and evaluation of factual material often becomes secondary, especially if the quantity of evidence is overwhelming and we have been given little guidance on how to weigh and judge it.

This is the context in which I discuss the Simpson criminal trial verdict, not as a unique event but as an exemplary event, and as exemplary not of racial issues but of what philosophers call epistemological issues, that is, our ideas and practices concerning how (and if) we arrive at our knowledge of things. The 1995 trial of O. J. Simpson was a seismograph on which were registered some of the deepest fault lines of our culture. All of these fault lines were affected by racial dynamics, as everything is in this culture. But not all of those fault lines are most adequately analyzed with racial dynamics at the forefront. I have always believed that trying to theorize everything at once does not permit us to *really* grasp anything at all (except, perhaps, for the sheer spectacle of diversity). I prefer the more analytic approach of pulling threads, one at a time, from the infinitely tangled complexity of things, *focusing* on each, and then "putting it all together" again. "All together" is the reality of things—a dense and woolly ball composed of a multitude of elements (such as race, class, gender, and history) that are not truly separable. But finite human minds are not equipped to see reality "whole"; we need to analyze, to take things apart and examine their relations, in order to come to whatever (partial) understanding of the complexity of things is possible for us.

This sort of multidimensional, analytical thinking about the Simpson case was continually discouraged by the media. Think about the way the verdict was described by commentators. It was "about" payback for white racism. About the purchasing power of the rich and famous. About bedazzlement by fame and glamour. About the jurors' lack of education and knowledge. Well, maybe it was "about" all these things and maybe about others too. But perhaps to speak of the verdict as "about" something—as though it were a movie or a novel with a theme rather than a complex historical event—is to reveal an unwillingness to analyze, evaluate, and adjudicate in precise and rigorous ways. Instead, the media goes with the most compelling "take," the story that will be readily digested, capture the imagination, entertain and emotionally appeal. Complexity doesn't sell.

"Either/or" reductionism was rampant throughout the media coverage of the trial and also, not surprisingly, in ordinary people's thinking. Either Mark Fuhrman was a contemptible racist or O.J. was a murderer. If you thought that Fuhrman was a contemptible racist, then that let O.J. off the hook. Either the trial was "all about race" or it "had nothing to do with race." And so on. At least some of the jurors reasoned in this way as well. Forewoman Brenda Moran said in a postverdict interview that she had found the domestic abuse evidence irrelevant—not just unconvincing, which would have been entirely appropriate reasoning, but *irrelevant*. "This was a murder trial, not domestic abuse," she insisted. "If you want to get tried for domestic abuse, go in another courtroom and get tried for that." Columnist Kathleen Parker commented that this was "akin to saying obesity is unrelated to eating. If it's eating you want to talk about, go somewhere else. This discussion is about fat."[2]

My focus in "Epistemology and O.J."—two words that probably have not yet appeared together in a sentence, even given the voluminous literature on the case—will be on fault lines that the Simpson case disclosed, not on racial politics but on how we reason, think, evaluate nowadays. In the last section of this essay, "Truth as Seeing Through Illusion," I *will* be looking at race—and gender as well—in connection with the Simpson trial. Here, using a class of my own as an illustration, I offer a model of truth seeking that is organized around neither the protection of eternal verities nor the mere representation of and respect for diversity. I believe that both the "old" canon and multicultural curricula have an important place in education. But they need to be supplemented by efforts to help our students learn to critically "see through" the sound bites and quick takes, the slick images and sensationalizing stories created by the media. We talked a lot about race and gender in the class I will describe, which for those who are looking for "P.C." behind the door of every feminist classroom is sufficient reason to call in the freedom fighters. But my aims were actually quite traditional. What we were doing in my class—as many others on the left are doing as well, sometimes despite their own rhetoric—was searching for truth.

JUST WHO HAS ABANDONED TRUTH HERE?

During the culture wars a concern for "truth" has come to be seen as the sole possession of those on the "right" flank. It wasn't always this way. An article from the September 2, 1987, *Chronicle of Higher Education* headlines "Humanities and Social Sciences: The Sound of Barriers Falling" and reports that "a new attentiveness to history, development and process" has disciplines questioning their traditional boundaries and narratives. Developments in black studies and women's studies are described as opening up entrenched paradigms, and scholars as diverse as sociologist Robert Bellah, philosophers Richard Bernstein and Samuel Gorovitz, theologian Martin Marty, classicist Gordon Williams, and feminist literary scholar Catharine Stimpson are quoted, speaking excitedly about the "new questions" and "challenged assumptions" in their fields.

Not everyone, of course, was equally thrilled with the new questions and challenges. The year 1987 also saw the publication of Alan Bloom's *The Closing of the American Mind: How Higher Education Has Failed Democracy and Improverished the Souls of Today's Students.*[3] Bloom's central premise was that contemporary academic "openness" was actually a shutdown of belief in reason, standards, enduring values. Feminists were not interested in truth or knowledge but in making sure that inferior women writers had their share of educational airtime. Ex-hippies and sixties politicos, now college teachers, were preaching cultural relativism and sexual liberation instead of teaching great books. This was perhaps the moment when the wars began. The immediate popularity of *The Closing of the American Mind* (it sold over a million copies in the first few months and remained on the best-seller list for a year) suggested that Bloom had hit a live nerve in directing attention to the state of higher education in America. He had also subtly politicized the terms of the conversation that was to ensue. The educational reforms that the *Chronicle* had spoken of in terms of *conceptual* and *intellectual* challenge, Bloom had redescribed as a *social* agenda. The educational tradition had not been challenged by new paradigms but by mindless educational egalitarianism, the misguided notion that democracy would best be served by teaching students equal respect for all cultures and lifestyles. The questioning of established knowledge (surely no new thing in the history of ideas) was on its way to becoming "political correctness."

In the last ten years the Bloomian representation of the academic left has come to dominate in the popular imagination. But with Reaganite polemicist Dinesh D'Souza the charges against the left mutated into a far more provocative form. In *Illiberal Education: The Politics of Race and Sex on Campus* (1991), D'Souza claimed that a totalitarian academic elite had emerged, forcing feminism and cultural diversity into the college curriculum, policing thought and expression on campuses, and fomenting a "victim's revolution" in the previously high-minded groves of academe.[4] The shift in the titles of Bloom's and D'Souza's books, from Bloom's imagery of closed minds and lost souls to D'Souza's complaints about "illiberal" politics, is significant. For Bloom, the cultural war (although he never uses the term "culture war," he is surely its paterfamilias) is between promiscuous relativism and fidelity to intellectual standards; for D'Souza it's all about "coercion" versus "freedom." Colleges and universities need to be protected, not (as Bloom had argued) from the dissolution of enduring values but from the enforcements of "political correctness." The popular media—*Harper's, Atlantic, Time, Newsweek*—had already been on this track. A 1990 *Newsweek* cover—a good indication of the popular media slant on events—reads: "Watch What You Say. Thought Police. There's a Politically Correct Way to Talk about Race, Sex and Ideas. Is This the New Enlightenment—or the New McCarthyism?" By 1992 the specter of "political correctness" had so infiltrated the contemporary imagination that when a Barbie-type doll appeared on the market with proportions more representative of the average female it was described by reporters as "a politically correct Barbie, a doll with a social agenda."

Indignation over "political correctness" was fueled by D'Souza's and later critics' continual conflation of curriculum reform with the movement for speech codes on college campuses; curriculum reform thus became associated with censorship. In 1993 the fire was fanned anew by

Camille Paglia and Katie Roiphe, who added the regulation of *sexual* conduct to the list of crimes against freedom committed by feminists and other members of the "correctness police" on campuses.[5] Now we were also puritans (an old charge against feminists) and whiners, crying rape and harassment rather than taking responsibility for our own behavior. Gradually, a collective nightmare-archetype of the academic left emerged. In 1994 Christopher Hitchens in *Vanity Fair* wrote of the "cult of P.C.":

> The cult of P.C. . . . . is probably best understood as a sort of mutation of the 60s, in which all the crappy aspects of that decade have been fused. The idealism and élan are defunct, while in hybrid form all the sectarian hysteria, all the juvenile intolerance, and all the paranoia and solipsism have been retained. And a toxic slogan of the period—*The personal is political*—has now spread like a weed, so that the undergraduate population of the country is being encouraged to turn into a generation of snitches, sneaks, and informers, running in tears to the dean at the least intrusion upon their "personal space."

While the notion that knowledge is at stake has recently again become prominent in the culture wars,[6] the spectre of P.C. continues to dominate the scene. From D'Souza on, the raison d'être of feminism and multiculturalism has been presented by critics not as a coherent vision of liberal education (however misguided, as Bloom believed) but as the subordination of truth to politics. In 1995 former chairs of the National Endowment for the Humanities William Bennett and Lynne Cheney "came out slugging" (as the *Chronicle* put it) against the NEH: "Many academics and artists," Cheney claimed, "now see their purpose not as revealing truth and beauty, but as achieving social and political transformation."[7] According to this construction of the feminist and multiculturalist "agenda," the chief, if not only, rationale for the inclusion of historically neglected perspectives within the liberal arts curriculum is to address and redress the grievances of oppressed groups. Thus, the goal is not education but curricular therapy for the wounded and marginalized, aimed—as George Will put it—at "making women and minorities 'feel good' about themselves."[8]

A few quotes will give a sense of how pervasive this construction is. The "issue" for multiculturalism, as described by Arthur Schlesinger, "is how to give various participants in America's drama *their due*"; the solution has been "therapeutic history," aimed at cultural affirmation and the nurture of self-esteem rather than the "exercise of intellectual disinterestedness." The National Association of Scholars has described multiculturalism as "oppression studies," a motif picked up by D'Souza, who writes of a widespread "victims' revolution" on campus, whose "mission" is to "advance the interests of the previously disenfranchised." In the *New York Review of Books* in 1991 historian C. Vann Woodward says that the "cause" being championed by multiculturalism is "minority rights," as minorities demand "a curriculum of their own."[9]

Enlivening the representation of multiculturalism as the political agenda of special interest groups are the numerous depictions of multiculturalists as "barbarians" (Hilton Kramer), "a tangle of squabbling nationalities . . . a quarrelsome spatter of enclaves, ghettoes" (Schlesinger), a "new tribalism," a "tower of babel" (*N. Y. Times* columnist Richard Bernstein, not to be confused with philosopher Richard Bernstein), "ethnic cheerleading" (D'Souza). Always, these racialized (and, in the case of D'Souza's metaphor, genderized) images of primitive, Hobbesian scramble and self-interest are juxtaposed to some unified, civilized "life of the mind," "common culture," or "universal heritage" that is under siege by the rabble. We clearly see this in Cheney's invocation of some mythical, apolitical time when artists and writers were devoted to "truth" and "beauty" in their pristine state.

These rhetorical tirades suggest, inaccurately, that feminists and multiculturalists are uninterested in truth or beauty—and that Bennett, Cheney, and their colleagues have no political agenda. They also conveniently overlook the fact that the "common" culture so nostalgically longed for was actually a monoculture whose much vaunted "objectivity" is a myth. Our dominant Western traditions have marked history as beginning and ending only with what is seen through the eyes of the European male—an exceedingly *subjective* understanding and one that has shaped the official conceptualizations of philosophy, religion, and literature. Why is telling the truth about this *bias* seen as "trashing" Western civilization, while hiding it is described as an exercise in "intellectual disinterestedness"? There's something fishy going on, surely, when protecting the Truth requires hiding the truth.

Far from being single-mindedly devoted to truth, as Cheney maintains, the history of the West—Western philosophy, for example—has usually been presented to students via a kind of de facto censorship of many important passages and ideas. So, when I was an undergraduate, my teachers simply omitted from our readings various philosophers' pronouncements on the lesser rationality of women, slaves, and Africans, viewing these ideas as irrelevant to their philosophical systems (or perhaps, at the other extreme, too threatening to the image of Western philosophy as universal in its concerns). Consider, as one example, Hegel on Africa, in his introduction to *The Philosophy of History* (1840):

> Generally speaking, Africa is a continent enclosed within itself, and this
> enclosedness has remained its chief characteristic. It consists of three
> parts, which are essentially distinct from one another. . . . The first of
> these is Africa proper, the land to the south of the Sahara desert. . . .
> The second is the land to the north of the desert, a coastal region which
> might be described as European Africa. And the third is the region of the
> Nile, the only valley land of Africa, which is closely connected with Asia.
>
> North Africa lies on the Mediterranean Sea and extends westwards
> along the Atlantic. . . . It could be said that this whole region does not
> really belong to Africa but forms a single unit with Spain, for both are

part of the same basin. . . . This portion of Africa, like the Near East, is oriented toward Europe; it should and must be brought into the European sphere of influence, as the French have successfully attempted in recent times.

Egypt . . . is one of those regions which we have described as constituting a focus, as destined to become the centre of a great and independent culture.

Africa proper is the characteristic part of the whole continent as such. . . . It has no historical interest of its own, for we find its inhabitants living in barbarism and savagery in a land which has not furnished them with any integral ingredient of culture. From the earliest historical times, Africa has remained cut off from all contacts with the rest of the world; it is the land of gold, forever pressing in upon itself, and the land of childhood, removed from the light of self-conscious history and wrapped in the dark mantle of night. . . .

In this main portion of Africa, history is in fact out of the question. Life there consists of a succession of continent happenings and surprises. No aim or state exists whose development could be followed; and there is no subjectivity, but merely a series of subjects who destroy one another. . . . We shall now attempt to define the universal spirit and form of the African character. . . . This character, however, is difficult to comprehend, because it is so totally different from our own culture, and so remote and alien in relation to our own mode of consciousness. . . . The characteristic feature of the negroes is that their consciousness has not yet reached an awareness of any substantial objectivity—for example, of God or the law—in which the will of man could participate and in which he could become aware of his own being. The African, in his undifferentiated and concentrated unity, has not yet succeeded in making this distinction between himself as an individual and his essential universality, so that he knows nothing of an absolute being which is other and higher than himself. . . . All our observations of African man show him as living in a state of savagery and barbarism, and he remains in this state to the present day. The negro is an example of animal man in all his savagery and lawlessness, and if we wish to understand him at all, we must put aside all our European attitudes. We must not think of a spiritual God or of moral laws; to comprehend him correctly, we must abstract from all reverence and morality, and from everything which we call feeling. All this is foreign to man in his immediate existence, and nothing consonant with humanity is to be found in his character. For this very reason, we cannot properly feel ourselves into his nature, no more than that of a dog, or of a Greek as he kneels before the statue of Zeus. . . .

We shall therefore leave Africa at this point, and it need not be mentioned again. For it is an unhistorical continent, with no movement or development of its own. And such events as have occurred in it—i.e. in its northern region—belong to the Asiatic and European worlds. Carthage, while it lasted, represented an important phase; but as a Phoenician colony, it belongs to Asia. Egypt will be considered as a stage in the movement of the human spirit from east to west, but it has no part in the spirit of Africa. What we understand as Africa proper is that unhistorical and undeveloped land which is still enmeshed in the natural spirit, and which has to be mentioned here before we cross the threshold of world history itself.[10]

I have quoted Hegel at length here to give some idea of the richness of a passage such as this and of what is obscured when it is written out of the curriculum. In the classroom one can use a quote like this in many ways. First of all, it provides a wonderful example of how facts can be ordered to accommodate belief (to my mind, one of the first epistemological lessons students should learn). Although Africa is described geographically as a "continent enclosed within itself," North Africa and Egypt do not "belong" to it, have no "part in it," but instead "belong" to Europe.

Why? Not by virtue of geography but because these were centers of "culture" and *Africa,* by definition, represents "barbarism and savagery" without "any integral ingredient of culture." "African" and "civilized" are mutually exclusive terms. Hegel goes on to provide a kind of blueprint of the paradigmatic cultural associations and images that go into the representation of the African as a primitive savage, living in a state of undeveloped consciousness, immersed in nature, and barely one notch above purely instinctual existence—"animal man," as Hegel puts it.

Students reading this quote recognize that such images are far from idiosyncratic to Hegel. But I don't like to leave such recognitions on the level of vague and impressionistic ideas about "racism" and "prejudice." Instead I lead students through some concrete cultural versions of the Hegelian paradigm—in later scholarly writings on Africa, in evolutionary accounts of racial difference, in art and literature, and in popular culture—from James Breasted to Joseph Conrad to discourse on AIDS to a recent *Vanity Fair* article on actor Laurence Fishburne, which described him as "a dangerous, magnificent beast" who is "not afraid to be savage." So too the image of the instinctual African savage is exploited (perhaps unconsciously) when Kramer, Bernstein, and others describe multiculturalists and Afrocentrists as squabbling tribes. In my classes we also look at the ways in which animal imagery is employed in other racist discourses, the literature of anti-Semitism, for example.

More general philosophical and conceptual issues can also be abstracted from the Hegel quotation and critically explored: the philosophical identification of humanness with certain forms of consciousness and self-awareness, the evolutionary conception of history as developmental, or the status of "race." On the last, the Hegelian notion that Egypt is not a part of Africa—later represented via European claims about the "whiteness" of the Egyptians—has continued to haunt us in the twentieth century, most recently in Afrocentric attempts to "correct" Hegel by insisting that the Egyptians *were* black. These attempts are misguided, as many race theorists would argue, because they retain the mistaken premise that what "race" the Egyptians were can be decided through recourse to some transparent set of biological facts. Race, while it partakes of biological traits, is not reducible to biology and always involves social decisions about how to cluster and categorize those traits. The Hegel text can function as an occasion to raise such timely and important questions.

Africa, of course, did *not* exist in a state of primitive, undifferentiated prehistory before European colonization (as Hegel argues) but had cultures and religions of its own. Intellectual rigor, not "political correctness," demands that we teach our students this. When I do so, my intention is not to discredit Hegel as a philosopher (if racism and sexism were enough to discredit thinkers, we'd be taking very few major historical figures seriously) but to show students the deep historical sources of still-living ideologies that may shape their own ideas and behavior and to trace the historical consequences, arguments, and debates they have generated. Philosophers, of course, participate in cultural events and ideas that are broader than the philosophical "conversation." Arguing that passages such as this from Hegel be included in the canon is *not* equivalent to "trashing" Dead White Males or giving African Americans a special history of philosophy "of their own." I examine this quote in order to provide *all* my students with a deeper, more culturally informed understanding of the elements that have shaped Western philosophical traditions, the disturbing ones as well as the glorious ones. It's about truth-seeking, not therapy.

BEYOND "DIVERSITY"

Unfortunately, some on the left in the culture wars *do* seem to view curriculum reform as therapy for the dispossessed and disenfranchised. Or at least they talk that way. Catharine Stimpson in a presidential address to the Modern Languages Association spoke of "the promise of bringing dignity to the dispossessed and self-empowerment to the disempowered";[11]

sociologist Renato Rosaldo, defending Stanford's curricular revision, asks how a Chicano student could be expected to find her identity in Plato and Aristotle.[12] Literary critic Stanley Fish's description of the multicultural curriculum as an "ethnic carnival or festival of cultures,"[13] it could be argued, simply looks at Schlesinger's "tangle of nationalities" through the eyes of a more appreciative sightseer. It's not that I don't hope, along with Stimpson, Rosaldo, and Fish, that wounds of exclusion will be healed (or at least addressed) by changes in our curriculum. But talking as though this is the *point* of such changes only reinforces the D'Souza/Cheney version of multiculturalism as about politics, not truth. It also identifies the representation of *diversity*—listening to "voices," attending to "difference"—as the main goal of educational reform.

This emphasis on diversity, to my mind, has been a big mistake. While there is undeniable value both in studying the culturally familiar (which will vary among students, of course) and in exposing students to worlds with which they are unfamiliar (and about which they may hold ignorant stereotypes or be dismissive), the question remains as to what they are going to *do* with all this "difference" beyond celebrating it, tasting all the dishes on the smorgasbord table. The world is not a collection of discrete and disconnected items, each existing in its own self-contained and self-justifying universe of values, but an infinite set of relations. Without analytical and critical tools to assess and evaluate those relations, why should our students prefer one set of cultural ideas or arguments to another, except on the basis of the whimsies of "taste" or individual comfort? If I had to choose, I'd much prefer that they learn to analyze, interpret, critique, and evaluate *one* thing (a classical text, a current event, a popular movie) in all its complexity—including issues of race, gender, history, and power—than that they be taken on a sightseeing tour of the globe.

Ideally, of course, a curriculum should provide places both for the cultivation of what philosopher Maria Lugones has called "world-travelling" habits of thought and for the development of critical, analytical thinking.

The two can and should support each other—as, for example, a critical analysis of the Hegel quote I presented can only be deepened by knowledge of actual African literatures and cultures, and vice versa. Our students need to be jostled awake from their culture-bound "arrogant perceptions"; they also need, however, to learn the historical origins of those perceptions, the social relations that sustain them, the systems of thought in which they are embedded, and so on. Simply introducing students to different voices is not enough, if only because Western culture has *not* been a celebration of diversity, and treating it as such cannot explain the actual inequalities of the world we live in. But the diversity model has tended to dominate—in the public face of the curriculum debates, if not in the reality of what's happening on campuses.

The diversity or "ethnic festival" model of education has enabled mono-culturalists like D'Souza, Bennett, Schlesinger, and Will to present themselves to the public as our culture's bastion of discriminative thinking, dedicated to objectivity and "rigor" rather than the uncritical, politically motivated advancement of marginalized peoples. And the academic left, for its part, has sometimes seemed all too content to let Bennett and company appropriate and carry the language and banner of "truth." Early on in the culture wars high visibility was bestowed on certain lit-crit gurus (often from Duke University) who delighted in aggressively challenging notions of "objective truth" and "standards" of discrimination, insisting that what one believed (on questions of whom to include in the canon, for example) was reducible to one's political *interests,* one's "stake" in things. Frank Lentricchia was quoted in the *Chronicle of Higher Education* as claiming that "nothing that passes through a human mind doesn't have its origin in sexual, economic, and racial differentiae."[14] Stanley Fish, similarly, argued that "once you have subtracted from the accidents of class, race, gender, and political circumstance, what is it that you have left?"[15] Statements such as this confirmed, in many people's eyes, that the right was accurate in describing the left as dismissing Western civilization as racist, sexist, classist, with nothing remaining to offer students. Fish has continued to fan the flames of right-wing caricatures; recently, commenting on the Sokol/ *Social Text* episode on the *New York Times* Op-Ed page, he compared scientific laws to the rules of baseball, suggesting that the principle of gravity is no less a matter of cultural "convention" and invention than what constitutes a fair or foul ball.

Houston Baker's much-quoted line that the choice between two literary works "is no different than choosing between a hoagy and a pizza" did a lot of damage too. "I am one," said Baker, "whose career is dedicated to the day when we have a disappearance of those standards."[16] Such ideas have been readily exploited in the many ridiculous imaginary choices that critics of multiculturalism pose in their caricatures: "To prefer Elizabeth Bishop to Judith Krantz is not of the same order as sanctioning the inequality of wealth in the United States," wrote Irving Howe. "To prefer Shakespeare to Sidney Sheldon is not of the same order as approving the hierarchy of the nomenklatura in Communist dictatorships."[17] There may be something to Howe's ridicule of the high-mindedness and heavy-handedness of some would-be academic guerrillas. But his satirical use of Judith Krantz and Sidney Sheldon as imaginary candidates for canon-inclusion trivializes and degrades the artistry and insight of those previously noncanonical writers who actually are now being included—for example, writers like Toni Morrison and Chinua Achebe, who, I would argue, meet any criteria one might care to propose.

My point is that the "hoagy/pizza" analogy doesn't allow for such an argument about Morrison and Achebe or any other writer. Surely this is throwing out the baby with the bathwater; it's excessive, it's unnecessary, and it kills the thing we love. In criticizing Timeless Truths we don't *need* to abandon all standards for distinguishing between edifying, moving, serious literature and fleetingly entertaining pulp fiction. The pragmatic strain in philosophy urges us to see truth, as Richard Rorty puts it, "not as a name of an authority" but as another way of describing a "search for stable and useful beliefs."[18] A *search,* not triumphant arrival at the finish line. *Stable* beliefs, not permanently enduring verities. Embracing the temporal, provisional nature of our conclusions, analyses, arguments does not entail descent into absolute chaos. In any given situation there are still reasons to believe some accounts over others, to deem some works "greater" than others. But these judgments are not to be seen as indelibly etched on a stone tablet, handed down to us from the heavens. They have to be defended, not simply buttressed by "tradition," and they can change.

In *retaining* evaluative distinctions—between, for instance, the superficial and the profound, the narrow and the broad, the mystifying and the credible—we are then also equipped to insist, against Cheney, that those who argue that the old canon is just fine as it is are not *necessarily* always on the side of "truth" and "beauty." Saul Bellow has written some dazzling novels, and if I were teaching a course on twentieth-century literature I would probably include him. But when he asked, "Where is the Tolstoy of the Zulus, the Proust of the Paduans?"[19] his profound cultural *ignorance* revealed itself. But we can't accuse Bellow of being ignorant unless we also believe that there is something he should *know.* And as long as knowledge is seen as merely a matter of political interests or ideology, then we are left only with the charge that Bellow is being "racist"—accurate perhaps, but not a sturdy basis on which to reorganize a curriculum.

EPISTEMOLOGY AND O.J.

Opening our students' minds cannot be conceived simply as equivalent to offering a broader menu of equally tasty cultural dishes—or equally valid interpretations. We have to provide contexts in which perspectives can offer themselves, challenge each other, and hold each other to responsible and mutually acceptable *intellectual* standards.

This is something of a new "cause" for me. When I was in college in the sixties, Thomas Kuhn's *Structure of Scientific Revolutions* had only just been published, academic feminism did not exist, and the disciplines were chugging along, blithely dispensing their racial and gender biases in the name of "methodology," "reality," "truth," "greatness," "clear thinking," and so on. Disciplines were not yet even conscious of themselves as having disciplinary idiosyncrasies or embodying paradigms or assumptions peculiar to themselves. Within many quarters of the discipline in which I was trained—philosophy—it used to be considered (and still is, by some) the highest sport to point out fatal flaws in the arguments of others: "patently false," "obviously groundless," "dead wrong," "spurious," "dreadful howler." Even as an undergraduate I was perplexed by the notion that ideas could suffer anything as simple or straightforward or final as a fatal wound, and I hated the dismissive bullying of the flaw detectors. They seemed to believe that they had a kind of X-ray vision into the truth of things, while those who didn't see things "correctly" were obviously blind. My early writings, like the work of many others of my generation of feminist philosophers, were devoted to challenging such arrogant, simplistic notions of truth and insisting on the perspectival, partial nature of all knowledge.

Our critique of the hubris of those who acted as though they had X-ray vision or a God's-eye view was, I believe, necessary and inevitable. But lately a historical corner has been turned which makes challenging the arrogance of philosopher-kings culturally redundant. Worse, talk about perspective and point of view has itself mutated into a new form of epistemological bravado. Feminist philosophers had argued that *having* a "point of view" was inevitable but had never claimed (Alan Bloom to the contrary) that all points of view are equal in legitimacy. (It would have been extremely difficult to mount a critique of sexism or racism on such grounds!) Today, to have a "point of view" has become equivalent to having "one's own truth." More and more of my undergraduate students no longer seem required to explain or defend their positions or interpretations against challenge; simply believing them strongly is good enough. Many of our students have learned, from talk shows, music videos, and unfortunately from some of their courses, that all realities are equal. When a colleague of mine corrected a student's spelling, the student objected: "Well, that's *your* way of spelling it; I have mine." But this is not much less absurd than Holocaust-deniers describing the "Nazi point of view" as offering a different "standpoint" on history, as though determining whether the Holocaust happened is equivalent to studying differing interpretations of a literary text.

In the spring of 1995, before the Simpson verdict, I asked my undergraduate students what they thought about Simpson's guilt or innocence. "Oh, he's innocent!" said one (a young white man). "On what basis have you come to that conclusion?" I asked. "Well . . . I don't know . . . He's a football hero, and handsome, and seems nice and friendly, and, well . . . I just sorta see it that way." When I pressed him further, he just kept repeating: "I just sorta see it that way."

"I just see it that way." This has always been a poor excuse for argument, but in a contemporary context, where images and statistics and texts can be so skillfully and often deceptively manipulated, it is particularly shaky grounds for decisions. I don't think that the left or right flanks of the culture wars, if they were to come down from their ideological or theoretical platforms, would find much cause for disagreement here. Some on the left may argue for infinite interpretations in *theory*, but I believe that most are just as appalled as I am when racist or sexist "interpretations" are swallowed whole by our students. The right may argue, for political reasons, that multiculturalists rather than television are responsible for our students' inability to discriminate in rigorous and responsible ways. But although they might thus quarrel with my analysis of who or what is to blame, they *do* recognize the power of cultural imagery—they have a *moral* critique of pornography, rock music, and so forth.

What the right fails to see (or doesn't want to see, since it implicates consumer capitalism) is how our culture of images and image-making (*whatever* the moral content) is undermining the *epistemological* resources of our culture. And what the left fails to see is that the notion that reality is a "text"—a notion that has now invaded nonacademic discourse—is only making the situation worse. In the discussion that follows I will be looking at how these elements affected the O. J. Simpson trial and public discussion about it.

Let me begin by saying that arguments about the infinite interpretability of texts are not very good bedfellows for those who care about social justice. Shortly after the first Rodney King verdict, in May 1992, an article appeared in the *New York Times* entitled "The Power of a Video Image Depends on the Caption." True enough, as the verdict had made clear. But the author then goes on to argue that because "photographic images of all sorts remain essentially ambiguous," the King videotape "remains open to interpretation."[20] Surely this is just what the defense had counted on the jury's believing! We cannot claim that the video is "open to interpretation" and condemn the verdict at the same time.

This is what distresses me so much about those commentators who after the Simpson verdict suggested that the life experiences of the jurors not only affected their judgment (nothing new there)[21] but led them to their own valid "version" of what happened. I'm not talking here necessarily about those who agreed with the verdict—they, of course, would find the reasoning of the jurors legitimate—but rather about a position taken by many who may even have *disagreed* with the verdict but who felt that whites had no right to criticize it. (Many who argued in this way were, by the way, white.) Blacks and whites, it was emphasized, saw the case differently, and that may have been true. (It must be noted, however, media commentators to the contrary, that other factors affected people's perception besides race. All-white sports teams, for example, cheered the verdict. And Simpson was *not* a hero to many black academics and professionals.) But some commentators went on to suggest that anger at the verdict was unwarranted, *because* the histories and life experiences of the jury legitimated their decision. Such an idea, as trial analyst M. L. Rantala notes, "clearly implies that there are multiple truths."[22] It is to view the Simpson case, as a friend of mine noted, the way postmodernists view literature: no interpretation can be incorrect.

Now, openness to multiple interpretations—as a regulative principle of deliberation and dialogue—is surely a good thing. The philosophical fatal-flaw police have no sense of the world as complex and multisided; that's what makes them such simplistic thinkers and intellectual bullies. But believing that no interpetation can be incorrect is as destructive of reasoned, communal dialogue as dogmatic single-mindedness. Those who *have* a strong opinion don't feel an obligation to justify their conclusions; at the same time, others back away from any judgment at all, overwhelmed by complexity and feeling that they have no "right" to impose their point of view on others. So, they just withdraw from the fray. Many undergraduate students today—particularly white students, who are also fearful of being seen as racists—refuse to offer any opinion at all about the Simpson verdict. (The media, which have contributed so much to fomenting racial polarization around the trial, have utterly ignored what is arguably a major generation gap in public reactions to the verdict.) In one sense, I don't blame them; we baby-boomers have presented such a spectacle of hot-headed, intransigent hostility in our "dialogues" about the verdict, it's no wonder generation X-ers want to retreat to their headphones. But clearly something must be done to bring them back, or we'll have no public dialogue at all.

For critics of racism and sexism, to view the world as a text with infinite legitimate interpretations is to open a dangerous door. To believe, based on a careful examination of the evidence, that the Simpson jurors reached the correct verdict would be one thing. But to exempt this particular jury from criticism on the basis of their special experience and history is not only condescending but opens the door to rejoinders from defenders of the Simi Valley jurors. For if there are "black and white" truths in the Simpson case, so too, it could be argued, were there in the Rodney King trial. If the life histories and expectations of the Simpson jurors legitimized *their* judgment—if they did not have a responsibility to put the "version" that made emotional or historical sense to them to one side, to be measured against a painstaking sorting and interrogating of the evidence before them—then, it could be argued, neither did the the Simi Valley jurors in the first King trial have a responsibility to interrogate the horribly racist "version" of events that made sense to them.

I am not suggesting that what happened in the Simpson trial and what happened in the first King trial are equivalent. I'm pointing to the dangers of justifying any such verdicts on perspectivalist grounds. Moreover, I believe—and here my position may differ from that of others who are critical of the Simpson verdict—that racial knowledge (unlike racism) has a legitimate role to play in such deliberations. I believe that the image of Mark Fuhrman the lying, racist cop planting a bloody glove had a persuasive "reality" for many blacks that it lacked for even the most antiracist whites, as did the history of railroading, scapegoating, and violence against black men in this country. Whites who were outraged about the Simpson verdict, as though it was the first time in our country's history that a guilty man was set free, should recall that a policeman's perjury kept Medgar Evers' killer, Byron De la Beckwith, out of jail for thirty years. For many of the jurors, arguably, the record of racism in this country in itself raised doubts about Simpson's guilt—and legitimately so. Our judgments of what to believe do not depend only on what lies before us; history is a reality, too, which lends or withholds plausibility and persuasiveness to various possibilities. The history of racism in this country is real, not a fantasy of the black jurors; it's a matter of historical record. It *ought* to have been considered in any reasoned judgment about the likelihood of a police conspiracy.

To recognize that oppressive history does not mean, however—and this is a big "however"—that after evaluating all the evidence it is reasonable to come to the conclusion that such a conspiracy took place *in this particular case*. Similarly, I don't believe that the prevalence of child abuse in this culture makes it reasonable to come to the conclusion—on the basis of the evidence of that particular case—that Lyle and Eric Menendez killed their parents out of fear for their lives. In the case of both these juries, and also the first King jury, it is my judgment that certain ideas and images, lent credence by the compelling nature of the narratives presented by the lawyers, overpowered reason. Of course, the content of those ideas and images was very different in each of these trials. The "plot to frame O.J." narrative was buttressed for the O.J. jurors by the realities of the history of racism, while the "Rodney King resisting arrest" narrative was buttressed by racism itself, by the ideology of blacks as savage animals, which furnished the language and metaphors (for example, King's groans as "bearlike") for the reconstructed video that encouraged the Rodney King jurors to see the beating from the policeman's "point of view." But in each case it was the power of image and narrative, not the examination of evidence, that generated doubt.

Simpson defense lawyer Barry Scheck was open about this strategy. "What people really do," he told Lawrence Schiller, "is listen to testimony and turn it into a story that makes sense to them . . . The key is to get the jurors to integrate all the information into *your* story line." As the defense team planned their strategy, Scheck wrote on a blackboard the story line that he believed would be most compelling: "Integrity of the Evidence: Contaminated, Compromised, and Corrupted."[23] Once that story was made vivid and "real" for the jurors, it would make little difference that even if one threw out *all* the evidence that the defense claimed was contaminated and compromised, one would still be left with more than enough evidence to convict O. J. Simpson.[24] The narrative won the day and relieved jurors of the responsibility to actually go through the evidence, sifting and weighing the relative strengths of each piece.

Lawyers have always traded in reality construction, of course. Yet gradually but significantly over the last several decades, new developments have made lawyers much more skillful at creating "virtual realities" and jurors more susceptible to accepting them *as* real. In helping us to understand the "consumer" end of this (the susceptibility of the jury), philosopher Jean Baudrillard is useful. He has described postmodern culture as one in which created images have become the only reality we have; the sheer proliferation of these images makes it less and less possible to refer to something "behind," "beneath," or exposing of their artifice. His point is not just that it's hard for us to discern the real from the fake but that we no longer care much about that distinction. (Think, for example, about the way political commentators now ceaselessly refer to "damage control" and "spin" and hardly ever talk flat out about events.)

Lacking a sense of any reality beyond the "appearances" of things, the seemingly most authoritative or most dazzling or smoothest appearance will always win. Here is where the "production" end enters. The image makers are now frighteningly adept at technologically manipulating elements to form seemingly unaltered new wholes (such as computer-generated bodies and reconstructed videos) and in general they seem to be ethically oblivious to the consequences. Our consumer culture has developed a virtual science of image making and illusion creating, which has radically changed the rules of the legal game. Nowadays, lawyers—given sufficient money—are infinitely more adept at diagnosing which realities will "play" to which jurors and in shaping materials to make those realities seem *real*. They have jury consultants, public relations firms, psychological advisors, technical experts, and graphic artists to help make their presentations as compelling—and selling—as an advertising campaign. Indeed, it is from this domain that all of these industries were generated. In this context notions like "evidence" and "reasonable doubt," which throughout history have *always* been vulnerable to jurors' prejudices (if there was bias in the Simpson verdict, there's certainly nothing new there!), are being even more undermined by some distinctively contemporary elements.

"Reasonable doubt," nowadays, has given way to a postmodern version of seventeenth-century philosopher Descartes's "hyperbolic doubt." Descartes, in an attempt to discover whether there are any absolutely indubitable truths, performed a thought experiment. He deliberately tried to infect everything he thought he knew with the poison of doubt, using elaborate and far-fetched hypotheses to shake up his ordinary reasoning about things. He even went so far as to imagine that everything he believed to be most certainly true—from geometrical truths to the fact that he is sitting before a fire in his dressing gown—is a grand illusion created by an evil genius bent on deceiving him. The point of this extreme, almost laughable skepticism was strategic: to allow Descartes to search for and ultimately arrive at one truth—which turns out to be "I Think"—which cannot be doubted even in a world in which everything else might be an illusion. He is then able to rebuild his structure of belief on surer ground.

The legitimate role of defense lawyers is to create *reasonable* doubt in the minds of jurors, that is, to lead them to the point where after they have sifted through all the evidence, they will have reason to doubt the proof of guilt presented by the prosecution. Nowadays, I would argue, what they try to do instead is to create a world of *hyperbolic* doubt in which nothing can be trusted because "everything is possible," leaving jurors unable to sift and weigh what is reasonable to believe and what is sheer speculation or fantasy. Like Descartes, jurors are led into a world of far-fetched hypotheses and dizzying doubt; unlike Descartes, however, they are not shown the path back to reason. That would be counterproductive to the lawyer's goal of getting the client off. Lawyers are aided and abetted in their efforts by the epistemological susceptibilities of contemporary juries. A friend of mine asked a student in his class if she would be willing to assert, if she were on a jury, that it is beyond reasonable doubt that the earth rotates on its own axis and revolves around the sun; she said no. When he asked her why not, she said she didn't know. Descartes's evil genius is at work here, clearly.

So: I am convinced that doubt *did* exist in the minds of the Simpson jurors. I do not believe that they cynically acquitted Simpson for strategic or political or racial motivations. But whether their doubt was *reasonable* is another matter. I don't think it was. I would call it irrational doubt rather than reasonable doubt—and by irrational I mean doubt generated by allowing ultimately immaterial elements to seize hold of the imagination and intellect and grow there to monstrous proportions, unimpeded by questions of relevance, empirical evidence, and even plain old logic. The prosecution contributed to this sorry state of affairs by continually focusing on the trees rather than the forest, thus suggesting in their own way that every little detail, no matter how trivial, counted as much as the most powerful pieces of evidence. And the defense constructed the fictional but compelling coherency—the plot to frame O.J.—to make "sense" of the clutter, providing the jurors with a narrative "logic" to replace the laborious sifting and weighing of evidence that they were either unable, unwilling, or too exhausted to perform.[25]

This kind of laborious evaluation, in a culture in which narrative and imagery decide what is "real," may ironically itself come to have the feel of *un*reality—a lot of dead, complex, abstract, factual stuff having very little to do with the living world. So, for example, one of the jurors found no problem in dismissing the DNA evidence because she "didn't understand the DNA stuff at all. To me, it was just a waste of time. It was way out there and carried absolutely no weight with me." But impressionistic snapshots *did* carry a lot of weight. Detective Philip Vannatter, as one juror explained, didn't look the jurors in the eyes and thus couldn't be trusted. The accuracy and dependability of criminologist Henry Lee's findings were settled positively for another juror by the warm smile he directed at the jurors as he approached the witness stand to testify. Certainly these sorts of "character" impressions have always played a role in jurors' assessments of whom to believe. But in the Simpson case they apparently counted far more than such extremely incriminating material evidence as DNA. Remember, for the juror quoted above, the DNA didn't count *at all*.

In allowing impressions and images to replace the examination of evidence, the reasoning of the Simpson jury was more indicative of contemporary habits of thought than unique. It seems to me that in focusing exclusively on issues of racial perspective, we have lost sight of this and in the process allowed perceptions that this jury was biased in some unprecedented and uniquely disgraceful way to blossom. If the Simpson jury "rushed to judgment" with their verdict (reaching it in a shockingly brief length of time that reminded me of the way some of my students take exams), so does the mass media rush to judgment every day, probably with far less sense of responsibility than the Simpson jurors brought to their job.

Thousands of people in this country were convinced, for example, that security guard Richard Jewell was guilty of the Olympic bombings because the media, exploiting the possibilities of a great story ("The Hero Turned Suspect") had so zestfully painted a portrait of him to fit the "profile" of a "lone bomber," "overzealous" in the commission of his duties, a frustrated police "wannabe," and (the coup de grâce) with duct tape under his bed and curtains drawn in his house. The "argument" generated by this image—it made such sense, the literary details all seemed to fit together so well, the constructed "text" was such a coherent and convincing one—utterly overshadowed the physical reality of the facts that proved Jewell could *not* have made the phone call warning of the bomb, could *not* have been the lone bomber whose "profile" he so vividly fit.

TRUTH AS "SEEING THROUGH" ILLUSION

Every age is required to meet its crises of relativism and skepticism in its own way. Plato challenged sophistic thinking by appealing to ideals beyond existing institutions, Descartes answered the skeptical crisis of the Renaissance and Reformation with a vision of a mathematically ordered universe. We could try to impose these historical answers on our students, in an attempt to cure their relativism. But I do not think it would work, for their skepticism has emerged from different historical upheavals and challenges than faced Plato or Descartes. Our students' sense of the "real" has been forged by the mass media; no wonder they are unable to sort out evidence, to discriminate good arguments from poor ones, to distinguish appearance from reality! As educators, we need to focus on the actual obstacles that lie in the way of their seeing things clearly or considering them intelligently. We need to help students develop an ability to "see through" the mystifications of cultural appearances—to the complex historical and social realities that don't necessarily make for good TV.

It's impossible to discuss the O. J. Simpson case without talking about the role of images. Media-generated images formed a constant screen through which our perceptions of the players in the drama were filtered. I recall my first reaction when the news of the murder of Nicole Brown Simpson and Ronald Goldman broke and it became clear that O. J. Simpson might be involved. It couldn't be, I thought. He's much too *beautiful*. Those warm eyes. That princely brow. That gorgeous mouth. Images of O.J.'s face—smiling, friendly, and impossibly handsome—flashed before me, images that refused to admit, to cohere with, certain loathsome scripts. During the Bronco chase I began to wonder. But if it were true—if O.J. actually *did* commit these horrible crimes—it surely must have come from a chaos and despair so deep as to befit a classic tragic hero. With reports that Simpson was holding a gun to his head, he became in my imagination the doomed protagonist of some distinctively modern fable, born out of the maelstrom of race, gender, sex, and stardom in this culture. My sympathies were with him. I knew nothing about Nicole or Ron; they were an abstraction for me, still faceless victims. But I knew O.J., I believed. *He* had a face for me, and it radiated good-nature, lack of pretention and guile, and—did I mention?—was very good-looking. If he did indeed murder, the poor man must be in hell now, I thought.

Ultimately this paradigm of the noble and doomed hero—an image predicated on the same sorts of foolish assumptions that people make when they have unprotected sex with wholesome-looking dates (good-looking = good, an equation that also got Ted Bundy's victims into trouble)—ceased being the sole screen through which I sifted all of the "evidence," turning anything ugly about O.J. into anomalous, irrelevant detritus. Beliefs and ideas can change. My point is that from the very beginning of the Simpson case, people's perceptions and judgments of what "really" happened and who O.J. "really" is had to contend with an already well-established, convincing, artificially created reality—a "virtual reality"—built up out of the commercially fabricated images of O.J. the sports hero, the spokesman, the movie star. (These were a powerful reality for O.J. himself: "Please think of the real O.J. and not this lost person," he begged in his "suicide" note; he then drew a happy face inside the O of "O.J.") As the case progressed, this virtual reality was joined by other media concoctions: the "dream team," Marcia the "tough and steely" (yet also too flirtatious) feminist, "smooth" and "silver-tongued" Johnnie Cochran, the numerous "devastating," "disastrous" turns of events deemed "critical" and "pivotal" by television's talking heads, the "eminent" and "unimpeachable" Dr. Henry Lee, and so on.[26] No matter what personal or racial histories we brought to our understanding and assessment of the case, these were the "realities" with which they interacted.

The Fall semester in 1995 when the Simpson trial was the subject of every tabloid and talk show, I taught a course on masculinity and femininity. I was extremely concerned that my students not be passive consumers of whatever the nightly news commentary was offering them. At the same time I saw the trial as providing an opportunity to go beyond a "diversity" model to one that would enable them to analyze the complex interconnections of history, gender, race, and class in this culture. This method, D'Souza and Cheney to the contrary, was not an exercise in "political correctness." We were on a quest for truth.

We did not focus, however, on discovering the truth of who killed Ron and Nicole. This was a course on gender, and it was not my job to sort through DNA and blood spatters with my students. It was my job to help them sort through the cultural images that stood between them and an informed assessment of this or any other public event in which the nature of a relationship between a man and a woman—in this case a black man and a white woman—was so pivotal. I subtitled the course "The True Untold Story of O.J. and Nicole"—an ironic nod to the tabloids but with a serious point. Television, newspapers, magazines, and radio pretended to "reveal all," to expose, to satisfy our "right to know." But in fact there was much missing from the stories they told, and I made it the job of the course to uncover and expose these gaps. What I was exposing, however, was not evidence of Simpson's guilt or innocence (although some of what we did in class had implications for such an assessment and I hope put my students in a better position to consider the case responsibly) but the historical, cultural, psychological, and political realities of the world we live in.

Those realities are far more complex than either defense or prosecution (or any news commentators) made them out to be. Take, for example, the defense's "frame-up" narrative, which (without even getting into its physical and logical impossibilities and incoherencies) asked us to accept the idea that O.J. was in the eyes of the police despicable and dispensable slime by virtue of his race. Just how persuasive is this notion? Did the police really "see" O.J. primarily as black? And just what does it *mean* to be seen as black? O.J.'s chromosomes won't give us an answer, but a historical analysis of cultural stereotypes and attitudes can help a lot.

Using documentaries such as Marlon Rigg's wonderful "Ethnic Notions,"[27] I led my students through a history of those stereotypes. They learned that there is a cultural storehouse of scientific theory, folklore, stereotypes, and imagery associating blackness with animality and aggression, images that do not merely exist on paper or on film but mediate perceptions of actual human beings. (The lawyers in the Rodney King case made liberal use of animal imagery in describing King's struggle with the police, and in this effort they drew on a rich legacy from both "high" and "low" culture.) But they also learned that the imagery of the savage black is not the only racial stereotype in our cultural storehouse. Images of the black male menace, which emerged postemancipation, were well suited to express white anxieties about the newly freed male slaves, but they were predated by the happy Sambo and Tom—childlike, smiling, singing folk who (it was suggested) are only too happy to serve and entertain master—proof that blacks were happy and content under slavery.

The various screens that mediate perceptions of the black male, my students learned, are more complicated than the defense team suggested (while never making explicit their assumptions). The black menace is one of those screens. But so too is the domesticated menial, so thoroughly identified with white culture, so desirous of pleasing it that he represents no threat at all. Far from it, he operates as a validation of the naturalness and rightness of a white-dominated order, and whites love to have him around. Sambo and Tom imagery has frequently been employed in the representation of black celebrities—Simpson among them—domesticating them, making them palatable and nonthreatening to white consumers. Their presence *sustains* and *supports,* it doesn't threaten, racist culture. Simpson's commercials and movie appearances follow the blueprint of Sambo and Tom imagery so exactly as to be painful to view. He leaps and prances, bug-eyed, smiling goofily; it's not hard to imagine a "Ya'suh" coming out of his mouth.

Further complicating this picture is the special position of the successful black athlete, the black athlete superstar, which my students read about in pieces by geographer Peter Jackson[28] and others. "Rodney King," Henry Louis Gates Jr. points out in the *New Yorker,* "was an unknown and undistinguished black man who was brutalized by the police; the only thing exceptional about that episode was the presence of a video camera. . . . Rodney King was a black man to his captors before he was anything else. O. J. Simpson was, first and foremost, O. J. Simpson."[29] (O.J. wanted it that way himself. In a 1968 interview with Robert Lipsyte of the *New York Times,* Simpson told Lipsyte, "I'm not black, I'm O.J.") Racism (and sexism) have always allowed for the exception that proves the rule: the Jew who is not pushy and loud (like the rest), the good feminist who is not a castrating bitch (like the rest). Black athletes, arguably, perform this function for white fans, particularly if they cultivate a persona that is non-threatening and assimilationist. Cheerful, friendly, physically energetic and talented, capable of evoking envy and desire without anxiety or hostility, these figures become constructed in the white imagination as exceptional, "untarnished" by their race (at the same time, whites get to prove, by liking them, that they are not racist). For blacks, however, as culture critic Michael Dyson points out, black superstars may remain marked, albeit in a highly positive fashion, by their race, often acquiring heroic dimensions as icons of "cultural excellence, symbolic figures who embody social possibilities of success denied to other people of color." When one of them goes down, it is a defeat for the race.

Analyses such as these put us in a much better position to intelligently approach the question of public and police perceptions of Simpson, to appreciate both why so many blacks identified with him despite his own lack of racial solidarity *and* why a white police conspiracy would have been highly unlikely. In fact, every action that the police took with O.J.—both in dealing (or rather, not dealing) with his abuse of Nicole and then later, after the murders, in deferential treatment that they showed him in the days prior to his arrest—suggests not that they saw him as a menace but that they were in fact star-struck. I want to stress here, against popular perception, that acknowledging the unlikelihood of a conspiracy against Simpson does not—as Cochran and many others implied—underestimate the racism of our culture. It recognizes its *complexity,* a complexity that was utterly ignored in the defense's simplistic use of the "race card" *and* in the prosecution's response. My students would never have got a sense of that complexity had they simply depended on the media coverage of the trial. For Johnnie Cochran wasn't interested in getting people to think in subtle or complex ways about race; he was interested in getting his client off. And commentators, themselves spinning around in the world of appearances, never challenged Cochran's construction of the way racism works. In my course, however, we were able to do so and to learn a good deal about racial stereotypes in the process.

We also learned about the interplay of race and gender. While race was continually in the air, gender was invisible in the courtroom and in media coverage. But the fact is that if there was a conspiracy at work, it was probably the unspoken gender solidarity that allowed the police to ignore or minimize Nicole's many calls for help. In not arresting Simpson for spousal abuse, the police seemed to be identifying with him "as a man" rather than despising him "as a black"—a point that never was raised, not even by the prosecution (who seemed to be avoiding the taint of feminism with a ten-foot pole). Lawrence Schiller reports, from a conversation with Shawn Chapman, a black female attorney working behind the scenes on the defense team, that on the day the jurors visited Simpson's Rockingham Avenue estate, O.J. himself loitered around outside the house with police deputies, "like guys hanging out on a street corner." Schiller recounts Chapman's description of the conversation she overheard as a "pretty alternate juror walks by, dressed casually in Levi's":

"Check out Fufu in jeans," one deputy cracks.

"Oh, man, look at her in those pants." Simpson is leering. "I want to get *at* her."

"Yeah, she's hot," another deputy agrees, "but she's so stupid."

"I don't care how stupid she is," Simpson says. "Look at her in those jeans!"

The usual nonsense, Chapman thinks. Just like guys everywhere. But one is a prisoner and the others are his guards.[30]

The reality is that we are never "just" black or "just" white, and gender played as profound a role in the trial as race. The woman who was killed, people seemed to forget, may have been as saddled with gender biases—held by the police and also by the jurors—as Simpson was saddled with racial biases. As culture critic bell hooks points out, Nicole was hardly seen as the virgin queen but more as a "a woman that many people, white and black, felt was like a whore. Precisely by being a sexually promiscuous woman, by being a woman who used drugs, by being a white woman with a black man, she had already fallen from grace in many people's eyes—there was no way to redeem her."[31] A Guess jeans ad that (shamelessly and shockingly) appeared while the trial was going on illustrates the "presence" of Nicole-the-temptress in the public imagination of the Simpson/Nicole relationship (figure 11). The caption on this O.J./Nicole looka-like advertisement reads: "If you can't be good, be careful." Is the suggestion that Nicole should have been more careful in dealing with volatile and violent O.J.? That O.J. should have been more careful and not dripped blood all over the place? That they were both reckless in getting involved with each other? In any case, the Nicole figure is hardly coded as an innocent victim (certainly not the virtuous abductee of the black savage, as in traditional racist images); rather, the ad presents her as someone whose sexual wantonness—her hunger for the phallic and powerful black man—contributed to her own demise.

The invisibility of gender at the trial contributed, I think, to the jurors' skepticism about the seriousness of Simpson's abuse. Simply put, they had no "theory" to help them understand why a woman might stay with an abusive man. Early in the trial the prosecution had written an eighty-five-page brief whose first words were "This is a domestic violence case involving murder, not a murder case involving domestic violence."[32] They argued that the case was "a domestic violence case at its core." Yet they presented only a handful of the many documented incidents of Simpson's seventeen-year-long history of beating, frightening, and stalking Nicole, and they called no experts to enlighten jurors about the psychology of abuse

FIGURE 11

"If you can't be good, be careful."

and—more important—being abused. The evidence is overwhelming that women have a difficult time leaving abusive husbands, and there is an extensive literature explaining why this is so. Why the prosecution presented none of this as evidence, I don't know.

The result was that the prosecution's case did not anticipate and answer the kinds of questions that people uninformed about the psychology of abuse might have. If it was all that bad, the jurors scoffed, why didn't Nicole just leave? Surely she of all people, a well-to-do white woman, a beauty with a family behind her, had the resources to do so. If the abuse was still going on, as the prosecution maintained, then why was Nicole thinking of reconciling with O.J.? Some commentators, falling into their own brand of "either/or" thinking, accused the jurors of being so emotionally identified with O.J. as a possible victim of a racist frame-up that they were unable to "see" gender issues at all, even when they had bearing on the question of motivation. But the prosecution never played a "gender card," they simply hoped that some instinctive female sympathy for Nicole would win out.

I encouraged my students not to see the jurors' attitudes as simply reflecting "racial identification" versus "gender identification" but as also indicative of an intellectual failure to *think* race and gender at the same time, let alone to analyze the interrelations between the two. Popular culture provides virtually no models of such multidimensional, analytic thinking but instead continually encourages us to take sides, assign villains and victims, come to the "bottom line," and so forth. (Which was more terrible, slavery or the Holocaust? The question is more than just polarizing and simpleminded; it does not enable us to "see" the similar cultural dynamics that were at work in both and so to understand the deep structure of racist thinking.)

We people our cultural dramas, too, with unidimensional identities. So, during the 1991 Clarence Thomas/Anita Hill hearings, Thomas's race was emphasized; that Hill was *also* black slid into the background. Hill was simply seen as "the woman" in the drama; that Thomas was a man as well as black was submerged. But as bell hooks continually points out, it is impossible to talk about the plight of black men in this culture without considering how dominant constructions of masculinity inform the dynamics of race. She points out that when Eldridge Cleaver, in *Soul on Ice,* describes rape as a means to "redeem my conquered manhood," he is drawing on cultural equations between masculinity and dominance over women which are hardly unique to Cleaver but which represent an all-too-common "sensibility" shared by black and white men. "Clearly both groups," hooks writes, "have equated freedom with manhood, and manhood with the right of men to have indiscriminate access to the bodies of women."[33]

Such equations, of course, are not held by all men (although they have survived remarkably intact within the sports culture that formed O. J. Simpson's sense of manhood and entitlement). My students not only read hooks's analyses of phallocentric black manhood but also her fond reflections on the gentle, caring men that she had known as a child growing up in the South. My students learned from these reflections, and from the work of historians, anthropologists, and sociologists, that notions of masculinity as dominance, virility, and raw power are not part of some timeless essence of being a man but vary from culture to culture. Nonetheless, such notions play a large—although certainly not unchallenged—role in modern and contemporary gender ideology, as we discovered from a close examination of advertisements, movies, and athletic culture. The idea that men are passionate beasts by nature, that they cannot be expected to control themselves—particularly when provoked by a woman—and that such lack of control is in fact a sign of their masculinity may be one key to understanding not only why O.J. seemed to feel that hitting Nicole was "no big deal" but also why the police did not arrest him, and—sad to say—why Nicole stayed with him. I do not mean to blame the victim here or minimize the helplessness or threat she may have felt. But women, as men have remarked, are often ambivalent about masculine dominance; we resent it in some areas and demand it in others. It would not be surprising if Nicole, despite her terror, continued to be captivated on some level by O.J.'s power and dominance (or a mythology of his power and dominance). His *masculinity*.

Race, of course, is far from irrelevant here, for images of the hypersexual superstud are very much a part of the mystique of black masculinity—the one piece of the ideology of black primitivity, as Gates points out, that black men have not been all that quick to disown, and from all accounts a part of what drew Nicole to O.J. Nicole, too, may well have embodied a racial feminine mystique for O.J. She was the blue-eyed blond prize, after all, the icon of the masculine success historically withheld from black men, and he had been with her since she was a teenager. (This is, of course, the sociosexual landscape that the Guess ad titillates, exploiting the iconography of blond beauty and black stud.) We can only imagine the complex resonances that Nicole's increasing independence may have had for O.J. These dynamics may be disturbing, but they are real.

The foregoing has provided just a sketch of some of the topics we discussed in my class in connection with masculinity; we studied femininity too, through an equally textured analysis. Like physicist Sokol, I insisted that we acknowledge the "reality" of the world, that it doesn't "all depend on how you see things." But reality, as the cultural critics that Sokol lambastes have emphasized, doesn't just consist of the laws of physics. Mine was the kind of class that Bloom, D'Souza, Cheney, and Bennett would no doubt dismiss as P.C. therapy. I don't mind having my course described as "therapy"; my course of treatment, however, was to encourage historical perspective, nonreductionist understanding, clear and rigorous thinking, skepticism about sound bites and slick images, the exercise of informed and reasoned judgment. But then I have a different diagnosis than Bloom and company of how and why our culture has impoverished the souls and minds of our students. Blaming feminists and multiculturalists is ideologically profitable for right-wing critics of higher education. Confronting the interrelations of media, consumerism, and professionalism would end the "culture wars" and force us to acknowledge the systemic nature of the problems we share.

BODIES AND FANTASIES

When Alicia Silverstone, the svelte nineteen-year-old star of *Clueless,* appeared at the Academy Awards just a smidge more substantial than she had been in the movie, the tabloids ribbed her cruelly, calling her "fat-girl" and "buttgirl" (her next movie role is Batgirl) and "more *Babe* than babe."[1] Our idolatry of the trim, tight body shows no signs of relinquishing its grip on our conceptions of beauty and normality. Since I began exploring this obsession it seems to have gathered momentum, like a spreading mass hysteria. Fat is the devil, and we are continually beating him— "eliminating" our stomachs, "busting" our thighs, "taming" our tummies— pummeling and purging our bodies, attempting to make them into something other than flesh. On television, infomercials hawking miracle diet pills and videos promising to turn our body parts into steel have become as commonplace as aspirin ads. There hasn't been a tabloid cover in the past few years that didn't boast of an inside scoop on some star's diet regime, a "fabulous" success story of weight loss, or a tragic relapse. (When they can't come up with a current one, they scrounge up an old one; a few weeks ago the *National Inquirer* ran a story on Joan Lunden's fifty-pound weight loss fifteen years ago!) Children in this culture grow up knowing that you can never be thin enough and that being fat is one of the worst things one can be. One study asked ten- and eleven-year-old boys and girls to rank drawings of children with various physical handi-

caps; drawings of fat children elicited the greatest disapproval and discomfort, over pictures of kids with facial disfigurements and missing hands.

Psychologists commonly believe that girls with eating disorders suffer
from "body image disturbance syndrome": they are unable to see themselves as anything but fat, no matter how thin they become. If this is a disorder, it is one that has become a norm of cultural perception. Our ideas
about what constitutes a body in need of a diet have become more and
more pathologically trained on the slightest hint of excess. This ideal of
the body beautiful has largely come from fashion designers and models.
(Movie stars, who often used to embody a more voluptuous ideal, are now
modeling themselves after the models.) They have taught us "to love a
woman's pelvis, her hipbones jutting out through a bias-cut gown . . . the
clavicle in its role as a coat hanger from which clothes are suspended."[2]
(An old fashion industry justification for skinniness in models was that
clothes just don't "hang right" on heftier types.) The fashion industry has
taught us to regard a perfectly healthy, nonobese body such as the one
depicted in figure 12 as an unsightly "before" ("Before CitraLean, no wonder they wore swimsuits like that"). In fact, those in the business have admit-
ted that models have been getting thinner since 1993, when Kate Moss
first repopularized the waif look. British models Trish Goff and Annie Morton make Moss look well fed by comparison,[3] and recent ad campaigns
for Jil Sander go way beyond the thin-body-as-coat-hanger paradigm to
a blatant glamorization of the cadaverous, starved look itself (see figure
13). More and more ads featuring anorexic-looking young men are appearing too.

The main challenge to such images is a muscular aesthetic that *looks*
more life-affirming but is no less punishing and compulsion-inducing in
its demands on ordinary bodies. During the 1996 Summer Olympics—
which were reported with unprecedented focus and hype on the fat-free
beauty of muscular bodies—commentators celebrated the "health" of this
aesthetic over anorexic glamour. But there is growing evidence of ram-

NEVER JUST PICTURES

pant eating disorders among female athletes, and it's hard to imagine that those taut and tiny Olympic gymnasts—the idols of preadolescents across the country—are having regular menstrual cycles. Their skimpy level of body fat just won't support it. During the Olympics I heard a commentator gushing about how great it was that the 1996 team was composed predominantly of eighteen- and nineteen-year-old women rather than little girls. To me it is far more disturbing that these nineteen-year-olds still *look* (and talk) like little girls! As I watched them vault and leap, my admiration for their tremendous skill and spirit was shadowed by thoughts of what was going on *inside* their bodies—the hormones unreleased because of insufficient body fat, the organ development delayed, perhaps halted.

Is it any wonder that despite media attention to the dangers of starvation dieting and habitual vomiting, eating disorders have spread throughout the culture?[4] In 1993 in *Unbearable Weight* I argued that the old clinical generalizations positing distinctive class, race, family, and "personality" profiles for the women most likely to develop an eating disorder were being blasted apart by the normalizing power of mass imagery. Some feminists complained that I had not sufficiently attended to racial and ethnic "difference" and was assuming the white, middle-class experience as the norm. Since then it has been widely acknowledged among medical professionals that the incidence of eating and body-image problems among African American, Hispanic, and Native American women has been grossly underestimated and is on the increase.[5] Even the gender gap is being narrowed, as more and more men are developing eating disorders and exercise compulsions too. (In the mid-eighties the men in my classes used to yawn and pass notes when we discussed the pressure to diet; in 1996 they are more apt to protest if the women in the class talk as though it's their problem alone.)

The spread of eating disorders, of course, is not just about images. The emergence of eating disorders is a complex, multilayered cultural "symptom," reflecting problems that are historical as well as contemporary, aris-

From left to right:

FIGURE 12
All our mothers needed
to diet

FIGURE 13
Wasted glamour

FIGURE 14
Advertising anorexia?

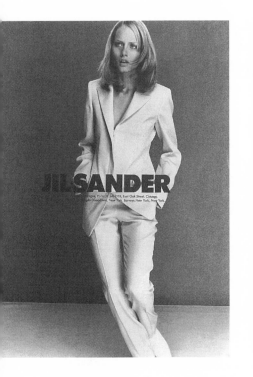 

ing in our time because of the confluence of a number of factors.[6] Eating disorders are overdetermined in this culture. They have to do not only with new social expectations of women and ambivalence toward their bodies but also with more general anxieties about the body as the source of hungers, needs, and physical vulnerabilities not within our control. These anxieties are deep and long-standing in Western philosophy and religion, and they are especially acute in our own time. Eating disorders are also linked to the contradictions of consumer culture, which is continually encouraging us to binge on our desires at the same time as it glamorizes self-discipline and scorns fat as a symbol of laziness and lack of willpower.

And these disorders reflect, too, our increasing fascination with the possibilities of reshaping our bodies and selves in radical ways, creating new bodies according to our mind's design.

The relationship between problems such as these and cultural images is complex. On the one hand, the idealization of certain kinds of bodies foments and perpetuates our anxieties and insecurities, that's clear. Glamorous images of hyperthin models certainly don't encourage a more relaxed or accepting attitude toward the body, particularly among those whose own bodies are far from that ideal. But, on the other hand, such images carry fantasized solutions *to* our anxieties and insecurities, and that's part of the reason why they are powerful. They speak to us not just about how to be beautiful or desirable but about how to get control of our lives, get safe, be cool, avoid hurt. When I look at the picture of a skeletal and seemingly barely breathing young woman in figure 14, for example, I do not see a vacuous fashion ideal. I see a visual embodiment of what novelist and ex-anorexic Stephanie Grant means when she says in her autobiographical novel, *The Passion of Alice,* "If I had to say my anorexia was about any single thing, I would have said it was about living without desire. Without longing of any kind."[7]

Now, this may not seem like a particularly attractive philosophy of life (or a particularly attractive body, for that matter). Why would anyone want to look like death, you might be asking. Why would anyone want to live without desire? But recent articles in both the *New Yorker* and the *New York Times* have noted a new aesthetic in contemporary ads, in which the models appear dislocated and withdrawn, with chipped black nail polish and greasy hair, staring out at the viewer in a deathlike trance, seeming to be "barely a person." Some have called this wasted look "heroin chic": ex-model Zoe Fleischauer recalls that "they wanted models that looked like junkies. The more skinny and fucked-up you look, the more everybody thinks you're fabulous."[8]

Hilton Als, in the *New Yorker,* interprets this trend as making the state-

ment that fashion is dead and beauty is "trivial in relation to depression."[9]
I read these ads very differently. Although the photographers may see themselves as ironically "deconstructing" fashion, the reality is that no fashion
advertisement can declare fashion to be dead—it's virtually a grammatical impossibility. Put that frame around the image, whatever the content,
and we are instructed to find it glamorous. These ads are not telling us
that beauty is trivial in relation to depression, they are telling us that depression is beautiful, that being wasted is *cool* (see figure 13). The question then
becomes not "Is fashion dead?" but "Why has death become glamorous?"

Freud tells us that in the psyche death represents not the destruction of
the self but its return to a state prior to need, thus freedom from unfulfilled longing, from anxiety over not having one's needs met. Following
Freud, I would argue that ghostly pallor and bodily disrepair, in "heroin
chic" images, are about the allure, the safety, of being beyond needing,
beyond caring, beyond desire. Should we be surprised at the appeal of
being without desire in a culture that has invested our needs with anxiety, stress, and danger, that has made us craving and hungering machines,
creatures of desire, and then repaid us with addictions, AIDS, shallow and
unstable relationships, and cutthroat competition for jobs and mates? To
have given up the quest for fulfillment, to be unconcerned with the body
or its needs—or its vulnerability—is much wiser than to care.

So, yes, the causes of eating disorders are "deeper" than just obedience
to images. But cultural images themselves *are* deep. And the way they
become imbued and animated with such power is hardly mysterious. Far
from being the purely aesthetic inventions that designers and photographers would like to have us believe they are—"It's just fashion, darling,
nothing to get all politically steamed up about"—they reflect the designers' cultural savvy, their ability to sense and give form to flutters and quakes
in the cultural psyche. These folks have a strong and simple motivation to
hone their skills as cultural Geiger counters. It's called the profit motive.
They want their images and the products associated with them to sell.

The profit motive can sometimes produce seemingly "transgressive" wrinkles in current norms. Recently designers such as Calvin Klein and Jil Sander have begun to use rather plain, ordinary-looking, unmadeup faces in their ad campaigns. Unlike the models in "heroin chic" ads, these men and women do not appear wasted so much as unadorned, unpolished, stripped of the glamorous veneer we have come to expect of fashion spreads. While many of them have interesting faces, few of them qualify as beautiful by any prevailing standards. They have rampant freckles, moles in unbeautiful places, oddly proportioned heads. Noticing these ads, I at first wondered whether we really were shifting into a new gear, more genuinely accepting of diversity and "flaws" in appearance. Then it suddenly hit me that these imperfect faces were showing up in clothing and perfume ads only and the *bodies* in these ads were as relentlessly normalizing as ever—not one plump body to complement the facial "diversity."

I now believe that what we are witnessing here is a commercial war. Clothing manufacturers, realizing that many people—particularly young people, at whom most of these ads are aimed—have limited resources and that encouraging them to spend all their money fixing up their faces rather than buying clothes is not in their best interests, are reasserting the importance of body over face as the "site" of our fantasies. In the new codes of these ads a too madeup look signifies a lack of cool, too much investment in how one looks. "Just Be," Calvin Klein tells us in a recent CK One ad. But looks—a lean body—still matter enormously in these ads, and we are still being told *how* to be—in the mode which best serves Calvin Klein. And all the while, of course, makeup and hair products continue to promote their own self-serving aesthetics of facial perfection.

EATING DISORDERS IN A CULTURE OF IMAGES

Fashion is never "just" fashion and the images are never "just" pictures. The mistake of regarding slenderness as a surface ideal, powerful but empty, is rampant in commentary and discussion of eating disorders, from scholarly journals to *People* magazine, and the mistake is as common among critics of popular imagery as it is among apologists for the fashion industry. Consider, for example, the position of groups such as BAM—the organization to Boycott Anorexic Marketing—which, when the waif look became popular in 1994, called for a boycott against marketers who employ hyperthin models.[10] Their argument, in a nutshell, is that these images have enormous power to imprint themselves on us, particularly on impressionable young girls. For BAM, the consumer is a tabula rasa, awaiting inscription, potentially vulnerable to any and all influences. The ubiquity of glamorizing images of the thin body, dictating the terms of beauty in this culture, shaping our perceptions of our own bodies and their (imagined) defects, is enough to account for the desperate lengths that girls and women go to achieve the desired look.

Before I go on to point out the limitations of BAM's argument, I want to note that the group is making an important point (one that had been sorely neglected for a long time in the literature on eating disorders)[11] about the role of cultural images in the spread of eating disorders. Most eating disorders, it has long been recognized, begin with a diet and escalate from there. But why do most of us diet nowadays if not to try to become the bodies in the images? Therapists tell me that their teenage clients bring photos of Kate Moss and others to therapy, to show their shrinks what they want to look like. I had a student who had to leave the classroom when I presented slide shows of contemporary advertisements. She was a recovering bulimic and in order to stay on the wagon could not even permit herself to *look* at the pictures of Moss and the rest. Some current therapeutic approaches, acknowledging (and seemingly capitulating to) the all-powerful role that images play in the lives of women with eating problems, encourage group participants to talk about the body styles that most attract them—waif look, athletic look, professional "superwoman" look—and then discuss the ways they can be achieved with more moderate dieting and exercise. (This sort of approach, I fear, only reinforces the authority of the images.)

It's also important to recognize, as I argue in the introduction to this book, that our susceptibility to cultural imagery has changed. When I was a teenager in the sixties, Twiggy's mascara-spiked stare and long coltlike legs represented our variant of the wide-eyed waif. We envied Twiggy's casual cool and boyish body. But few of us imagined that Twiggy was a blueprint for the ordinary adolescent girl to pattern herself after. She was a high-fashion mannequin after all, and we all knew that models had to be skinny "to photograph well." Today, teenagers no longer have the luxury of a distinction between what's required of a fashion model and what's required of them; the perfected images have become our dominant reality and have set standards for us all—standards that are increasingly *un*real in their demands on us.

With some insightful and brave pioneers as notable exceptions,[12] it has taken a long time for clinicians working in the field of eating disorders to acknowledge the central role that cultural images play in women's problems with food, eating, and body image. To acknowledge that role is arguably to admit that anorexia and bulimia—although they both do terrible damage to individual lives and may respond favorably to many different kinds of individual psychotherapy—need to be understood not as individual psychopathology but as *social* pathology. It's understandable that there is professional resistance to the implications of the enormous evidence now establishing that eating disorders (like hysteria and neurasthenia in the nineteenth century) are culturally produced and culture-bound, and on a continuum with normative female behavior. A whole industry in the conceptualization and treatment of eating disorders—distinguished by professionals, journals, conferences, treatment centers, paradigms and concepts (such as "Body Image Disturbance Syndrome," "Bulimic Thinking," "Anorexic Personality Type")—has been organized, it now seems, around highly questionable premises. Conceptual transformation is not just about ideas, it's about personal and professional investments. Change is usually arduous and slow.

Most frequently nowadays, clinicians are willing to grant that cultural images may contribute to or "trigger" eating disorders, but they insist that underlying psychological, familial, or biological factors are the true cause of eating disorders. "There has to be a predisposing vulnerability," says Michael Strober, director of the eating disorder center at UCLA's Neuropsychiatric Institute. "A *real* anorectic suffers from extreme self-doubt, inadequacy concerns and self-esteem anxieties that are far more extreme than other people's. The average person will not be induced into anorexia because they see Kate Moss."[13] Dr. John Mead, director of the eating disorders clinic at Chicago's Rush Presbyterian-St. Luke Medical Center, adds that "girls who have a healthy self-image and come out of a good parent-child relationship do not fall victim to eating disorders."[14] In such arguments the role of the family is often emphasized. Clinical psychologist Rhoda Lee Fisher, for example, considers cultural messages far less potent than those sent by parents: "A mother saying 'Don't take that food. You've been a bad girl' is a powerful message to a female child."[15]

Medical professionals are right to insist that eating disorders are multidimensional and that many of those with severe eating problems have serious psychological and familial problems too. But in positing culture as a "contributory" factor and families as the "real" cause they forget that families do not exist outside cultural time and space. The destructive family dynamics they cite prove rather than dispute the importance of culture. In Fisher's example a mother scolds her daughter for eating too much food. But what made this mother so anxious about her daughter's eating? Such anxiety, after all, is not universal; families living in poverty probably have more anxiety over their children's *not* getting enough to eat than eating too much. And even in conditions of greater economic security, "old" cultural associations relating to food, eating, and the body may persist in families. My own mother, who was born in poverty in Poland early in the century, became concerned when I *didn't* eat every scrap on my plate. Her own body was lush and clearly admired by my father and by their friends (figure 15). When, at age eight or so, I began to eat compulsively and gained a significant amount of weight, my parents were troubled; the kids at school were teasing me and I was becoming withdrawn and depressed. But I never got the impression from them that food was sinful, that appetite was ugly, or that in order to be attractive a female body needed to be pruned of all excess flesh. Far from it.

I grew up, like many women who were born just as the mass visual media were taking off as dominant cultural forces, with serious body-image problems. My weight, which has tended to go up and down within a range of about twenty-five pounds (no doubt the result of dieting from an early age), has been a central struggle in my life. But my problems have never escalated into severely disordered eating, and I think that one of the reasons for this is the "alternative" set of values I grew up with, values that remained in competition with those becoming increasingly dominant during my youth. My parents, in their own way, were a countercultural force in my life. Today few mothers and fathers of teenagers and preteens (that is, the generation of parents my own age or younger) represent such a force; in an increasingly image-dominated culture, the presence of countercultural body ideals has become diluted.

Increasingly the values communicated by today's younger parents are likely to be representative of the popular culture of slenderness worship. Many are counting calories themselves, complaining to their own friends about their weight, and almost undoubtedly bound to feel anxiety over the possibility that a child is getting fat (or even chubby). We know that no one dates fat people, that they lose out on jobs, that they become the butt of cruel jokes. Parents of young women with eating problems often suffer from severe eating and exercise problems themselves. If they are overbearing in their demands for physical perfection from their children, why is this a "family" problem rather than a "cultural" problem? The dichotomy won't hold.

FIGURE 15

Regina and Julius Klein

ca. 1955

When a father teases his daughter for getting "chubby," when parents encourage their teenagers to become mini-superwomen who get the best grades but never forget the importance of looking good, they too are responding to (and perpetuating) messages sent to them from their culture.

Families exist in cultural time and space. So does "peer pressure," "perfectionism," "body-image distortion," "fear of fat," and all those other elements of individual and social behavior that clinical models have tended to abstract and pathologize. In a culture in which dieting, bingeing, purging, and compulsive exercising are virtually normative behavior for college women (that is, *most* young women engage in them; they are the norm not the exception), surely Strober and others are wrong to consider the most extreme cases as their model and to make such a sharp demarcation between these "real" anorectics and all the others. Are the majority of my students suffering from self-doubt, inadequacy concerns, and self-esteem anxieties far more extreme than those of most women? It's hard to believe that their problems are anything but fairly representative of the experiences of other working- and middle-class women attending a coed state institution. If so, then according to Strober they could not have "real" eating disorders, since the underlying vulnerabilities of those with "real" disorders are by definition more extreme than the norm. But what then do my students have?

Dr. Mead says that girls who have a healthy self-image do not fall victim to eating disorders, and he may be right. But how many women in this culture *have* a healthy self-image? Women, as study after study has shown, do not feel very good about their bodies.[16] They regard themselves as too fat even when they are too thin, consistently overestimate the size of their bodies, and suffer from deep depression over their perceived physical inadequacies. Many of my students have a terror of gaining a pound or losing a day of exercise. One of them revealed to me that she had eaten nothing but a jar of baby food, one peanut butter and jelly sandwich, and a piece of fruit every day for ten years. She often purged as well. Yet she rejected the idea that she had an eating disorder, and so did the student who recently told me that she eats only every other day (because, as she explained, she just doesn't feel comfortable when she has food in her stomach). They have read the medical articles and on the basis of the profiles contained in them have excluded themselves. They weigh too much, or aren't purging enough, or are eating too much to have a "real" eating disorder.

Thanks to the arguments of feminist writers and consumer groups like BAM and because of the unfortunate worsening and increasing visibility of the problem, the popular media and the therapeutic community are finally beginning to confront the power of cultural images over women's lives. A few years ago *People* ran a much publicized cover story showing a picture of Kate Moss alongside the question: "Is a Dangerous Message Being Sent to Weight-Obsessed Teens?" The article, which made sure to include "experts" from the fashion industry to give their opposing point of view (as well as the views of Strober, Mead, and other semi-skeptical therapists), answered the cover question with a highly qualified "Yes, but . . ." (the "but" insisting that "no one gets sick just from looking at a picture"). More recently another *People* cover story ("Too Fat? Too Thin? How Media Images of Celebrities Teach Kids to Hate Their Bodies") was much less equivocating in its indictment of mass imagery:

> In the moral order of today's media-driven universe—in which you could bounce a quarter off the well-toned abs of any cast member of *Melrose Place* or *Friends,* fashion magazines are filled with airbrushed photos of emaciated models with breast implants, and the perfectly attractive Janeane Garofalo can pass for an ugly duckling next to Beautiful Girl Uma Thurman in the current hit movie *The Truth about Cats and Dogs*—the definition of what constitutes beauty or even an acceptable body seems to become more inaccessible every year. The result? Increasingly bombarded by countless "perfect" body images projected by TV, movies and magazines, many Americans are feeling worse and worse about the workaday bodies they actually inhabit. The people being hurt most are the ones who are most vulnerable: adolescents.[17]

From my point of view—and for the moment ignoring the fact that the preceding month's issue of *People* had been completely devoted to airbrushed coverage of "the fifty most beautiful people in the world"—the new story was a big improvement over the old. But the fashion industry, as might be expected, is not too happy with such a shift in perspective and is especially scornful of groups like BAM. Coopting the rhetoric of "power feminism," Peggy Northrop, senior editor at *Vogue,* charges her critics with minimizing women's active agency and also misunderstanding what fashion is all about. She insists that to suggest that "women are so utterly victimized by the way they are portrayed that they go on a diet, starve themselves and become sick" is to see women as passive, helpless pawns of the media.[18] Surely, the implication is, feminists must grant women more independence of mind, more individualism than that!

Moreover, as designer Josie Natori argues (in a *Harper's Bazaar* magazine article specifically "answering" feminists and others who protested when the waif look came into fashion), anyone ought to know that "fashion is not about reality. It's about ideas and vision."[19] On this argument it's as inappropriate to emulate Kate Moss as to try to look like the Mona Lisa, or—perhaps more relevant—like a Rossetti or Beardsley waif. These ideas have been recycled in a recent *Vogue* rejoinder to Swiss watch manufacturer Omega's charge that the glamorization of "skeletal" models like Annie Morton and Trish Goff promotes eating disorders. *Vogue* wants to know why we just can't get it through our heads that these are *models* (and hefty eaters, too, as the designers are always quick to insist).[20] They are incredulous that any ordinary girl would think they should or could look like them.

In one sense, of course, Josie Natori is right. Fashion images are not "reality" but an artfully arranged manipulation of visual elements. Those elements *are,* however, arranged precisely in order to arouse desire, fantasy, and longing, to make us want to participate in the world they portray. That is their point and the source of their potency, and it's in bad faith for the industry to pretend otherwise. If we were content to admire the pictures in some mildly interested, aestheticized way and then put down the magazine, personally unaffected, our bubble of fantasy time over and done with, ready to get back to "real" life, it is unlikely that we would be as hot to buy the clothes and products advertised as the industry obviously wants us to be. And if they truly want us to regard the models as belonging to an unattainable world of artifice and illusion, why do they so often publish makeup and hair-styling features telling us how to achieve "the look" of popular models as well as diet and exercise "tips" on how models keep their bodies in shape?

I do agree that no one gets sick just from looking at a picture, and I share Peggy Northrop's irritation with BAM's depiction of women as pawns of the media. But there are other ways of looking at how we experience these images, as I will now argue, than as a choice between acknowledging that we are victimized dupes unable to resist the images or insisting that we are autonomous free spirits who can take them or leave them.

JUST BODIES?

Although BAM and the fashion industry seem to be standing on opposite sides of the fence in the debate about cultural images and eating disorders, they (and *People* and therapists Mead and Strober) share an important and defective assumption about the way we interact with media imagery of slenderness. Because these images use bodies to sell surface adornments (such as clothing, jewelry, footwear), the images are taken to be advertising, at most, a certain "look" or style of appearance. What that "look" or style might project (intelligence, sophistication, childlikeness) is unacknowledged and unexplored, along with the values that the viewer might bring to the experience of looking. Throughout the literature on eating disorders, whether "fashion" is being let off the hook or condemned, it appears as a whimsical, capricious, and socially disembodied force in our lives.

This trivializing of fashion reflects a more general failure to recognize that looks are more than skin deep, that bodies *speak* to us. The notion that bodies are mere bodies, empty of meaning, devoid of mind, just material stuff occupying space, goes back to the philosopher Descartes. But do we ever interact with or experience "mere" bodies? People who are attracted to certain sizes and shapes of bodies or to a particular color of hair or eyes are mistaken if they think their preference is only about particular body parts. Whether we are conscious of it or not, whether our preferences have their origins in (positive or negative) infant memories, culturally learned associations, or accidents of our histories, we are drawn to what the desired body *evokes* for us and in us. I have always found certain kinds of male hands—sturdy, stocky hands, the kind one might find on a physical laborer or a peasant—to be sexually attractive, even strangely moving. My father had hands like this, and I am convinced my "aesthetic" preferences here derive from a very early time when my attitudes toward my father's masculinity were not yet ambivalent, when he existed in my life simply as the strong, omnipotent, secure hands that held me snugly against harm.

Once we recognize that we never respond *only* to particular body parts or their configuration but *always* to the meanings they carry for us, the old feminist charge of "objectification" seems inadequate to describe what is going on when women's bodies are depicted in sexualized or aestheticized ways. The notion of women-as-objects suggests the reduction of women to "mere" bodies, when actually what's going on is often far more disturbing than that, involving the depiction of regressive ideals of feminine behavior and attitude that go much deeper than appearance. I remember Julia Roberts in *Mystic Pizza* when she was still swinging her (then much ampler) hips and throwing sassy wisecracks, not yet typecast as the perpetually startled, emotional teeter-totter of later films. In order for Roberts to project the vulnerability that became her trademark, those hips just had to go. They suggested too much physical stability, too much sexual assertiveness, too much womanliness. Today the camera fastens on the coltlike legs of a much skinnier Roberts, often wobbly and off balance, not because she has "great legs" in some absolute aesthetic sense (actually, when they do aestheticized close-ups of her legs, as in *Pretty Woman,* they use a body double!) but because her legs convey the qualities of fragility that directors—no doubt responding to their sense of the cultural zeitgeist as well as their own preferences—have chosen to emphasize in her.

The criticism of "objectification" came naturally to feminism because of the continual cultural fetishization of women's bodies and body parts— breasts and legs and butts, for example. But these fetishes are not mere body parts. Often, features of women's bodies are arranged in representations precisely in order to suggest a particular attitude—dependence or seductiveness or vulnerability, for example. Heterosexual pornography, which has been accused of being the worst perpetrator of a view of women as mute "meat," in fact seems more interested than fashion layouts in animating women's bodies with fantasies of what's going on inside their minds. Even the pornographic motif of spread legs—arguably the worst offender in reducing the woman to the status of mere receptacle—seems to me to use the body to "speak" in this way. "Here I am," spread legs declare, "utterly available to you, ready to be and do whatever you desire."

Many women may not like what this fetish, as I have interpreted it, projects—the woman's willing collapsing of her own desire into pleasing the male. Clearly, my interpretation won't make pornography less of a concern to many feminists. But it situates the problem differently, so we're not talking about the reduction of women to mere bodies but about what those bodies *express.* This resituating also opens up the possibility of a non-polarizing conversation between men and women, one that avoids unnuanced talk of "male dominance" and control in favor of an exploration of images of masculinity and femininity and the "subjectivities" they embody and encourage. Men and women may have very different interpretations of those images, differences that need to be brought out into the open and disinfected of sin, guilt, and blame.

Some feminists, for example, might interpret a scene of a man ejaculating on a woman's face as a quintessential expression of the male need to degrade and dominate. Many men, however, experience such motifs as fantasies of unconditional acceptance. "From a male point of view," writes Scott MacDonald, "the desire is not to see women harmed, but to momentarily identify with men who—despite their personal unattractiveness by conventional cultural definition, despite the unwieldy size of their erections, and despite their aggressiveness with their semen—are adored by the women they encounter sexually."[21] From this point of view, then, what much (soft) heterosexual porn provides for men is a fantasy world in which they are never judged or rejected, never made to feel guilty or embarrassed. I think that all of us, male and female alike, can identify with the desire to be unconditionally adored, our most shame-haunted body parts and body fluids worshipped, our fears about personal excess and ugliness soothed and calmed.

From the perspective of many women, however, the female attitudes that provide reassurance to MacDonald—although he may, as he says, "mean no harm" by them—*are* demeaning. They are demeaning not because they reduce women to *bodies* but because they *em*body and promulgate images of feminine subjectivity that idealize passivity, compliance, even masochism. Just as women need to understand why men—in a culture that has required them to be sexual initiators while not permitting them the "weakness" of feeling hurt when they are rejected—might crave uncomplicated adoration, so men need to understand why women might find the depiction of female bodies in utterly compliant poses to be problematic. In our gender history, after all, being unstintingly obliging—which in an ideal world would be a sexual "position" that all of us could joyfully adopt with each other—has been intertwined with social subordination. When bodies get together in sex, a whole history, cultural as well as personal, comes along with them.[22]

In *Unbearable Weight* I attempted to "unpack" the range of meanings embodied by the slenderness ideal. I found them to be complicated and often contradictory, suggesting empowerment in some representations and feminine passivity in others. I continue to believe that the appeal of slenderness is *overdetermined* in this culture; we worship the slender body because it evokes so many different qualities that we value. Here I would like to explore the appeal of slenderness as reflecting anxiety about women as "too much." This metaphor, I discovered, struck a chord with more women than any other idea or image in *Unbearable Weight* and so it deserves a closer look. We need to reflect on its specific meaning for younger women today ("generation X," those in their early thirties and younger) and its connection with racial images and ideology. I emphasize, though, that my discussion here will only follow the trail of this one metaphor and is not meant to be an exhaustive analysis of either the images or the current situation of women.

When we admire an image, a kind of recognition beyond a mere passive imprinting takes place. We recognize, consciously or unconsciously, that the image carries values and qualities that "hit a nerve" and are not easy to resist. Their power, however, derives from the culture that has generated them and resides not merely "in" the images but in the psyche of the viewer too. I recently asked my students why they found Kate Moss so appealing. It took them a while to get past "She's so thin! And so beautiful!" I wanted to know what *made* her beautiful in their eyes and how her thinness figured into that. Once they began to talk in nonphysical terms, certain themes emerged again and again: She's so detached. So above it all. She looks like she doesn't need anything or anyone. She's in a world of her own, untouchable. Invulnerable. One of my students, who had been struggling unsuccessfully with her bulimia all semester, nearly moved me to tears with her wistful interpretation. "She looks so cool," she whispered longingly. "Not so needy, like me."

These are not mere projections on the part of my students. The unfocused princess of indifference whom Kate Moss impersonates in fashion photos is also part of the "real" persona created by Moss and those who market her. Her detachment is always emphasized (and glamorized). "I like doing the [fashion] shows," she told *People* magazine, "but I don't need to at all." The quotation was the apt caption for an image of slouching, blank-faced Moss, cigarette in hand, in a dazed world of her own (figure 16.) Worries about lung cancer? It wouldn't be chic to be concerned about one's health. And although many models admit to smoking in order to hold their weight down, Moss denies that she ever frets over her diet. "It's kind of boring for me to have to eat," she said in an *Esquire* interview. "I would know that I had to, and I would." How many times have we read statements like this in interviews with supermodels? "I guess I'm just one of those lucky people who doesn't have to count calories. . . . But I've never really been all that interested in food, anyway." Then, we are often treated to an accounting of the model's daily routine, recited with supreme casualness. "I'll catch some pasta at Spago's . . . " Frankly, I find these comments rather sadistic. How many girls and women would give their eye teeth to find food boring or something you "catch" on the fly! Most of my students are in a constant and often bloody battle with their appetite. And they associate that struggle with their own (as they see them) gross desires.

In my discussion of "heroin chic" I briefly explored the glamorization of being beyond desire in general cultural terms. Now, as I look specifically at the gender-related dimension of such ideals, I begin by reemphasizing my students' responses to Moss and the way she is presented in fashion spreads and stories. To the degree that a "message" is being sent by her body, it is not only or primarily about the desirability or attractiveness of being thin. Rather, thinness is a visual code that speaks to young women about the power of being aloof rather than desirous, cool rather than hot, blasé rather than passionate, and self-contained rather than needy. They

FIGURE 16

Kate Moss: too cool to care

don't learn to value these qualities, of course, from the images alone (although the images do contribute); thus, BAM's suggestion that images simply imprint themselves on passive viewers is inaccurate. My female students are drawn to Moss—as my male students are drawn to Julia Roberts—because she embodies a fantasy that answers *needs* they have. Their interaction with the images is more like a conversation than a one-way imposition of views.

But the outcome of this conversation is predictable. Neither the images nor their projected values are arbitrary; they are a function of the world in which we live and our understanding of the kind of person we must be like in order to negotiate it most safely. My students don't feel they can choose to defy either the images or the qualities embodied—and, of course, they are right. The fashion and advertising industries know this and count on it. They *exploit* it in the way they package and promote their products (and models such as Moss). Clearly, they are merely being self-serving and disingenuous (or in profound bad faith) to insist that people are utterly free to accept or reject their "ideas and vision" as they please.

The values that animate my students' perceptions of Moss—whether they are anorexic or not—are on a continuum with "anorexic thinking." "People think that anorexics imagine ourselves fat and diet away invisible flab," writes Stephanie Grant in her autobiographical novel, *The Passion of Alice:* "But people are afraid of the truth: we prefer ourselves this way, boiled-down bone, essence . . . Anorexics differentiate between desire and need. Between want and must. Just to know where I begin and end seems, in this day and age, a remarkable spiritual achievement."[23] And if the thin body represents a triumph over need and want, a stripping down to some clear, distinct, essence of the self, fat represents just the opposite—the shame of being too present, too hungry, too overbearing, too needy, overflowing with unsightly desire, or simply "too much." Often the fear of being "too much" will have a strong sexual dimension, an association that is present in the stories of women with anorexia and bulimia, disorders that often arise after episodes of sexual abuse, sexual taunting, or rejection by fathers who are uncomfortable with their daughter's maturation.

These sexual associations are cultural as well. From Eve in the garden to the many voluptuous movie stars who have found themselves typecast as sex bombshells, female eating, sexual voraciousness, and expansive flesh have long been associated with each other. (Even Cindy Crawford, who is hardly *zaftig,* is continually hypersexualized and cast as a temptress, at least in part because she falls on the curvaceous end of the supermodel spectrum.) When *Cosmopolitan* ran a story aimed at striking a blow against the tyranny of slenderness and rehabilitating voluptuousness, it advised "big, beautiful, Junoesque girls" that their "style is best enhanced with classic courtesan looks: upswept hair (leaving some tendrils hanging), flowing fabrics and décolleté necklines, sultry eyes. . . ." The story was illustrated with photos of "Famous Love-Goddess Bodies": Ann-Margret, Sophia Loren, Mae West, and Jayne Mansfield. If Helen Gurley-Brown imagined that this article would help stem the tide against eating disorders, she no longer has her pulse on the modern woman. The last thing most women with eating disorders want is a body that blatantly advertises female sexuality. Jayne Mansfield is *not* their ideal!

The associations of fat, voraciousness, and excessive sexuality are also frequent in the life experiences of fat women: "Being fat meant that I had uncontrollable desires, that I was voracious. It was a clear danger sign to men: stay away, this woman will eat you up. . . . Appetite equals sexual appetite; having a sundae is letting go. Eating that cake and ice cream meant I wasn't getting sex, and look how much sex I must need if I had to eat so much to compensate. Since I couldn't control myself around food I wouldn't be able to control myself around men; since no food ever satisfied me, no man ever would."[24]

But being fat is not a prerequisite for experiencing these equations. A few weeks ago, while looking through old diaries of mine, I came across an entry that revived disturbing memories for me. It was written during a time when I had been ill and depressed and had consequently lost a great deal of weight. I was thin to the point that I no longer felt I looked very good, and I was withdrawn and anxious most of the time. I wrote:

> I've suddenly realized that deep inside me, I am convinced that men will find me more attractive in my diminished state. X's cousin this past week-end mentioned how good I looked, and I felt that he found me attractive. Here's how I was: skinny, no makeup, hair lank and dirty. I remember when I was so depressed that other time, got down to 114 pounds, and could barely do anything; Y wanted to have sex with me all the time. . . . Here is the way I used to be: robust and Jewish, brainy, forceful, demanding, conscious, conscious, conscious. Now I am so much less, both physically and in terms of assertiveness . . . and I'm aware of how drawn men are to me.

Reading this entry was chilling. I had forgotten about those moments when I suddenly realized that some man was attracted to me because I was "less." Remembering those moments, I was reminded of a truth that is hard to face, about the personal price women may pay for increased presence and power in the world, and the personal rewards they receive for holding back, keeping themselves small and tentative. Let me make what I'm saying here very clear: I'm not claiming that these attitudes are characteristic of *all* men and I'm not blaming men *for* them (any more than I blame those women whose libidos are fixated on muscles and macho). My male friends and students did not create the long-standing notions that shape their attractions and desires, that underlie their conception of what it means to be a "real" man or woman. They often feel as harassed and humiliated by them as women do. The images of beautiful female bodies that bombard them at every turn in this culture can feel, as writer/activist Timothy Beneke has pointed out, *intrusive,* invasive of their personal space and equanimity, challenging to their manhood.

I am not castigating those men who prefer Julia Roberts to the women of Rubens. I am sounding a note of caution, in this era of "power feminism," that there are old but still operative notions about femininity that subsist alongside the briefcases and Nikes. These notions create "glass ceilings"—in the institutional world, in relationships, and in the female psyche—that can hold women back even as they advance in the world.[25] Feminist writer Susan Brownmiller has described femininity as an aesthetic of limitation. If that aesthetic still survives—and I believe it does—it will of course affect notions of what is sexually desirable or beautiful. We cannot evade or deny these attitudes or drown out their reality in a pumped-up rhetoric, announcing the coming of a new age, "beyond" feminism. Men and women stand to gain a lot by talking candidly about them and their effects on sexuality and relationships.

Anxieties about women as "too much" are also layered with racial and other associations that, contrary to the old clinical clichés, set up black, Jewish, lesbian, and other women who are specially marked in this way for particular shame. According to the old clichés, those who come from ethnic traditions or live in subcultures that have historically held the fleshy female body in greater regard and that place great stock in the pleasures of cooking, feeding, and eating are "protected" against problems with food and body image. There is an element of truth in this understanding. Certainly, many cultural heritages and communities offer childhood memories (big, beloved female bodies, sensuous feasts), places (the old Italian neighborhood, the lesbian commune kitchen), and cultural resources (ethnic art, woman-centered literature) that seem diametrically in opposition to everything Kate Moss stands for.

Feminist writers have also worked to reconceive the uneasy relationships between women, sexuality, food, and eating as well as the stereotypes associated with them. Among the charms of Laura Esquivel's *Like Water for Chocolate* is the evocation of a sensual and magical world in which female sexuality, food, and power are knit together but celebrated rather than feared. Audre Lorde, in *Zami,* also yokes food—the erotically described preparation of a Jamaican dish—with her sexual coming of age and increasing self-knowledge. Alice Walker, putting a new spin on the Aunt Jemima stereotype, describes in *Ms.* her delighted recognition of the goddess imagery latent in caricatures that have usually been criticized as only representing the powerlessness, subservience, and sexlessness of the black mammy.[26]

These "alternative" images may provide comfort, delight, inspiration. But each of us also lives within a dominant culture that not only surrounds us with its versions of what is beautiful (still Anglo-Saxon, despite the allowance of "exotic" touches like full lips) but often recoils from what we are. We may grow up sharply aware of representing for that dominant culture a certain disgusting excess—of body, fervor, intensity—which needs to be restrained, trained, and, in a word, made more "white." (Recall that in describing my "former," more assertive self in my journal, I listed "Jewish" among my attributes.) A quote from poet and theorist Adrienne Rich speaks to the bodily dimension of "assimilation": "Change your name, your accent, your nose; straighten or dye your hair; stay in the closet; pretend the Pilgrims were your fathers; become baptized as a Christian; wear dangerously high heels, and starve yourself to look young, thin, and feminine; don't gesture with your hands. . . . To assimilate means to give up not only your history but your body, to try to adopt an alien appearance because your own is not good enough, to fear naming yourself lest name be twisted into label."[27]

Clearly we can no longer regard serious problems with food and body image as solely the province of pampered, narcissistic, heterosexual white girls. To do so is to view black, Asian, Latin, lesbian, and working-class women as outside the loop of the dominant culture and its messages about what is beautiful—a mistake that has left many women feeling stranded and alone with a disorder that they weren't "supposed" to have and that clinicians dismissed. Indeed, as I am arguing, there are reasons why racial and sexual "Others" might find themselves to be more, not less, susceptible to the power of cultural imagery.[28] I include myself here, as a Jewish woman whose body is unlike any of the cultural ideals that have ruled in my lifetime and who has felt my physical "difference" painfully. I have been especially ashamed of the lower half of my body, of my thick peasant legs and calves (for that is indeed how I represented them to myself) and large behind, so different from the aristocratic WASP norm. Because I've somehow felt marked as Jewish by my lower body, I was at first surprised to find that some of my African-American female students felt marked as black by the same part of their bodies. I remember one student in particular who wrote often in her journal of her "disgusting big black butt." For both of us our shame over our large behinds was associated with feelings not of being too fat but of being "too much," of overflowing with some kind of gross body principle. The distribution of weight in our bodies made us low, closer to earth; this baseness was akin to sexual excess (while at the same time not being sexy at all) and decidedly not feminine.

But we didn't pull these associations out of thin air. Racist tracts continually describe Africans and Jews as dirty, animal-like, smelly, and sexually "different" from the white norm. Our body parts have been caricatured and exaggerated in racist cartoons and "scientific" demonstrations of our difference. Much has been made of the (larger or smaller) size of penises, the "odd" morphology of vaginas. In the early nineteenth century Europeans brought a woman from Africa—Saartje Baartman, who came to be known as "The Hottentot Venus"—to display at sideshows and exhibitions as an example of the greater "voluptuousness" and "lascivity" of Africans. European drawings from the period show a woman with extraordinarily large nipples, broad hips, and buttocks so protuberant that one could balance a glass on them. Baartman was exhibited as a sexual monstrosity, her prominent parts an indication of the more instinctual, "animal" nature of the black woman's sexuality (a motif that continues in commercial advertisements today).

When the female "dark Other" is not being depicted as a sexually voracious primitive, she is represented as fat, asexual, unfeminine, and unnaturally dominant over her family and mate—for example, the Jewish Mother or Mammy (figure 17). These stereotypes appear not only in cartoons and situation comedies but in contemporary academic texts, such as David Gilmore's *Manhood in the Making,* in which Gilmore describes "secular, assimilated Jewish-American culture" as "one of the few in which women virtually dominate men."[29] (This would have been a real surprise to my mother!) It isn't surprising then that when black, Jewish, and other racially marked groups talk about their eating problems, ethnic "shame" is a prominent theme, with slenderness and fat coming to stand for successful assimilation versus the taint of "difference."

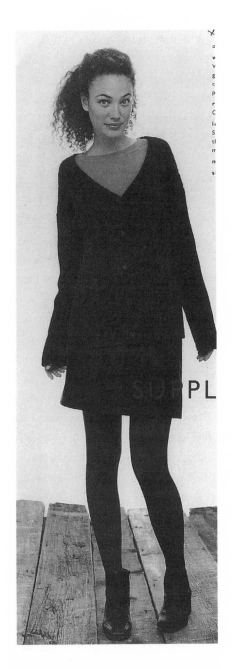

FIGURE 17

Scarlett and Mammy: fashioning femininity as white

FIGURE 18

"Power feminism"?

The associations are loaded even more when sexuality enters in. As one woman notes, "As a Fat Jewish Lesbian out in the world I fulfill the stereotype of the loud pushy Jewish mother just by being who I am (even without children)!"[30] The same woman remarks that the culture of the nineties has "brought a new level of fat hatred within many lesbian communities . . . [an] overwhelming plethora of personal ads which desire someone fit, slim, attractive, passable, not dykey, athletic, etc." That "not dykey" and "slim" are bedfellows here is not surprising. An older generation of lesbians who dressed in overalls and let their hips spread in defiance of norms of femininity may be as much an embarrassment to young nineties lesbians as the traditional Jewish mother is to her more assimilated daughters.

A similar desire to disown the "too much" mother, I believe, motivates many young women today in their relation to feminism and to the stereotypes of my generation's feminism which they have grown up with. Young women today, more seemingly "free" and claiming greater public space than was available to us at their age, appear especially concerned to establish with their bodies that, despite the fact that they are competing alongside men, they *won't* be too much (like their strident, "aggressive," overpolitical feminist mothers). In conversation, they lower their heads and draw in their chests, peeking out from behind their hair, pulling their sleeves over their hands like bashful little girls (see figure 18). Like Julia Roberts, Meg Ryan, and the other young stars who model this culture's versions of vulnerable femininity, they talk in halting baby voices that seem always ready to trail off, lose their place, scatter, giggle, dissolve. They speak in "up talk," ending every sentence with an implied question mark, unable to make a declaration that plants its feet on the ground. They often seem to me to be on the edge of their nerves and on the verge of running away. They apologize profusely for whatever they present of substance, physically or intellectually. And they want desperately to be thin.

CAN A WOMAN HARASS A MAN?

SEX FIENDS AND SCHEMING FEMALE EXECUTIVES

In 1991 Anita Hill charged Supreme Court Justice nominee Clarence Thomas with sexual harassment, which she alleged had taken place while Thomas was her supervisor at both the Department of Education's Office of Civil Rights and later at the Equal Employment Opportunity Commission. The televised hearings that followed initiated a new genre of entertainment—the now familiar teledrama of real-life "justice" in action— and had viewers, as journalists put it ad nauseam, "riveted to their sets." As people lined up on the side of Hill or Thomas, our culture was pressed into a long overdue conversation about gender, power, and sex in our workplaces and educational institutions. That conversation began in a promising fashion, with an unprecedented attention to how commonplace sexual harassment is and how subtle its dynamics can be. I recall with fondness a telephone call from my father, then eighty years old and as suspicious of feminist politics as ever. He had called specifically to find out my views (in itself an unusual occurrence) on the hearings. He didn't believe Hill; like many men (and some women) he was genuinely puzzled by the fact that she had continued to work for Thomas. "Why didn't she just quit? Why did she follow him to the EEOC?" I thought I could answer those questions; I had been harassed myself, knew many other women who had also been harassed, and understood that mixture of intimidation, pragmatics, and training in feminine comportment that keeps one from "making a fuss."

By the end of the phone conversation my father, remarkably, had "gotten it." I rarely had felt so hopeful about the possibilities of communication between men and women about the politics of gender.

Since 1991 such communication has had the dismissive label of "politically correct" affixed to it, men are being encouraged to reclaim their alpha status and stop letting women push them around, and the public conversation about sexual harassment has degenerated to sound bites and stereotypes. Sexual harassment is no longer being explored as a troubling but unremarkable outgrowth of sexual inequality. Instead, the popular imagination has been filled with sensational images that portray the harasser as sex-obsessed and power-mad, his or her behavior far outside the pale of the everyday; in this way we are discouraged from looking at how unfortunately "normal" harassment actually is. I begin this essay by looking at some of those pathologizing images. My first illustration is from the world of pure fiction—Michael Crichton's best-selling novel *Disclosure* and the blockbuster film based on it; my second example is from the world of semifiction—journalistic accounts of the real-life drama of Senator Bob Packwood, who in 1995 was charged with seventeen charges of sexual misconduct and forced by the Senate Ethics Committee to resign from his seat. I open with these images (with side trips revisiting the Thomas/Hill hearings) as a way of beginning to diagnose what has gone wrong with current discussions of sexual harassment.[1]

"Can a woman harass a man?" Providing an affirmative answer to this controversial question was the covert, political agenda behind *Disclosure,* an otherwise conventional thriller about a bureaucratic takeover. The film version, directed by Barry Levinson and starring Demi Moore and Michael Douglas, was widely touted as a provocative "role reversal" in which, to quote the *New York Times,* a "cool, smart and ferociously ambitious" female executive, Meredith Johnson (played by Moore), sexually harasses Tom Sanders, a male in her employ (played by Douglas). The centerpiece of the movie is a scene in which Meredith aggressively presses herself on Tom sexually and then seeks revenge when she is rejected. (Just in case the viewer is in doubt over whether her advances are "welcome," the scene has Douglas whimpering "no" a full thirty-one times as Moore performs oral sex on him.)

Levinson has insisted that the film is "just a movie, not a polemic."[2] He claims that the gender reversal is not intended to exploit and incite the suppressed rage of contemporary male viewers but to get viewers to "pay attention" to issues of power abuse and victim helplessness. Nonetheless, both the novel and the film read like a litany from the white male hell of contemporary gender politics: to begin with, Meredith is not only Tom's boss but occupies precisely the job Tom had coveted—and she's got it, as the president of the company openly declares, in order "to break the glass ceiling." After Tom rejects Meredith, not only does she try to sabotage him at meetings and the like but—in a reversion to more traditional stereotypes—falsely accuses *him* of sexual harassment. In the interrogation that follows, Tom's faithful Asian secretary likewise accuses him of touching her in "inappropriate" ways. The book and movie thus hit all the current raw male anxieties, both warranted and fantastical, from legitimate concerns about behavior being interpreted as harassment to nightmares of sexually castrating, scheming executives and rage at imagined injustices of affirmative action policies. (But remember: it's just a movie, not a polemic.)

Crichton's book, too, refuses to own its politics. The following speech—put into the mouth of Tom's glamorously tough-as-nails, scrupulously egalitarian, and vehemently anti-P.C. Latina attorney—states the point that Crichton *claims* he is making about the protean, neuter nature of power:

> Harassment is about power—the undue exercise of power by a superior over a subordinate. I know there's a fashionable point of view that says women are fundamentally different from men and that women would never harass an employee. But from where I sit, I've seen it all. I've seen

and heard everything you can imagine—and a lot that you wouldn't believe if I told you. That gives me another perspective. Personally, I don't deal much in theory. I have to deal with the facts. And on the basis of facts, I don't see much difference in the behavior of men and women. At least, nothing that you can rely on. . . . The fact is, harassment is a power issue. And power is neither male nor female.[3]

Crichton clearly means here to strangle with its own rope the feminist insistence that sexual harassment is "about power" by yoking that claim to a view of power as "neither male nor female," as gender-neutral. Although unnamed as feminism, the "fashionable point of view" referred to is obviously some version of the caricature created by polemicists such as Christina Hoff Sommers and Katie Roiphe: the "gender feminist" who believes that woman's "different" and superior nature is what's needed to transform an unregenerately ugly and abusive male culture. This is the imagined position that Crichton uses lawyer Fernandez, his "equity" feminist mouthpiece (who is probably against affirmative action too), to knock down with her disdain for fashionable "theory" and her more clear-eyed experience of the "real world." (Someone should inform Crichton that the position Fernandez refers to is hardly fashionable among academics today.)

Putting his ideas in the mouth of an ethnic female, of course, allows Crichton both to be politically correct himself and to get revenge against "political correctness." But it's all a setup, based on that caricature of feminism currently circulating in popular culture to which the "good feminist" Fernandez is contrasted. In the much more diverse actual feminist world, the available positions are not so dichotomous. One can believe, as I do, that sexual harassment is indeed "about power," insist that the kind of power it is "about" requires a specifically feminist analysis, and yet *not* subscribe to the view that "men and women are fundamentally different and that a woman would never harass an employee." In other words, a lot of fertile analytical feminist territory lies between an essentialized and idealized notion of female purity and the conceptualization of power as a sexless and bodiless abstraction. These are simply not our only choices.

In apparent contrast to the Crichton quote is the following narration, from a *Newsweek* story containing excerpts from Bob Packwood's diary and represented as an example of his sexually harassing behavior:

> On Nov. 21, 1989, Packwood began his diary describing a staffer he referred to as "S-1," a "very sexy thing" with "bright eyes and hair and that ability to shift her hips." After a few glasses of wine that evening, "I finally said to her," 'S-1, would you like to dance?' She says, 'I'd love to.' So I slipped around the side of this gigantic desk and we danced. . . . Well, I won't bore you with all the details of the evening. S-1 and I made love, and she has the most stunning figure—big breasts. . . . They stand at attention." As Packwood was lying with S-1 on the floor of his office, she said, "You have no idea the hold you have over other people." "What is it?" asked Packwood. "Well, I think it's your hair," she replied. "We both laughed," recorded Packwood. "Now bear in mind that this is an hour and a half after we've made love and we're both still nude and lying on the rug." Packwood gleefully observed ("Get this," he wrote) that two of his aides were right outside the door the entire time.
>
> Packwood seemed quite pleased with his hairdo. On March 20, 1992, after 20 minutes in the hot tub, he recorded, "I just blew my hair. I didn't use any gel on it at all. I just blew it until it was about dry, combed it, and if it didn't come out looking just right. It had just the right amount of bounce to it, and wave to it."[4]

The *Newsweek* writers who constructed this narrative make no attempt to disentangle the salacious, sophomoric, and merely silly excesses of Packwood's sexual life as revealed in these diary passages from his more clearly harassing behavior. Packwood, we know, did a lot of invasive grabbing and groping of staff assistants, hostesses, and elevator operators. But having sex with a woman who felt relaxed enough to tease him about his hair does not seem to fall into quite that category. An argument can be made, of course, although I'm not inclined to make it, that simply having a sexual relationship with a staff member, no matter how apparently consensual, was an abuse of power. Even so, surely writing gushingly in one's own diary about bodies to which one is attracted, no matter how juvenile or sexist the aesthetic, is not sexual harassment. And what abuse is involved in Packwood's pleasure at having got his hair to have "just the right amount of bounce"—"after 20 minutes in the hot tub," as we are reminded? The only crime he commits here is to expose a narcissism that our culture has generally deemed unmanly, feminine. In fact, these passages are embarrassing precisely because Packwood seems less an adult man and more a perpetually excited adolescent boy who can't get over the fact that he is actually having sex with women.

The press, for their part, huddle around these passages like a bunch of kids who have stolen another kid's notebook and are giggling over the dirty stuff inside. Of course, the secrets they discover are their own; we all have our sexual and bodily shame over less-than-correct desires, embarrassing vanities, humiliating exposures. Packwood affords the classic relief of projection—the excesses of his behavior allow us to disown and distance ourselves from our own. But only, of course, if we represent his behavior as shocking and repulsive, outside the pale of anything that *we* would do. The obvious delight of the press in passages such as the one in *Newsweek* has very little to do with how clearly they expose Packwood's abuses of power and much more to do with the opportunity they afford our culture to identify sexual harassment with a sexuality that has not been properly normalized and so with a deviant "Other." This happened over and over in the Thomas/Hill hearings, as the senators seized on details like "Long Dong Silver" and pubic hairs on coke cans, with pious displays of disgust and overheated speeches—Orrin Hatch was particularly disposed to these—about how only a "psychopathic sex fiend" would engage in such behavior. The strategy served their political purposes admirably, since finding Thomas guilty of harassment would then require that he be acknowledged as a psychopath and sex fiend, which I don't think even Anita Hill believed he was.

But not only narrow political purposes were being served here. As feminists outside the building talked to the press about the commonness of sexual harassment, an alternative portrayal—of the sexual harasser as the inverse of normality rather than its mirror—was emerging. The Bob Packwood of the diaries is a triumph for this construction, and for all its rhetoric to the contrary so is *Disclosure*. Meredith Johnson's sexuality is as crude and insatiable as Packwood's; she's just less juvenile, more glamorous. (After all, she's fully fictional rather than semifictional.) These cultural images of the harasser as slavishly obsessed with sex operate as a powerful, if unarticulated, argument both against the feminist insistence on the everydayness of sexual harassment and against the fact—not underscored enough by feminists—that sexuality, although it may be one of the mediums of harassment, is not its essence.

During the Thomas/Hill hearings, defenders of Thomas argued that he couldn't possibly have been sexually interested in Hill because of the other romances he was pursuing at the time he was supposed to have harassed her. The implication here is that harassment is fueled by sexual or romantic desire and represents an inept, insensitive, overinsistent attempt at seduction. But Hill's description (and Angela Wright's, whose testimony never made the light of day) emphasized that although Thomas may have begun with hopes of romance, the worst harassment occurred after these hopes had been dashed. The real spice of the harassment, both Hill and Wright believe, was not a fantasy of overcoming the reluctance of the women but the pleasure of unnerving and humiliating them. When Hill made her discomfort at his talk of oral sex and penis size clear to him, she sensed "that it urged him on, as though my reaction of feeling ill at ease and vulnerable was what he wanted."[5] Thomas's coin was sex talk. But his aim, as Angela Wright's friend Rose Jourdain saw it, "was making people uncomfortable, you might say harassing them. I think the only thing he was in love with was the conquest of power."[6] Here, of course, "the conquest of power" refers not simply to institutional or political or interpersonal power but to the pleasures of using such power to reduce and demean others, to the pleasure of dominance over others. This is what we should be focusing on in our definitions of harassment: the harasser as *bully,* not sex fiend.

The "sex fiend" scenario is fed not only by contemporary psychological and political currents but by a Puritanism that has set its stamp diversely and profoundly on U.S. history, politics, and culture. (Consider, for example, that Heidi Fleiss and Mel Reynolds will be serving time in jail for consensual sex while O. J. Simpson's wife-battering was dismissed by jurors in the criminal trial as trivial and "irrelevant.") The sensationalizing mass media, attempting to appeal to a population that still views sexuality as the great illicit delight, has created a "discursive explosion" (as French philosopher Foucault would put it) about sexual harassment, in which dirty words, body parts, and gropes and grabs are continually given center stage, as they also clearly are in the headline of a recent story in the German magazine *Bunte:* "What Do I Do If My Boss Wants to Kiss Me? Or Give Me a Pat on the Butt? The Modern Anxiety of Men in the Workplace." Although viewing harassment as exclusively about sexual grabs and gropes does not further a feminist analysis of harassment, the squeamishness of feminists has sometimes aided and abetted such a view. Cultural critic Ellen Willis points out: "Some recent harassment complaints sound like heavy-handed satire: a male professor is charged with using a sexual comparison to make a point in class; another is enjoined from keeping a picture of his bikini-clad wife on his desk; a female professor demands the removal of Goya's Naked Maja from her classroom wall; a teaching assistant, supported by her professor, warns a student she considers him a harasser for handing in a paper containing an 'inappropriate' sexual analogy. . . . Can covering piano legs be far behind?"[7]

In this climate, confusion and anxiety over how one's behavior may be interpreted is entirely justifiable, and many people have felt the safest course is simply to avoid all sexual references, compliments, touching, glances. For those of us who have grown up in families or ethnic communities that use touch to communicate empathy, humor, and playful mutual recognition, this is a tall—and grim—order. But it seems to many the surest way to guard against causing offense. Correlatively, many people believe that sexual harassment *can't* possibly have taken place *unless* a physical "pass" has been made or the body touched in a sexual way. This abstract, acontextual view of bodies and the meaning of their sexual gestures also underlies fantasies of gender reversal like *Disclosure,* in which it is imagined that all that is necessary to make a woman's harassing a man believable is simply to switch the sex of the bodies involved.

MASCULINITY AND "DOMINATING SUBJECTIVITY"

While nightmare fantasies of gender reversal may jangle powerful chords in the cultural psyche, the excesses of the narratives are really far more instructive than their purported "arguments." For at the same time as Hollywood has found it impossible to depict a woman who won't let go as anything other than deranged (as in *Fatal Attraction*) or power-mad (as in *Disclosure*), it continues to churn out romantic comedies in which the persistent suitor is rewarded in the end with the girl. While popular culture stokes male paranoia about unwanted advances, it continues to look tolerantly, even admiringly at the man who won't take no for an answer.

Another mundane and meaningful gender asymmetry ignored in fantasies of reversal is the different responses that men and women tend to have to gestures of affection from bosses and teachers of the opposite sex.

In brief, women feel demeaned by such gestures far more than men do. Men may even feel ill-treated when women do *not* bestow a certain degree of warmth and affection on them. Indeed, studies of perceptions of teacher/student harassment have revealed that while as many men as women complain of being "harassed" by their teachers, the men usually describe the harassment as a female instructor's "being cold and un-friendly."[8] (In my experience such complaints do far more damage at tenure time than women's charges of sexism and discrimination.)

Contrary to what is suggested in the *Bunte* headline, heterosexual men do not generally feel "anxiety" about sexualized and sexualizing gestures from women, unless they are experienced as specifically undermining their masculinity. A young male philosopher once reflected on why he did not feel demeaned when an older woman, who was also his chair, told him he was "cute." I had just shared with him my own experience of "cute," which was that when I was younger I had constantly had to work against being perceived as "cute" at job interviews for fear of not being taken seriously as a philosopher. His reaction had been very different. He had not for a moment felt that the comment reduced or demeaned him in any way; his self-conception as serious philosopher was untouched. He did believe, however, that if the remark had been made by a colleague his own age, he would have felt somewhat sexually diminished, being regarded (as he put it) as a "puppydog rather than a Sean Connery."

Despite such asymmetries in the experiences of men and women, not to mention the added complications of race, ethnicity, age, and sexual ori-entation, the belief that there can be a simple "reversal" of subject posi-tions, even subject positions with a long and deep history, is widespread in our culture. This is evident in the popularity of arguments about "reverse discrimination" and "reverse sexism." I now want to look more closely at one version of such an argument, not with a view to demonstrating that women are too virtuous or disempowered to engage in harassment or to accuse all men of being "Packwoods waiting to happen" (as

Newsweek put it) but to confront a particular construction of masculinity that plays a large role in the social "production" of harassment.

Let me begin by pointing out, first, that studying masculinity is not equivalent to studying *men*. Rather, what is at stake are ideologies and representations of gender, idealizations that affect (and that may also be resisted by) actual men in varying ways, that may be aspired to and embodied by women as well, and that may even come to be incorporated in dominant notions of femininity. (I'll present a concrete example of this last point later in this essay; see "Light My Lucky" ad, figure 26.) Second, while I speak of "masculinity" (rather than the more currently popular "masculinities"), this does not imply that I consider there to be one unchanging and universal form of masculinity or that one can adequately analyze cultural forms of masculinity without also considering race, class, or sexuality. Third, I emphasize that constructions of masculinity are not smooth or seamless but contain internal tensions and contradictions of many sorts.

Men's bodies, no less than women's, are battlegrounds of conflicting requirements about sex roles. Double messages about what it means to "be a man" are communicated even in the most seemingly innocuous children's cartoons. In Disney's version of *Beauty and the Beast,* for example, the beast-hero is represented as the keeper of the flame of civilization. He owns a ceiling-high library full of books, which he presents to heroine Belle, and he is continually contrasted in the film with the provincial, arrogant, ferociously anti-intellectual hunter, Gaston, whom Belle describes at one point as "primeval." (Gaston's room is decorated with antlers; even his furniture is made of antlers.) Gaston, who is a "normal" man, is portrayed as the truly uncivilized beast of the story. It would seem, then, that a statement is being made by the Disney people—that macho isn't cool, that kindness and gentleness are in.

But at the same time as the film extols the virtues of masculine civility, the fierce, animal nature of the beast-hero is romanticized and sexualized. He growls impressively, rears up on his hind legs in phallic splendor, and has a wild passionate nature that seems the cartoon equivalent of Mel Gibson's portrayal of Scottish rebel William Wallace in *Braveheart*. (Wallace is also a scholar, as the film makes sure to emphasize, no doubt anticipating complaints about its otherwise *Animal House* version of masculinity.) The beast's aggression, like Wallace's, is well intentioned and pure of heart. But it's pretty potent, ferocious—and admirable, the Disney cartoon makes clear—when it gets going. Such admiration for man-the-beast abounds in contemporary America—in movies, ads, songs. Don't hold back. Be a man. Be a wild thing. The requirement that men behave like gentlemen orders them, however, to act in a contradictory fashion.

Think, for example, of the instruction in raw aggression that football provides and how it encourages the player to think of his body as a fierce, unstoppable force of nature. Think of how this aggression is rewarded— with scholarships, cultural admiration, romantic attention. Now imagine the young quarterback at a workshop on date rape, held by the counseling center of the same high school that is encouraging him to be an animal on the football field. At that workshop he's told that he must learn that he is not an animal, that his body is not an unstoppable force of nature, that it must yield, in fact, to one little word: "No." Now, which is this young man supposed to be: an animal or a gentleman? The answer, of course, is that he is supposed to be both. Add layerings of race and class ideology and this paradoxical condition becomes even more vexing.

Gender may be complex and changing. However, we do not yet live in a post-gender age. Avant-garde magazines may offer images that unsettle and challenge dominant ideas about masculinity and femininity and that ultimately may alter them. But most of us live in social contexts that exact stiff penalties for resisting or failing to conform to existing conventions, and that offer significant social and material rewards (in jobs, sexual desirability, and the like) for those who successfully obey them. Part of what I try to do in my work is "track" the persistence of notions of gender which we may believe we have gone beyond but with which we are actually still struggling. Often it is the body that reveals this struggle. "Power feminism" celebrates women with social and physical muscle, yet teenagers starve themselves into wispy, dreamy waifs. Men are encouraged by the women in their lives to be more emotionally responsive; at the same time we swoon over rock-hard film heroes and a "soft" man like Bill Clinton is mocked in the press for not knowing how to play "hard ball," for being a negotiator and consensus seeker rather than taking a "firm" stand on issues. This equation of masculinity with "hardness" has dogged Clinton's body too; during his campaign and his first year in office, the press made nasty fun of his doughy physique, treating it as a symbol of how "unpresidential" he was.

Let's now examine what some have claimed to be a major "gender reversal" in the representation of men's bodies in order to determine just how far this reversal goes. When Lucky Vanos took off his shirt in a Coke commercial, editorials sprang up everywhere either complaining about or celebrating the fact that heterosexual male bodies (or perhaps more accurately, bodies being represented as heterosexual) were now being equally as "objectified" as female bodies. The commercial depicted an office full of women setting their watches and running to the window at the precise time every day when Vanos, playing a construction worker, would take off his shirt and drink a Coke. Its joke was the gender turnaround of the familiar trope of male spectator and female spectacle. Examining both classical Western art and contemporary ads, art critic John Berger had noted a pervasive formula: "Men act and women appear." That is, the rule of representing men has been to show them in action, instrumental and effective, seemingly unconcerned about how they appear to others (even when undressed). The rule for representing women, in contrast, has been to depict them only as objects of sight, existing for the pleasure of an imagined spectator, and aware that to be a spectacle is the domain of their value, even when walking to work on a city street. Note this contrast in the ads in figures 19 and 20.

FIGURES 19 AND 20

"Men act and women
appear."

STRIPES GO EVERY WHICH WAY
on this dazzling suit, a three-season winner
because it's made of cotton. Both jacket and
skirt are cropped short. By Charles Chang-
Lima. Boots and shoes these pages by Nine West.

ne Copeland
Ryan Murrayshow
: Hiromi Ando
Samuel Salon

This visual formula reflects certain cultural notions about femininity and masculinity and the differing subjectivities—modes of experiencing oneself, in relation to other people and to the surrounding world—required by those notions. Where femininity is measured and evaluated on the basis of appearance, women are expected to be conscious of and concerned about how they look to others. A degree of vanity is acceptable, even desirable; women who don't seem to care about how they look are suspect (of lesbianism, man-hating, wanting to be men themselves, and so on). Correspondingly, where masculinity is associated with activity, the "manly man" is supposed to embody a subjectivity that is only concerned with "getting the job done." It's narcissistic and feminine to worry about how you look (and thus may be considered a "gay thing" in some cultures). Of course, the notion that heterosexual men are unconcerned with their appearance is a fiction, especially nowadays when magazines on men's fitness and grooming multiply and the industry in cosmetic surgery for men blossoms. I would bet that any "hero"—whatever his sexual orientation—who has developed a chest like the one depicted in the Matchabelli cologne ad is aware of how his muscles look with the sun glinting off them, even as he is "immersed" in baling that hay. The difference that Berger describes is not necessarily a "real" one, reflecting how men and women actually behave or experience themselves, but a *representational* one. That is, the asymmetry has to do with cultural *ideas* about sexual difference and how these ideas are expressed in visual depictions of men and women. These images, of course, have tremendous impact on people's lives. But they do not necessarily accurately mirror reality.

The Coke commercial made Lucky Vanos a celebrity—for his allotted five minutes of cultural time. But simply depicting an undressed male body as the object of the female gaze is not in itself an indication that the representational asymmetry Berger described has been overcome. A 1994 *New Yorker* cover (figure 21) brings the point home humorously. What the Spiegelman cartoon (with or without intent) lampoons is that the male body, insofar as it is represented in terms of an aggressively self-defining authority, oblivious to and unresponsive to other meanings that might be bestowed on it by the gaze of another person, remains powerfully and only a commanding *phallic subject,* capable of forcing the other person to cower before it. Here I am making a distinction between the sexualization of male bodies and the depiction of male bodies as dependent on the look of another to confer or acknowledge value. In a certain sense, as long as the male body is "dressed" in the phallic power to author all definitions and evaluations of its situation, it is not really undressed (or, perhaps more precisely, it is undressed but not naked).

A Fruit of the Loom ad does in earnest what the *New Yorker* cartoon depicts humorously (figure 22). "Yeah, I'm in underwear," the model seems to declare. "Wanna make something of it?" The underwear itself is specifically associated with self-definition, with "making a statement . . . about his style, his way of thinking," and with "bold colors." The ad's ironic play on the word "understatement" winks at the notion that anything about this man could be associated with a diminished or recessive or dependent state, even when he is in his skivvies—or perhaps *especially* when he is in his skivvies. Everything about this ad—the model's muscularity, his bodily stance, his expression—works to code his (semi-)revealed genitals in terms of phallic armor rather than fleshly exposure.[9]

Now I want to explore some of the deeper meaning of the subjectivity depicted in this ad, and I ultimately want to suggest that we look to that subjectivity, not to fantasies of reversal or women's patting men on the butt, for insight into the question that is the title of this essay: "Can a Woman Harass a Man?" The short, uninteresting answer to this question is "Of course." Women are not angels and men are not devils, and both are capable of abuse of power. But men and women are still generally subject to different instructions on how to *be* in the world, and these may help us to understand harassment. The capacity to harass is not written on the Y chromosome. But this doesn't mean that masculinity, as a *cultural* ideology, plays no role in the social production of harassment.

Positing a relationship between masculinity and harassment is not as distinctively modern or feminist as it might seem. The elaborate rules of sexual conduct which regulated relations between men and boys in ancient Greece suggest an implicit recognition of the potential for abuse in otherwise idealized social constructions of masculinity as dominance. The sexual (and social) realization of dominance, of course, requires a dominated "Other," which created no ethical problem as long as the subordinate part-

From left to right:

FIGURE 21
Cover drawing "Brief Encounter" by Art Spiegel-man. © 1994 The New Yorker Magazine, Inc. All rights reserved.

FIGURE 22
Undressed but armored

FIGURE 23
Masculinity without domi-nance

FIGURE 24
Sleep as feminine

ner was a woman, believed to be passive and inferior by nature. But when the beloved was another free man, even if a not yet fully developed free man, the enactment of his lover's masculinity became problematic. How could the older partner fully exercise his masculinity without compromising the nascent masculinity of the younger male, without degrading and reducing and shaming him, without turning him into a woman?

This is not the place to detail the formal and informal rules to protect nascent male subjectivity in classical society. But the Greek "problem of loving boys" (as Foucault calls it)[10] does highlight some important issues for the purposes of this essay. For one, it underscores that bodily gestures and postures—what is invasive, what is demeaning—can only be understood within a larger context of cultural meaning. Gender roles, ideology, and associations are a part of that context. Thus, sexual penetration of the younger man by the older was ethically problematic not because the act of penetration is inherently dominating and demeaning but because receptivity was viewed as a kind of passivity, the mark of inferior, feminine being. Such associations are alive and well today, for example in some contemporary Latin cultures, where whether an individual is considered a "real man" is determined not by whether he sleeps with women or men but by whether he is the active, dominant, penetrating partner or the receptive one. For the "active" *machisto* partner, no stigma attaches. Indeed, as sociologist Thomas Almaguer describes it, "No clear category exists in the popular language to classify him [the active partner]. For all intents and purposes, he is just a normal . . . male." But to play the receptive, "feminine," *pasivo* role is to be regarded with disdain.[11]

With these constructions of gender in mind, let us look again at the model of masculinity suggested by the "Understatement" ad—this time by way of contrast with alternative depictions of the male body which attempt to challenge or subvert that ad's central taboos. Consider, for example, the "2(x)ist" advertisement (figure 23). The model's body here, like that in the "Understatement" ad, is muscled and well-endowed. His body size and shape, by themselves, suggest phallic power. But his reclining, open pose neutralizes any suggestion of aggression or threat. His eyes are closed, his head turned away from the viewer. Instead of being stared down and glowered at, we are invited to survey the model's body, to be the more active partner in the relationship. It is perhaps most significant that the model is asleep—a powerful trope in art and advertising for depicting narcissistic, unconscious immersion in the passive pleasures of the body. Most often it is women who are depicted in this way. In numerous paintings and ads (figure 24) women are shown dreaming, half-smiling over some private secret, happily absorbed in a fantasy world, permitted to withdraw from the responsibilities that require men to stay alert, ready to spring into action at a moment's notice.

Because sleep is generally coded as passive and feminine, depicting male sleep has been uncommon in Western representations. In classical art we do find some languorous Adonises and sleeping fauns. But most male nudes are heroically posed like the Prince Matchabelli man; they look out and beyond, their bodies suggesting movement into the world rather than retreat into dream. There is, however, a still deeper meaning to the aversion to representing men as asleep. Recall the Fruit-of-the-Loom ad's metaphor of "making a statement," projecting one's own definition of self (through one's choice of underwear!). Awake and alert, one can assert such definition. When one is asleep, it is the gaze of the other that is in control, as Jean-Paul Sartre emphasizes in his discussion of Proust's hero Marcel, who only "knows relief" when his lover is asleep.[12] Consciousness defines, lack of consciousness leaves us radically open to the definitions of others. Of course, for Sartre, it is not only when we are asleep that we are vulnerable to what he calls "the look" of the Other. The simple fact that we have bodies that appear to others as objects in the world means that we are forever haunted by our inability to know ourselves in the objectifying mode that others know us. Our vulnerability in sleep is only a particularly concrete reminder of our condition as humans.

Sartre does not consider gender in his discussion of "the look." But there is a provocative difference in the way that Sartre and Simone de Beauvoir approach the subject. For Sartre, our vulnerability to the objectifying and defining look of the Other is an occasion for shame, the "hell" that other people represent. But it is striking that Beauvoir describes this vulnerability as a necessary condition of self-worth—for women. In *The Second Sex,* seemingly unaware that she was providing a counterexample to Sartre's position, she describes "the woman in love" as "hating" her lover's sleep for the very reason that Sartre has Marcel welcoming it: "For the woman," she says, "the absence of her lover is always torture; he is an eye, a judge . . . away from him, she is dispossessed, at once of herself and of the world." We can, of course, question the cultural universality of this construction of femininity. Even so, it presents a challenge to the ungendered universality of the anxiety that Sartre describes, especially when that anxiety is viewed alongside the Greek and Latin constructions of masculinity just discussed. Perhaps Sartre's recoil from the "the look of the Other"—described by him as a "possession" and a "stealing" of his being —is better understood not the way Sartre presents it, as a universal feature of the human condition, but as the consequence of an ideology of masculinity that abhors being gazed at because of the passive, feminine positioning that observation entails. The anxiety is over being penetrated, as it were, by the look of the Other.[13]

Who can stare the other man down? Who will avert his eyes first? Whose gaze will be triumphant, turning the other man into a "woman"? Such moments—"facing up," "facing off," "staring down"—as anthropologist David Gilmore has documented, are a test of machismo in many cultures.[14] "Facing off" is also a common trope for masculine confrontation in movies. "Don't eyeball me!" barks the sergeant to his cadets-in-training in *An Officer and a Gentleman;* the authority of the gaze is a prize to be won only with full manhood. Before then, it is a mark of insolence or stupidity, a failure to understand the codes of masculine rank. In *Get Shorty,* an unsuspecting film director challenges a mob boss to look him in the eye; in return, he is hurled across the room and has his fingers broken. So too in the "Understatement" ad, the gaze of the model stares the viewer down, defies any attempt on the part of the viewer to project definition onto him, insisting that the imagined spectator "take him as he is." I will call this stance that of a "dominating subjectivity," with an emphasis on the subject's discomfort with and unwillingness to be on the receiving end of the defining gaze of another.

The depiction of such a "dominating subjectivity" remains a key feature in popular cultural images of the "real man," easily tailored to various race, class, and sexual codes (as the following ads demonstrate: figures 25–29). It is no longer exclusively reserved for men, however. When the

Marlboro Man appeared in the early sixties, his counterpart was a seduc-tive-looking plaything, blouse unbuttoned, being offered a Tiparillo by a "gentleman." "Light my Lucky" clearly reveals a major transformation in the degree of autonomy and sexual assertiveness deemed appropriate for women.

The old representational asymmetries don't give up without a fight, however. As women pump up, men must bulk up even more. As women compete alongside men, depictions of men must show that males still have the "natural," aggressive edge. So male underwear ads have begun to fea-ture amazingly endowed models who aggressively direct the viewer's atten-tion to their frontal bulges (figures 30 and 31). Some ads show men cupping their genitals, virtually in the same pose taken by street toughs challeng-ing each other. In others the penis appears fully erect, advertising its potency. These ads—which have appeared in "mainstream" publications such as *Vanity Fair* and the *New York Times Magazine*—are remarkable in that erect penises (or penises so large as to suggest erection even when flaccid) have usually been reserved for homoerotic photographs and art. In most West-ern representations the erect penis has been a symbol of an excessive sex-uality (on statues of satyrs, for example) that doesn't fit with the heroic ideals men are supposed to uphold. Typically, in classical art, the conven-tion has been to represent the mature male body as muscular and "phal-lic" but the actual penis as tiny.

These new images—undoubtedly an attempt to grab the gay and straight markets with tropes of masculinity that will have appeal to both groups—have taken our culture from near censorship of the male organ to blatant advertisements for its potency. The uncloseting of the penis is thus a cul-turally mixed bag. On the one hand, it's wonderful to have beautiful, sex-ualized male bodies recharging the experience of reading the Sunday *Times*. The first time I saw one of these ads, a Calvin Klein number that featured a young man with long hair, head lowered and eyes peeking out à la Princess Di, hip seductively posed in the S curve more typically reserved for women

FIGURES 25–29

CAN A WOMAN HARASS A MAN?

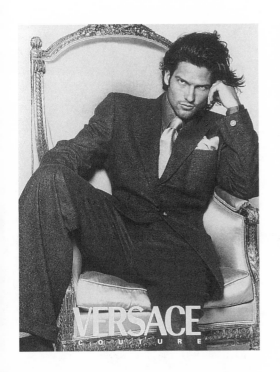

but with rippling torso and torn, form-fitting briefs, it nearly took my breath away. But underwear ads that show men in seductive poses are rare. Most often, the model stares challengingly into the camera, as if daring the viewer to see him as a passive, sexual "object." These ads, while they may be experienced as erotic, are martial in their eroticism, and their message is certainly not one of emotional exposure or penetrability. The penis functions as an assertion of man's "natural" dominance, his unwillingness to be bossed around.

RECONCEPTUALIZING HARASSMENT

The dominating subjectivity depicted in these ads is not linked to men in any essential, universal, or exclusive way. *Of course* women can embody a dominating subjectivity, and in some socially prescribed roles—being a mother, for example—the ability to "stand firm" may even be considered an asset. As the "2(x)ist" and "Light my Lucky" ads show, conventional notions about what postures, gestures, attitudes are appropriate to masculinity and femininity are heterogeneous and often in flux.

CAN A WOMAN HARASS A MAN?

But the ability to mark off one's territory, define the situation, and stand one's ground remains strongly associated with "real" manliness in representations concerned to perpetuate such notions.[15] Recent films like *Braveheart, Legends of the Fall,* and *Independence Day* celebrate this conception of masculinity (allowing some of their female characters to embody it as well). In *Wolf* the hero's transformation from ineffectual, mild-mannered book editor to "natural" man/wolf is represented in several scenes showing him "squaring off" with other men, not letting himself be pushed around. In one scene, in a Bernard Goetz white-man retribution moment, the hero bites off the fingers of a black gang member who had tried to rob him in the park. In another scene, which must have delighted Camille Paglia, he pisses on the shoes of his assistant: "Just marking my territory and you got in the way," he says. In a 1994 issue of *Esquire* devoted to the topic "How to Be a Man," men are urged to abandon the feminized "*faux male*" ideal—"Mr. Sensitive"—foisted on them by women (as the article theorizes) and demand "the freedom to be guys again."[16] Although the article discusses sports, girl chasing, and other activities that the "post-sensitive man" ought to reclaim, it is clear that what defines him is that "he is no longer allowing women to dictate the terms in the ongoing exchange between the sexes."[17]

This quotation speaks powerfully to me about the subjective contours of harassment, particularly when I remember my own experience when I was in graduate school, in the days when we didn't have a word for such things. The relevant set of events had begun with a professor expressing more than professional interest in me over lunch. But I want to emphasize that I do not consider that overture in itself to have been harassing. I wasn't interested and I indicated so, but I didn't feel offended, compromised, degraded, or vulnerable. That I was enrolled in one of his classes didn't concern me, for up to that point I had no reason to believe that what had occurred at lunch would affect his treatment of me as a student. We were more naive in those days, true. But I also do not believe, even today, that emotional complications of this particular nature necessarily compromise teacher/student relations more, say, than unexpressed fantasies or covert resentments.

In any case, the situation rapidly changed for me when the man, having been told "no," then began to sprinkle virtually every conversation we had with references to my gender and/or personal life. After I passed my comprehensive exams, he told me that he was shocked to discover, when the names were revealed, that my exam had been written by a woman, because it had been so rigorously argued; in another conversation he suggested that I was doing my translation in Russian only to please my boyfriend, a professor of Russian. And so on. I swallowed all of this, not because I was afraid of him but because it all seemed to fall into the category of the garden variety, routine forms of sexism I had learned to expect as a normal part of life. Moreover, I had been taught, along with many woman of my generation, that being nice to people, trying not to expose their failings or make them feel bad, particularly if they were men, was more important than standing up for myself. Thus do constructions of femininity and masculinity work to reinforce each other.

But when this professor jovially instructed me that it was "time for class, dear" as he patted me on my rear end at the open doorway of a classroom full of other students, mostly male, his actions entered a qualitatively different realm, even for well-socialized me. My first impulse, believe it or not, after I had run down the hall in humiliation, was to tell him how degrading that gesture had been to me, with what economy and precision he had reduced me, in front of my colleagues, from fellow philosopher-in-training to . . . to what? I'm not sure I can say exactly what, perhaps to a child, perhaps to a piece of meat, perhaps to a being so inconsequential that her personal boundaries and integrity were meaningless. When I tried to explain, the professor laughed and told me that I ought not to be so sensitive, a further humiliation that I didn't even try to explain to him. Instead, I sought understanding from my fellow students. My closest friends were males; they told me, "Well, what did you expect? You don't exactly dress like a nun!" Even at the time, I knew that the professor's gesture, although it involved physical contact with a culturally sexualized part of the body, was not in the nature of an unwelcome sexual advance. That part had taken place weeks before. What was going on now was an attempt—conscious or otherwise—to put me back in my place.

What was that place? My transgression had been that I had answered back, had said "no" to him. In one sense, of course, my behavior was in keeping with the gender rules, for modern constructions of femininity and masculinity have allotted to women the power to accept or reject potential suitors. This is a power that men feel acutely as a source of *their* vulnerability and potential shame in the face of an evaluating and possibly dismissive *female* gaze. But one way to foreclose on being dismissed is to pursue those who are less experienced, less fully formed in their opinions, structurally subordinate, dependent, tentative, more likely to be dazzled by authority. I was a student, I had been counted on to defer—if not to accept, at least to be rattled or flattered—yet instead I dared to assert the evaluative gaze of a grown-up woman, an equal.

My teacher's response was remarkably effective in restoring a balance of power more comfortable to him. We understand and perform the grammar and semantics of bodily gestures as effortlessly and with as little thought as we put together sentences from our native language. With one eloquent gesture, my own ability to define myself—as student, intellectual, future philosopher, sexual subject—was stripped away with a flourish and replaced by his preferred construction of relations. The same dynamics, if we believe Anita Hill, were at work when Clarence Thomas shoved pornography under her nose. Yes, he was counting on Hill's proper upbringing to ensure that she would feel humiliated. But the manipulation of Hill's sexual mores here should not confuse us into thinking that this was a crude attempt at sexual seduction. Thomas's actions and those of my professor were not the actions of men confused about the rules of sexual courting. They were the actions of gender bullies, trying to cut uppity women down to size.

We make a great mistake, then, in equating harassment with specifically sexualizing gestures. I do not deny that sexuality and abuse of power are often married in this culture. It may be that it is through sexualizing gestures that women most frequently get defined, reduced, and stripped of their subjectivity. When Bob Packwood grabbed an elevator operator and shoved his tongue into her mouth, he invaded her professional and bodily space with a sexual weapon. But clearly one can willfully reduce and disempower *without* the use of sexual weapons. Although some racial harassment, for example, is sexualizing, not all of it is; being called "boy," in fact, disempowers and demeans the black male by desexualizing him, by neutralizing his adult masculinity. And much of what we call sexual harassment is really more properly speaking *gender* harassment; that is, comments and behaviors that, like my professor's snide remarks about women's lesser intellect and the "personal" nature of my scholarly choices, continually make a point of gender "difference"—often (although not always) with a view of that difference that is derogatory to women—and thus have the effect of making women feel like less than full persons in that classroom or workplace.

In the same way that one can disempower without sexualizing, initiating sexual "looks" and gestures are not in themselves disempowering. But how do we begin to draw useful distinctions here? I'm afraid that I can only offer complexity, issues to mull over rather than codes to install. One place to begin, taking off from my notion of "dominating subjectivity," is with the question of whether each person in the relationship in question (and "relationship" here can refer to the glance that passes between two strangers) can tolerate and accommodate the other's subjectivity responding, "answering"—and not necessarily with the response that is desired or expected. Packwood, of course, didn't even give the elevator operator and many others a chance to respond, to protest; that perhaps was the essence of what was so degrading about what he did to them. On this analysis, a boss's putting a calendar with naked women on the wall of an office is not in itself necessarily harassing; nor is a teacher's putting an arm around a student. Rather, harassment becomes a relevant category only when the demeaning or disturbing nature of gestures or materials is evident or, if it is not evident, has been pointed out by the person who is feeling uncomfortable. When that "definition" of the situation is deliberately ignored by those who control the environment, when *their* constructions continue to prevail, we can meaningfully talk of harassment.

But "having knowledge of the demeaning nature of gestures" can become a sticky or slippery criterion. We might want to insist that some knowledge of this sort—for example, of the degrading effect of gross racial and sexual epithets—should come with being an ethically responsive and responsible member of the culture and shouldn't *require* instruction from employees or students. More important, subordinated subjects are not always—perhaps rarely—in a position to freely offer such instruction. Their jobs and grades may be at stake, but more subtly and profoundly they may experience themselves as overwhelmed by the sheer cultural power held by their bosses and teachers: their power to construct and control the operant language, the interpretations, the "reality" of the situation. Those who hold this power may be the last to recognize it because it is as natural and invisible as the air they breathe. Here David Mamet's *Oleanna,* for all that may be problematic about its portrayal of campus politics, is much more sophisticated than Crichton's *Disclosure* in exploring the dynamics of disempowerment. In one of the play's most trenchant moments, the male teacher reduces the female student, who had just been nervously about to reveal a painful personal secret, to virtual nothingness by cavalierly taking a phone call on a real-estate matter. Throughout their appointment such calls had interrupted their conversation, the teacher thinking nothing of conducting his business loudly, the way adults talk to each other at dinner parties, oblivious to their children's presence. Mamet's point, as I interpret it, is not that this is harassment but that we annihilate each other in myriad ways other than through "unwelcome sexual advances." The professor, however, is totally oblivious to the impact of his behavior, in part because he tacitly assumes that he "owns" the universe they inhabit and that any time, space, and intimacy he offers is a magnanimous gift the student should feel honored by, and in part because he is so engrossed in himself that her reactions simply don't register with him.

Disclosure's hypothetical reversal obscures the historical reality that with male privilege—which not all men possess equally, of course—comes a sense of implicit (and often unconscious) ownership of public space and its definitions and values, a sense of ownership that women typically do not feel. When that implicit ownership is challenged by women, when women claim the right to share the power to define and control the rules of the game, sexual and otherwise, men may feel baffled and uncertain about the new rules. They may also feel threatened by the loss of manhood implied in relinquishing the right of sole ownership of public space to women. But easy and unconscious familiarity with the privileges of such ownership is not a prerequisite for being threatened by equality with women. Men who come to some position of power from groups historically deprived of the masculine privilege of defining and controlling public space—men *manqué* is the term sociologist Richard Majors suggests in *Cool Pose*[18]—may have just as intense an investment in their phallic authority, hard-won and precarious as it is. Throughout the Thomas/Hill hearings, Clarence Thomas's need to maintain a proud and controlled presence (a "cool pose," as Majors would call it) seemed to go far deeper than the exigencies of politics; it was not hard to imagine how difficult it would have been for this man to tolerate Anita Hill's own coolness and self-composure in her previous dealings with him. In the "natural" (read: phallocentric) order of things, women look *up* to men, they do not answer men's gaze as equals. Having finally achieved a public place in that order, Thomas was not about to relinquish its privileges without a fight. Around such "manhood" issues, the white senators could feel a genuine sense of pained empathy with Thomas.[19]

I do not mean to say that such defensive, dominating, and phallocentric behavior is characteristic of men, black or white. My purpose is rather to identify that piece of masculinity that sanctions and encourages such behavior. But femininity plays a role here too. For both men *and* women in this culture may have deep problems with women "answering," talking back, asserting their definitions of reality. Many women, for their part, put up with and attempt to ignore demeaning behavior, as I did when I was a graduate student, because femininity demands protecting male egos and subordinating the needs of self to the care of others. We may also feel it is our job to keep the calm in a situation where a male might display anger or violence. Such constructions of femininity, although challenged by Nike ads and calls to "power feminism," are still very much alive in this culture. When Anita Hill was lambasted by some African Americans for exposing Clarence Thomas, the charge was her lack of racial solidarity and consciousness. Many white women had a hard time accepting the fact that some of Thomas's defenders were black women; these white women failed to appreciate how painful it was for black women to see yet another black man reduced to a man *manqué,* and in public view of the nation. But in their protective responses to Thomas, the racial identifications of black women were clearly aided and abetted by gender socialization. For Hill's dignity was at stake too, and Hill was no less black than Thomas. Why should protecting Hill's integrity and dignity be any less required of "racial solidarity and consciousness" than protecting Thomas's? And why should Hill but not Thomas have been required to subordinate her interests to a larger community good? Would the same have been required of another black man bringing forth evidence that Thomas had been racially or physically abusive to him?

The cultural landscape, while complex, argues against the notion, as Crichton's equity feminist lawyer puts it, that "power is neither male nor female." Understanding harassment, as I hope to have shown, does not require us to replace the mystifications of *Disclosure* with a scenario of essentialized male villains and female victims but to recognize the ways in which ideologies of masculinity and femininity inform the historical realities of power in this culture. As the Clarence Thomas example makes clear, gender ideology is not alone in this. Although Clarence Thomas and my professor may have shared a certain notion of the deference due them as men, they surely came to that notion with different expectations, frustrations, and investments. Power has racial, class, and other features as well as gender features. But above all it is never faceless, never neuter, and the fantasy that it is operates as an obstacle to our beginning a more candid, culturally informed conversation about harassment.

BRINGING BODY TO THEORY

There's nothing like reading interpretation and criticism of one's own work to confirm the mundane reality of the postmodern pronouncement that the author is dead. The work itself, however, often feels all too alive, slippery and wiggly as it is handled and given shape by other people's psyches and concerns, other political and intellectual agendas than one's own. It's an unnerving and challenging experience—I imagine not too different from a parent's recognition that her children have minds of their own—in which one has to learn to accept with grace exactly what all one's efforts have been aiming at: a once intimate part of you is out there, going its own way, able to exist quite well without you.

Sometimes, though, there *is* the pleasure and relief of feeling understood (which does not necessarily mean receiving praise; some of the most admiring readings of my work discuss a text I barely recognize): "Yes, that's it, you've got it, that's what I was trying to say, that's the thing that's most important to me." The author may be "privileging" her reading of the text in feeling that these are moments of truth, recognition, clarity. But that's an author's privilege, and it's irresistible in any case. Susan Hekman's intelligent, nonideological, perceptive, and integrative reading of my work and Judith Butler's not only takes extraordinary care to read the texts with a view to discovering our projects as *we* have conceived and pursued them (perhaps, at times, as they have pursued us) but also places the texts in a broad perspective that allows them to speak to each other in a way that they haven't before.[1] I felt understood by her reading, and I also learned

173

about my work from it. I believe Hekman's essay is one of the most useful, difference-respecting but polarity-busting discussions of feminist theory I have read.

In addition to tracing differences and points of connection between Butler's work and my own, Hekman raises some questions for each of us. The challenges she poses to me—to make explicit both my conception of the "materiality" of the body and my theory of "resistance"—have frequently been posed to me by philosophers and theorists. My reaction to them has been ambivalent. On the one hand, I want to say (and sometimes have said, when pressed too hard): "Leave me alone! I don't do that kind of thing and don't want to!" I have always considered myself a phenomenologist and diagnostician of culture who uses diverse theoretical tools to excavate and expose hidden or unquestioned aspects of concrete forms, occurrences, texts, practices. Although my work is highly theoretical in that it is always analyzing and interpreting (always "reading into things," as my students sometimes complain), it is not aimed at articulating or defending an overarching theory of body, resistance, or anything else. I don't consider that I "do theory" or "have" a theory but rather that I *use* theory, fairly promiscuously but with a decided preference for certain types.

On the other hand, I have sometimes felt—precisely because I have preferences among theories and have invoked them in order to criticize other approaches—that it is disingenuous of me to disown my theory in this way. Moreover, silence on these issues would allow certain common misinterpretations (from my point of view) of my arguments and ideas to flourish unchecked. But more important issues are at stake too, and they go beyond the interpretation of my work. My critique of theory, like all my work, is cultural criticism, that is, it is directed at particular styles of theorizing, not at "theory" in general. Theorizing, like all human activities, has taken many different historical forms and served many different purposes. My criticisms of postmodern theory have been very specific. First, I have often taken issue with the baroque obscurity of postmodern prose. I love Foucault's image of ideas as intellectual "hand grenades" and I personally value culturally lobbed disturbance over hot-house scholarly conversation. Second, I have argued that despite postmodern theory's infatuation with "the body" it often seems to be scaling the heights of abstraction with pure mind. I am not "antitheory." But my criticisms of *certain kinds* of theorizing—as excessively aestheticized, pretentious, or unhinged from social context—have sometimes been mistaken as indicating that I am. This impression, in turn, has led to characterizations of my work as "practical" rather than "theoretical," perpetuating one of the (gender and race-coded) dualities I most abhor and contributing to the notion that the only "real" theory is what I would describe as "metatheory."

Nowadays few academics engage in general theory building, an enterprise that has been criticized (often unfairly) as "totalizing."[2] But many academics do engage in metatheory and regard it as the most rigorous form of scholarship. Metatheory is talk *about* theory: about the presuppositions, implications, and complexities of various theoretical formulations, about conflicts between theories, internal contradictions, and unintended alliances (for example, with essentialism, foundationalism, relativism), and so forth. Metatheory is important and interesting and is accorded a privileged place by philosophers and social theorists. But theory need not be the object of analysis in order for a discussion to qualify as theoretical; it can be an animating force "behind" an analysis. What theory animates can vary widely; the analysis may be social, political, or historical, a piece of cultural criticism, or even an exploration of personal experience. Among those who see themselves as "theoreticians" (especially philosophers), however, there has been a tendency to view these approaches hierarchically; the more particular one gets—and certainly, the more personal one gets—the less "theoretical" one's work is considered. Work that theorizes about the body by exploring the situation of women, particularly if it makes use of personal experience, has rarely been accorded the privileged status of "theory." Such has been the fate of much early feminist writing (before we learned to gussy our discussions up with sophisticated jargon drawn from male theorists).

So: I have come to realize that by not taking responsibility for the theoretical commitments of my *own* work, I may be contributing to some of the intellectual assumptions and biases I complain about most bitterly. Perhaps it's time for me to embrace the theory in my work, not as a temporary partner providing solace or excitement for the night but as a serious and committed relationship that deserves acknowledgment and legitimization. On to "materiality," then, and a key quotation from Karl Marx:

> In direct contrast to German philosophy, which descends from heaven to earth, here we ascend from earth to heaven. That is to say, we do not set out from what men say, imagine, conceive, nor from men as narrated, thought of, imagined, conceived, in order to arrive at men in the flesh. We set out from real, active men, and on the basis of their real life process we demonstrate the development of the ideological reflexes and echoes of this life process. The phantoms formed in the human brain are also necessarily sublimates of their material life process, which is empirically verifiable and bound to material premises. Morality, religion, metaphysics, all the rest of ideology and their corresponding forms of consciousness, thus no longer have the semblance of independence. They have no history, no development; but men, developing their material production and their material intercourse, alter, along with this, their real existence, their thinking, and the products of their thinking. Life is not determined by consciousness, but consciousness by life. (From Karl Marx, *The German Ideology*)

Marx was my first intellectual hero, and while I do not consider myself a Marxist, my own "materialism" has roots in his. Despite Marx's own pronouncement that he is standing idealism on its head, I have never understood him to be "reversing" Hegel by elevating some *other* realm of human activity (call it the "material realm") to a position of priority over the realm of "consciousness." What drew me to Marx was what I took to be his insistence on the *concreteness* of human existence—consciousness included—against such abstract conceptions as Man, Reason, and Freedom. Consciousness, while it may fancy itself in league with Platonic forms or transcendental subjectivity, does not fly with the angels but walks the earth. Its biography is as concrete and historical as any other feature of human life.

In "Feminism, Foucault, and the Politics of the Body,"[3] I discuss the important role that historical thinking—which developed out of my participation in feminism and later also drew me to Foucault—played in my intellectual development: "As a philosopher and a feminist," I wrote, "historicism was for me the great liberator of thought, challenging both the most stubborn pretensions of my discipline (to the possession of eternal truths, atemporal foundations, universal reason) and enduring social myths about human nature and gender by showing them to be, in Nietzsche's words, 'human, all too human.' " But claims to privileged foundations or absolute truth can take other forms than that of the Platonic or Cartesian (or Hegelian) overseer of Reality. My earliest critiques were aimed at these "masculine" forms of philosophical hubris (*cultural* forms, not to be simply equated with the work of Plato, Descartes, or Hegel but representing dominant traditions of philosophizing grounded in particular interpretations of their work). I later found cultural overseers exercising their muscles in areas closer to home.

I vividly recall the first time I insisted on the "materiality" of the body at an academic conference. It was not a pleasant experience. It was 1988, "textuality" was still the rage, "essentialism" was the horror of horrors, and the word "material"—since become so fashionable—was decidedly *not* "comme il faut." The paper I was presenting was an early version of "Material Girl: The Effacements of Postmodern Culture,"[4] and when the word "material" came out of my mouth it was as though I had farted in public. This is no exaggeration. I felt the atmosphere in the room shift palpably, as those who had been comfortable in the assurance that I was a right-minded person (after all, I was working out of Foucault, wasn't I?) all at once felt something unexpected and foul enter the room. During the discussion period some feminist scholars generously gave me the opportunity to clarify and save myself, with questions like "You aren't *really* positing, *are you,* a body that is unmediated, 'natural,' outside of language and discourse, which is not open to a multiplicity of interpretive readings, *are you*?" I tried to explain what I was doing, but it was no use. None of my explanations were able to cleanse me of the taint of the retrograde notion of a "material body." I was not invited to dinner after the talk with the rest of the feminist theorists, and when I came upon one of the conference organizers speaking to a keynote speaker outside the hotel, they fell into awkward silence.

The incident was a watershed for me and nearly drove me out of academia. Instead, I decided that I had my work cut out for me. "Material" and "matter" are no longer dirty words, and I like to think that I have played a role in bringing about that change and in encouraging open criticism of some of the dogmas that once reigned in feminist theory. In attaching itself to certain intellectual fashions, feminist theory has been, of course, no different from any other scholarly culture; what's different, perhaps, is feminism's responsiveness to challenge and its willingness to change. That responsiveness has been enormously gratifying to witness. I now see graduate students insisting that theory be tested against their insights and experiences as embodied beings, I see them incorporating cultural criticism and personal experience into theoretical dissertations, I see them wanting to write in accessible styles—and I see feminist faculty encouraging them while trying to break through some old habits and dogmas of our own.

In the eighties I had absolutely no use for biological or evolutionary paradigms of the body, and I was just as phobic about "genes" as any other self-respecting social constructionist. The word "natural" elicited lectures from me on ideology and mystification. Today I am more agnostic and humble—and less politically trigger-happy—about the role of biology and evolution. I continue to insist, along with other social critics of scientism, that what constitutes our knowledge of biology is always mediated by the conceptual frameworks—cultural as well as scientific paradigms—that we bring into the laboratory. But for me, this does not distinguish science from any other human enterprise and thus should occasion no more prima facie suspicion of science than anything else. For me, there is a big leap from acknowledging that the science of biology is mediated by historically located, conceptual frameworks (an acknowledgment that adds a cultural dimension to what Kant argued) to reducing the concept of "biology" to the status of "fiction." If biology is a "fiction," so too is every other framework for understanding the body, social constructionism and performative theories included.

I think that Butler would agree with my last statement—in theory. In practice, though, she is what I would call a "discourse foundationalist." For the discourse foundationalist, insights into our embeddedness in discourse—the signs and symbols we use to depict and categorize the world—function as a "bottom line," a privileged framework that is used to deconstruct other frameworks of understanding to its own preferred elements (that's why I offer the image of a "theoretical pasta machine" that converts everything passing through it into a "trope") and, having done this, dispense with them as so much detritus. Certainly, we are embedded in language. We are also creatures with a physiology that limits us, even in the kinds of languages we have developed. Humanists are appalled when evolutionary biologists reduce our "privileged shrine" (as Maxine Sheets-Johnstone jibes) of language to merely one variant of primate "vocal and facial display." Is it any less reductive when poststructuralist theorists evaporate concepts like "genes" (or "matter") into "tropes" of scientific fiction?

These reductions (with guilt equally distributed on both sides, as far as I can see) have played a large role in fomenting the hostile polarization of the sciences and the humanities at universities today and perpetuating the fragmenting Cartesian division that has structured the disciplines. The humanities (with literature and philosophy at the forefront) have perfected an identification with disembodied pure mind (read, for much contemporary lit theory and philosophy: "language"), while the sciences have reduced experimental rigor to the study of *res extensa,* mindless bodies. (Anyone who doubts the latter should try to find entries for "consciousness," "mind," "experience," or even "thinking" in the indexes of most texts on biology and evolution.) These "academically propagated creatures," as Sheets-Johnstone states, "mindless bodies on the one hand and disembodied minds on the other . . . are profoundly unnatural species."[5]

Let's agree we cannot "get outside" the (historically sedimented) discourses and representations that shape our reality. Does this mean that all we are legitimately permitted to talk about is our reality *as* discourse and representation? And what makes "matter" an "effect of discourse" and the "trope" a foundational explanatory concept? The "trope" has a history, too, and is no more "prior to discourse" than "matter." And in any case, whatever we believe on a "meta" level, we all still go on talking and arguing (and hopefully evaluating and discriminating and thoughtfully considering) as if there were more than just competing fictions at stake, and this is how it must (and should) be for embodied beings. For myself, today I am less inclined than I used to be to dismiss the claims of geneticists. As I grow older and fall prey to the same disorders as everyone else in my family, I feel my own genetic inheritance more acutely than I did when I was younger and naively convinced of my power to "resist" becoming anything like my father and mother.

This evolution in my thinking doesn't mean that I'm not still suspicious of arguments about the biological basis of homosexuality, or race, or differences between men and women. But historical vigilance is not a metaphysical position, it's a critical attitude. And it's one that needs to be applied toward all our intellectual attachments, not just science. All disciplines, all scholars, all scientists, all social policymakers need to be critically aware of the cultural assumptions we bring to our work and of the cultural uses being made of our work. The problem with many scientists who have recently inveighed against "cultural studies" is not that they insist on the "reality" of the world or scientific objectivity as a regulative ideal—both of which I and many other cultural theorists insist on too—but that they take their *own* objectivity as an accomplished and unquestionable premise and refuse to look at their own beliefs and practices through culturally and historically informed eyes. But then so too do many postmodernists.

These issues are intimately related to my conception of "materiality," which for better or worse has not changed much over the last ten years. First, the obvious (or hopefully obvious): In speaking of "materiality" I am neither invoking some "matter" of the body to oppose to its "form" nor am I insisting on the primacy of the brute "matter" of things or the "natural" or the instinctual against the culturally overlaid or linguistic. "Materiality," for me, is not *stuff,* not substance, not nature. (It is not even exclusively about "the body," except insofar as "the body" has been imagined as the cultural repository for the features of human existence on which I am insisting, shortly to be described.) So much for what "materiality" is *not* for me. What it *is,* as Susan Hekman rightly says, is less clear. This doesn't surprise me, because I invoke the concept as a kind of umbrella metaphor or governing image that embraces a cluster of values—epistemological, dialogical or conversational, political, existential, perhaps even ethical—that I am advocating.

"Materiality," in the broadest terms, signifies for me our finitude. It refers to our inescapable physical locatedness in time and space, in history and culture, both of which not only shape us (the social constructionist premise, which I share with postmodernists) but also *limit* us (which some postmodernists appear to me to deny). As Nietzsche rightly insisted, we are always standing *someplace* and seeing from *somewhere,* and thus we are always partial and selective thinkers. But the desire, the anxiety, to get "above and beyond" our finite selves (as Dewey, mincing no words, put it) is intense. Intellectuals have different ways of enacting such a fantasy. The presumption that one has attained a "view from nowhere" is the classic philosophical one, and it is the subject of *The Flight to Objectivity*[6] and my early writing on the hubris and self-deception of philosophical fantasies of escape from the body (for example, "The Cultural Overseer and the Tragic Hero").[7] What I call the "dream of being everywhere" is the postmodern version, discussed in my critiques of contemporary theory ("Feminism, Postmodernism, and Gender Skepticism,"[8] "Feminist Skepticism and the 'Maleness' of Philosophy").[9] Neither image of transcendence admits the finiteness of our condition as knowers or the historical nature of its own existence. When I was studying philosophy, in a discipline in which the Cartesian overseer was still king, his gender, race, and class biases yet to be challenged, the "view from nowhere" ruled the roost. But today I sometimes wish, dazed and confused by some slithery, postmodern conversation, that the Cartesian overseer would make a return appearance and "clear" the air. (Of course, he hasn't actually gone away, he's just in another room.)

Our materiality (which includes history, race, gender, and so forth as well as the biology and evolutionary history of our bodies and our dependence on the natural environment) impinges on us—shapes, constrains, and empowers us—both as thinkers and knowers and also as "practical," fleshly bodies. The latter has been an important focus of my work on eating disorders, contemporary technologies of reshaping the self, and now my current work on masculinity. But my conception of the socially constructed body tends to be more "materially" inclined than that of many other contemporary academic writers. This is not because (as some critics have charged) I invoke some "essential female subject" or "gender core" as a ground. I don't even believe, as Hekman says in one of the few places where I believe she has misinterpreted me, that feminism as critical practice "must be grounded in the sexed specificity of the female body." In my view, that has been *one* of feminism's key critical projects, but (like everything else) its vitality and efficacy are dependent on historical, cultural context.

Drawing on Ann Snitow's satirical but telling distinction between "Red Bloomer" feminists (who emphasize, even revel in, sexed specificity) and "Transcenders" (who want to deconstruct gender, even sex), I argue that each of these poles is "necessary to feminist struggle and change." My criticism of the postmodern feminist infatuation with "transcendence" concerns the discrepancy that I see between the currently dominant theory (deconstructing gender) and the bodily, institutional, practical realities of our culture. These are very much organized around the "fictions" of gender and race, and, as Hekman correctly points out in explicating my conception of "material," their inscriptions cannot be simply evaporated, for they "cause pain and suffering for 'real,' 'material' women." Here Hekman understands what those critics who have charged me with "essentialism" have missed: In insisting on the materiality of gender I am not invoking "nature" or importing covert essences. Our materiality includes our biology, but that is for scientists to explore. As a cultural critic and philosopher of the body, I explore and urge that we not lose sight of the concrete consequences—for "our bodies, ourselves"—of living in a gendered and racially ordered world.

My work on the body is more "material" than that of many other philosophers because I believe that the study of representations and cultural "discourse," while an important part of the cultural study of the body, cannot by itself stand as a history of the body. Those discourses impinge on us as fleshly bodies, often in ways that cannot be determined from a study of representations alone. To make such determinations, we need to get down and dirty with the body on the level of its practices—to look at what we are eating (or not eating), the lengths we will go to keep ourselves perpetually young, the practices that we engage in, our emulation of TV and pop icons, and so forth. Our assessments of gender and race inequities must consider not only the most avant-garde images from *Details* or *Interview* magazine but also what people are doing to their bodies in the more mundane service of the "normal"—the kinds of cosmetic surgeries they are having, the hours they spend on the StairMaster, what they feel about themselves when they look in the mirror. In studying masculinity we must not only study the "phallus," symbol of masculine power and authority and capable of being assumed by women as well as men, but also *men's* bodies in their historical diversity and concrete, fleshly vulnerability.

Such talk makes many philosophers queasy. The first time I said the word "thigh" in a talk to (mostly male) philosophers, the gulps were audible; now that I'm working on male bodies, I expect them to be even louder. But it's not just prudishness that makes philosophers blanch at mention of body parts. Many philosophers have been drawn to philosophy or "theory" because of the promise of a high, heady, and "untouchable" (as Dewey puts it) realm of ideas where they can imagine themselves as masters rather than creatures of the universe. As bodies, as Dewey points out, we are most definitely not masters of our own lives, let alone the universe.

Keeping track of the practical life of our bodies is important to keeping us intellectually honest. Intellectuals tend to grossly conflate the articulation of an idea or argument to their own satisfaction or excitement (or the excitement and satisfaction of their academic cohorts) with the "reality" of things outside the domain of their own activity. It's a kind of idealism, and image makers do it too. Ingrid Sischy, editor of *Interview* magazine, proclaims in a recent editorial that we are living in an age in which beauty has had "its chains taken off." Pardon me? Sischy may view the difference between a skinny eighties model in a tailored suit and a skinny nineties model with a nose-ring as the difference between repression and liberation, but teenagers are still starving themselves, all the same.

Our ideas, of course, are a part of reality, and they can change it. Imaginative interpretations (and images) excite and inspire, they start important cultural conversations going; if our ideas were limited to mirroring reality (as if that were possible), things would be pretty dreary. But just because an idea or image—of the body, say—is thrillingly "transgressive" to a bunch of artists or academics does not mean we should start trumpeting the dawn of a new age. We can, of course, argue anything we want "in theory." But only an examination of concrete historical situations can determine whether the body is being "rewritten" or dualisms are being "transcended." This is why *Unbearable Weight* insists that assessing where we stand vis-à-vis the dualisms of mind/body, male/female, black/white, and so on requires concrete exploration and critique of the many practical, institutional, and cultural arenas (including the aesthetics and ethics of the body) that have been and continue to be shaped by those dualisms. We cannot make the mistake of imagining that they have been transcended or "transgressed" just because we can "destabilize" them in theory. I believe that many postmodern readings of the body become lost in the fascinating, ingenious (and often, prematurely celebratory) routes that imagination, intellect, and political fervor can take when looking at bodily "texts" without attention to the concrete contexts—social, political, cultural, practical—in which they are embedded. And so they need to be reminded of the materiality of the body.

This, in a nutshell, was my problem with Butler's original reading of drag as parody and the reason why I have questioned (in "Postmodern Subjects, Postmodern Bodies")[10] whether "there is a body" in her *Gender Trouble*. The body's materiality, for me, is first and foremost about concreteness and concrete (and limiting) *location*. In *Gender Trouble* Butler claims a great deal for the destabilizing power of parodic bodies, a power that for her derives from highly general and abstract features of parody, one might say from its grammar. She does not concretize and specify the "body-in-drag" itself or locate it in the concrete contexts that, from my point of view, will determine just where and how "destabilizing" the parody is. Yet she concludes that drag "effectively mocks . . . the notion of true gender identity" and "displaces the entire enactment of gender significations from the discourse of truth and falsity."

Queer theorists are now doing exciting work complicating Butler's position by looking at diverse forms of drag in concrete social contexts. And Butler has since modified her own position. I have mentioned my critique of *Gender Trouble* here in order to clarify a common misunderstanding about the nature of my criticisms of that book. I do *not* see Butler as arguing that "we choose our gender much as we choose our clothes." That would be a crude and silly reading of Butler (although accurate with respect to some other postmodern authors), and it is not mine. (For me, the act of choosing clothes is hardly the best metaphor for an act of autonomy, anyway!) What I charge Butler with is a philosophical abstractness that, combined with a postmodern taste for the "instability" of texts, leads to what is perhaps an overestimation of the degree of subversion of norms that is taking place at any time. As I have argued against *Gender Trouble*'s abstract theory of parody: "Subversion is contextual, historical, and above all, social. No matter how exciting the destabilizing potential of texts, bodily or otherwise, whether those texts are subversive or recuperative or both or neither cannot be determined in abstraction from actual social practice." Butler has since acknowledged (in *Bodies That Matter*) the importance of such considerations.

Perhaps another point of confusion about my position has been that for me—although apparently not for many other theorists—questions of "autonomy" and questions of "resistance" are separate ones. That is, whether our actions can be said to be autonomous or "free" is distinct from the question of which of those actions can be said to "resist" a social norm. Questions concerning free will, determinism, and autonomy are either metaphysical questions I couldn't begin to imagine *how* to answer or they are so dependent on definition that they can be answered in any number of equally arbitrary ways. In neither case do they provide information about the sort of cultural diagnoses that interest me.

Am I behaving autonomously when I choose my clothes? If I imagine autonomy as having to do with interpretation and creative interraction with cultural forms, I would say that I have "autonomy" in choosing my clothes. But if this is my definition of autonomy, then it applies as well to just about every conceivable human activity beyond the purely instinctual, including many of those performed in conditions of outright servitude. If, however, I define "autonomy" as requiring that I act without the mediation of culture, then no, I certainly do not have "autonomy" in picking my clothes. But what actions *would* qualify as autonomous in this way? However I define autonomy, the cultural world is impinging on me in the same *concrete* ways, and these are what I am interested in assessing.

Nowadays academics may be more likely to speak of "agency" rather than "autonomy" or "freedom." But usually they are after the same prize. "God made man but not the sin in him," Augustine said, trying to salvage "free will" for Christians. Academic attempts to prove that human beings have "agency," I believe, are no less motivated by extraintellectual investments. We want to believe that our choices are "ours," we don't like to feel that we are being pushed around. For some reason, although I am quite rebellious when it comes to concrete cultural interactions, I have never felt the need to assert my metaphysical autonomy. I resent many of the norms of our culture and I resist obedience to them. (The more normative cosmetic surgery to "correct" aging becomes, the less likely I am to have it.) But I am quite willing to grant that my defiance is as "determined" in me (by my genes, upbringing, moment in history) as another person's conformity. The difficult issue, for me, is figuring out the meaning and consequences—both personal and political—of my actions. In having a face-lift or in having my "Jewish" nose bobbed, what norms would I be servicing? What effect will these actions have on my sense of who I am? On my acceptance of my finitude, my mortality? On the values I am communicating to those who look up to me for guidance? On shaping, in my own small way, the culture of the future?

In assessing resistance—as I understand that activity—I am not asking questions about whether an action is "free" or "determined," chosen or culturally coerced, performed by agents or automatons. I am looking at the concrete consequences of actions, trying to assess in what direction(s) they are moving (or reproducing) the institutions and practices of society. This assessment will always be an enormously complex cultural determination, which can only yield a provisional and perhaps ambiguous conclusion, and it *will* require theory. Examining what's going on in the material realm, Marx's comment in *German Ideology* to the contrary, is never a matter of purely "empirical" verification. For we need to learn to "see" what is around us, as Marx was well aware, and for that we need tools that will bring what is obscured (and sometimes deliberately mystified) into clear relief. Even so, the map is seldom clearly marked.

As Hekman insightfully points out, both Butler and I (following Foucault) view resistance as produced from "within" rather than outside a dominant order. This is an important commonality in our work. We share a view of power that recognizes that precisely when an order seems at its peak, it is releasing the lava that may bury it (or, at least, heat things up for it). The seeds of transformation are indeed everywhere, always. But how can we determine the status of our own activity within these (historical) processes? This is a question that is frequently posed to Foucaultians, and Butler asks it of herself in *Bodies That Matter:* "How will we know the difference between the power we promote and the power we oppose?" Susan Hekman poses a similar challenge to me: "If our resistance to the cultural construction of the body cannot appeal to a 'real' or 'natural' body, and thus, that resistance is also a cultural construction, then how can it be effective as resistance?" And she poses a variant of this to Butler as well: "If the excluded, the abject, is as much a discursive product of the law of sex as the hegemonic heterosexual norm, then how can the abject be defined as a realm of resignification that destabilizes the hegemonic? How can it be the site where disruption will occur?"

It's interesting (and makes a great deal of sense) that, for all our differences, in the final analysis Butler and I are presented with the same sort of challenge. Perhaps more strenuously than most, Butler and I have each insisted—while focusing on different arenas, hers the discursive/linguistic, mine the practical/material—on the impossibility of "getting outside" history. I believe that this is a core conviction that goes to the heart of what drives both of us as philosophers, and—parodoxically but predictably—it may be where we have each seen the other lacking, slipping in the rigor and consistency of her dedication. But in this particular challenge to both of us our similarity emerges in clear relief. I would like to end this piece by responding, perhaps in a way that applies to both of us.

Sometimes I have heard variants of this challenge posed in terms such as "How is resistance possible in a Foucaultian world?" This formulation reveals what is wrong with a whole set of questions that academics have been asking recently. In "Rehabilitating the 'I' " Mario Moussa and I describe such questions as a postmodern return of Zeno's paradox: "For Zeno, the problem was how to account for movement; for many postmoderns, it is how to account for political action. Of course, movement occurred no matter how much it puzzled the philosophers, and the same goes for action. Yet academics continue to write as though action is impossible without the adequate theory."[11] Foucault himself never asked how resistance is possible. Instead, he asked other, more concrete questions, concerning how to interrupt various entrenched discourses, how to excavate their human origins so their "necessity" will be exposed as a lie, what cultural edifices need to have an intellectual hand grenade tossed their way. He also took part in political movements, as do many academics (even as they ask these questions about the "possibility" of resistance).

Theories of resistance can indeed function at certain historical junctures as intellectual hand grenades. But theories of resistance are not *required* for social or cultural change. It has always amazed me when critics comment that *Unbearable Weight* underestimates or "does not account for" resistance. Sometimes that criticism will be accompanied by the complaint that the picture I paint is too grim or depressing. I wonder when making people feel good became a criterion for the adequacy of social criticism? My point in the book is precisely to *encourage* resistance to certain discourses and practices by breaking up some of the illusions that permit them to function smoothly. I do indeed find certain aspects of our situation grim; if I didn't, why would I want to resist them? If I put a more cheerful face on it all, would that make resistance to them more "possible"? Postmodernists like to see resistance "acknowledged" in texts and "accounted for" by theories. But texts and theories can also function as *practices* of resistance, which work in a variety of ways to help instigate change.

Resistance can be produced in many ways. How it is produced, whether it is imagined as a cultural construction or an act of pure freedom, whether it appeals to a natural body or a cyborg or no body at all—these, to me, have no bearing on the issue of effectiveness. The fact that resistance is produced from within a hegemonic order does not preclude it from transforming that order, any more than the fact that we are our parents' children precludes us from living lives very different from theirs. But clearly, so long as we think our parents' lives were swell, we will do little to break away. So I think of the development of an oppositional or critical attitude as more important than the question of where resistance originates or what it appeals to.

There are lots of wells from which to draw an oppositional spirit and project—the experience of cultural exclusion being an extremely powerful one, as Butler and I agree. Sometimes that experience can result in a conscious politics, sometimes not. Those of us who do philosophy in an oppositional or critical mode could be described as trying to make explicit the elements that would enable a sharper consciousness of what philosopher Marilyn Frye calls the "politics of experience." But often there are no clear diagrams for the excluded to appeal to, yet they become agents of social transformation. Sometimes our bodies resist even without our conscious participation.

Certain and conclusive knowledge of the effectiveness of our actions, however, is not available to us. That would only come at the end of the line—and we are not standing there. We are standing in concrete bodies, in a particular time and place, in the "middle" of things, *always*. The most sophisticated theory cannot alter this limitation on our knowledge, while too rigid adherence to theory can make us too inflexible, too attached to a set of ideas, to freshly assess what it is going on around us, to stay alert in what Foucault called an attitude of "hyper and pessimistic activism."[12] Thus, my answer to Butler's question "How can we know the difference between the power we promote and the power we oppose?" We *cannot* know with certainty. But this merely means that we are fallible, our assessments provisional, our actions subject to revision. It should not be taken as cause for fatalism or passivity. (Actually, I believe it is mostly philosophers who respond with despair to the impossibility of certainty; most people become fatalistic and passive when they despair of *changing* things and do not require certainty in order to try to do so.) To act responsibly and with hope, it's not necessary that we know the final outcome of our actions. We assess what we take to be the chief dangers or needs of a situation—the practices that require demystification, criticism, transformation—and we *act,* both individually and collectively, ready to change course if we discover something we didn't notice at the outset or something that has emerged since we began. "The essence of being radical is physical," as Foucault said in a late interview; "the essence of being radical is the radicalness of existence itself."[13]

THE FEMINIST AS OTHER

The terms masculine and feminine are used symmetrically only as a matter of form, as on legal papers. In actuality, the relation of the two sexes is not quite like that of two electrical poles, for man represents both the positive and the neutral, as is indicated by the common use of man *to designate human beings in general; whereas woman represents only the negative, defined by limiting criteria, without reciprocity. In the midst of an abstract discussion it is vexing to hear a man say: "You think thus and so because you are a woman"; but I know that my only defense is to reply: "I think thus and so because it is true," thereby removing my subjective self from the argument. It would be out of the question to reply: "And you think the contrary because you are a man," for it is understood that the fact of being a man is no peculiarity. . . . There is an absolute human type, the masculine. Woman has ovaries, a uterus; these peculiarities imprison her in her subjectivity, circumscribe her within the limits of her own nature. It is often said that she thinks with her glands. Man superbly ignores the fact that his anatomy also includes glands, such as the testicles, and that they secrete hormones. He thinks of his body as a direct and normal connection with the world, which he believes he apprehends objectively, whereas he regards the body of woman as a hindrance, a prison, weighed down by everything peculiar to it.*

SIMONE DE BEAUVOIR *The Second Sex* (1949)

FEMINISM AT THE MARGINS OF CULTURE

As cultural critics, feminist theorists have produced powerful challenges: to dominant conceptions of human nature and political affiliation, to norms of scientific, philosophical, and moral reason, to ideals of spirituality, to prevailing disciplinary identities and boundaries, to established historical narratives. Yet how often do we see feminist theorists listed alongside Foucault, Derrida, Rorty, Taylor, Kuhn, or Fish as critics and reshapers of the Disciplines, Science, Philosophy, Culture? The answer is rarely. More often, we encounter a version of Edward Said's formulation: "There are certainly new critical trends . . . great advances made in . . . humanistic interpretation . . . We *do* know more about the way cultures operate thanks to Raymond Williams, Roland Barthes, Michel Foucault, and Stuart Hall; we know about how to examine a text in ways that Jacques Derrida, Hayden White, Fredric Jameson, and Stanley Fish have significantly expanded and altered; and thanks to feminists like Elaine Showalter, Germaine Greer, Helene Cixous, Sandra Gilbert, Susan Gubar, and Gayatri Spivak it is impossible to avoid or ignore the gender issues in the production and interpretation of art."[1]

So because of Barthes, Derrida, and colleagues we "know more" about culture and texts. "Thanks to feminists," we are unable to "avoid" or "ignore" gender. I don't want to make too much of the construction of the European male contribution as that of increasing *knowledge* while feminists apparently have simply harangued and harassed to the point where they cannot be "avoided" or "ignored." I know that Said didn't *really* mean to suggest that unfortunate, reverberant contrast. Nor do I wish to emphasize, although I would point out, the inaccuracy of Said's description of Gayatri Spivak, who is as much concerned with issues of race and class as with gender. What I *do* want to insist on, however, is the importance of Said's juxtaposition of "gender"—what all feminists are concerned with, in his description—and the general interrogation of "culture" and "text" attributed to the men. The juxtaposition construes feminists as engaging in a specialized critique, one that cannot be ignored, perhaps, but one whose implications are contained, self-limiting, and of insufficient general consequence to amount to a new knowledge of "the way culture operates." One does gender *or* one engages in criticism of broad significance; pick one.

In this essay I will argue that Said's characterization of feminist criticism is not merely an annoying bit of residual sexism but a powerful conceptual map that keeps feminist scholarship, no matter how broad its concerns, located in the region of what Simone de Beauvoir called the "Other." De Beauvoir argued that within the social world, there are those who occupy the unmarked position of the "essential," the universal, the human, and those who are defined, reduced, and marked by their (sexual, racial, religious) difference from that norm. The accomplishments of those who are so marked—of the Other—may not always be disdained; often, they will be appreciated, but always in their special and peripheral place, the place of their difference. Thus, there's "history" and then there's "*women's* history," and women's history—unlike military history, for example—is located outside what is imagined as history proper. There are the poststructuralist critiques of reason, which are of "general" interest, and then there are the feminist critiques, of interest to those concerned with gender. Said's juxtaposition of those writers who teach us "about the way culture operates" and those who make it "impossible to avoid or ignore gender issues" applauds the feminist—as Other.

As Simone de Beauvoir recognized, gender is not the only cultural form of Otherness. I had a non-Jewish colleague who, having found out that I am Jewish, became unable to have a conversation with me that didn't revolve around the brilliance, historical suffering, or sense of humor of "the Jewish people." On one occasion the conversation turned to our mutual love of Broadway show tunes. For a moment I thought I would be spared, but then he piped: "And what did you think about *Fiddler on the Roof?* I bet you loved that one!" Every time black authors are quoted only for their views on race—expertise about "general" topics being reserved for white males, who are imagined to be without race and gender—the Otherness of the black is perpetuated. On college campuses the specter of Otherness has dogged efforts to establish multicultural curricula, efforts which continually get represented *not* as an attempt to bring greater historical accuracy and breadth to a Eurocentric curriculum but as subordinating "general" educational ideals to the special needs and demands of particular groups.

Otherness thus has many faces. De Beauvoir's insight, indeed, is probably the single most broadly, deeply, and enduringly applicable insight of contemporary feminism. It has shaped numerous critical discourses—on race, colonialism, anti-Semitism, and heterosexism, for example. Yet ironically (although perhaps predictably) de Beauvoir's profound philosophical contribution itself fell victim to the dynamic that she describes. To begin with, a zoologist (rather than a philosopher) was chosen to do the English translation of *The Second Sex*. The philosophical term "L'expérience vécue"—lived experience, a central category of phenomenological thought—was rendered as "woman's life today." Only men do philosophy; women are fit to write, if at all, about the facts of our own condition. This construction of *The Second Sex* pursued the book throughout the press's marketing and the book's subsequent critical reception. *Time* even headlined its review with the birth announcement: "Weight: $2\frac{3}{4}$ Lbs,"[2] in one brilliant, if unconscious, stroke associating the book with the materiality of the body, the heavy immanance that is woman—"weighed down by everything peculiar to [her]," as de Beauvoir puts it—and woman's "natural" role of childbearer. And so de Beauvoir, that most unnatural of creatures, a woman philosopher, was put in her rightful place. Today, admittedly, we are more apt to see *The Second Sex* as having theoretical and philosophical import, but only for feminism; its more general cultural influence remains unacknowledged. Thus *The Second Sex,* generally remembered as a book "about women," is consigned to play the role of gendered Other in our narratives of philosophical history. The truth of de Beauvoir's insight is borne out ironically by the marginalization of de Beauvoir herself.

Simone de Beauvoir was not the last feminist to suffer such marginalization. Said's construction of the contemporary feminist as engaged in gender critique rather than general cultural critique, far from being anomalous, is typical of the role assigned feminism in our collective narratives of intellectual challenge and change. Consider, for example, the twentieth-century conception of the body as socially constructed. Such notions owe much to feminism, not only to the scholarly writings of academic feminists but to the more public challenge to biological determinism and essentialism that was raised by the activist feminism of the late 1960s and early 1970s, that is, in the demonstrations, the manifestos, the consciousness-raising sessions, the early, popular writings.[3] At the center of "personal politics" was the conception of the body as profoundly shaped, both materially and representationally, by cultural ideology and "disciplinary" practice. But it is Foucault who is generally credited (perhaps with a backward nod to Marx) as the father of "the politics of the body."

Feminist theorists, too, have exalted the philosophical contribution of the father and imagined our feminist mothers as in a more primitive, naive association with the body. Linda Zerilli, for example, while crediting Foucault for having shown us "how the body has been historically disciplined," describes Anglo-American feminism as holding an "essentialist" view of the body as an "archaic natural."[4] In my own 1980 review of Foucault's *History of Sexuality* (volume 1) (1978) I pointed out that Foucault's notion of a power that works not through negative prohibition but proliferatively, producing bodies and their materiality, was not itself new.[5] But I had in mind here Marcuse's notion, in *One-Dimensional Man,* of the "mobilization and administration of libido." Not for a moment did I consider the relevance of the extensive feminist literature on the social construction and "deployment" of female sexuality, beauty, and femininity, for example in the early work of Andrea Dworkin:

> Standards of beauty describe in precise terms the relationship that an individual will have to her own body. They prescribe her motility, spontaneity, posture, gait, the uses to which she can put her body. *They define*

THE FEMINIST AS OTHER

precisely the dimensions of her physical freedom. And of course, the relationship between physical freedom and psychological development, intellectual possibility, and creative potential is an umbilical one.

In our culture, not one part of a woman's body is left untouched, unaltered. No feature or extremity is spared the art, or pain, of improvement . . . From head to toe, every feature of a woman's face, every section of her body, is subject to modification, alteration. This alteration is an ongoing, repetitive process. It is vital to the economy, the major substance of male-female differentiation, the most immediate physical and psychological reality of being a woman. From the age of eleven or twelve until she dies, a woman will spend a large part of her time, money, and energy on binding, plucking, painting, and deodorizing herself. It is commonly and wrongly said that male transvestites through the use of makeup and costuming caricature the women they would become, but any real knowledge of the romantic ethos makes clear that these men have penetrated to the core experience of being a woman, a romanticized construct.[6]

Is this "essentialism"? A view of the body as an "archaic natural"? Or is the collapsing of Dworkin *on* female bodies with Dworkin *as* a female body responsible for our inability to read her as the sophisticated theorist that she is? When I wrote my review of Foucault, I was working on a dissertation historically critiquing the duality of male mind/female body. Yet, like the zoologist who translated *The Second Sex,* I expected "theory" only from men. Moreover—and here my inability to move beyond these dualisms reveals itself more subtly—I was unable to recognize *embodied* theory when it was staring me in the face. For in Dworkin's work, as in feminist writing of the sixties and seventies more generally, theory was rarely abstracted and elaborated, adorned with power jargon, and made into an object of fascination in itself; rather, theory made its appearance as it shaped the "matter" of the argument. Works that perform such abstraction and elaboration get taken much more seriously than works that do not. Dworkin, to make matters worse for herself, has consistently refused to tame and trim her own material body, to enact the cultural control of the flesh—through normalizing diet, dress, and gestures—that would align her with disciplined mind rather than unruly body.

But, as de Beauvoir argues, no matter how we dress ourselves or our insights, we will almost always be mapped into the region of the Other. Thus, when feminists such as Dworkin talk about the discipline of the body required by the "art" of femininity, their work is read as having implications only for women and the "peculiarities" of their bodies. But when Foucault talks about the discipline of the body involved in the training of a soldier, it is read as gender-neutral and broadly applicable. The soldier body is no less gendered a norm, of course, than the body-as-decorative-object. But this fact is obscured because we view the woman's body under the sign of her Otherness while regarding the male body—as de Beauvoir puts it—as in "direct and normal relation to the world." The ironies engendered by this asymmetry are dizzying. The male body becomes the Body proper (as in: "Foucault altered our understanding of the body") while the female body remains marked by its difference (as in: "Feminism showed us the oppressiveness of femininity"). At the same time, however, the male body *as* male body disappears completely, *its* concrete specificity submerged in its collapse into the universal.[7] Thus, while men are the cultural theorists *of* the body, only women *have* bodies. Meanwhile, of course, the absent male body continues to operate illicitly as the (scientific, philosophical, medical) norm for all.

READING AND MISREADING FEMINIST PHILOSOPHY

When we turn to cultural narratives about philosophical modernity and "postmodernity," the ghettoization of feminist insight is even more strik-

THE FEMINIST AS OTHER

ing. From de Beauvoir herself—the *first* philosopher to challenge the notion that there *is* one "human condition" that all persons share—to feminist critiques of modern science, to contemporary feminist skepticism over the continuity and unity of identity, feminist theorists have been at the forefront in challenging the presumed universality, neutrality, and unity of the modern "subject." The challenge began with the specific exposure of gender, as feminists pointed out that Man really *is* man, albeit covertly. And *as* an embodied, en-gendered being, he could no longer be imagined to have an elevated, disinterested, "God's-eye view" of Reality. Thus began the widespread questioning throughout the disciplines of the established paradigms of truth and method which had set the standards for philosophical and ethical reasoning, scientific rigor, literary and artistic values, historical narrative, and so on.

This questioning has hardly been the canon-bashing "assault on reason" that contemporary polemics make it out to be. With few exceptions, the point has been to reveal what dominant models have *excluded* rather than to attack the value of what they have *offered*. Yet a sort of cultural castration anxiety continually converts any criticism of canonical thought into the specter of Lorena Bobbit-like academic feminists, wildly lopping reason, logic, and Shakespeare right off at the quick. For those who suffer from this anxiety—and this includes women as well as men—there appear to be only two choices: phallocentrism or emasculation. But for many feminist critics of modernity (and I include myself here), dethroning the king is *not* equivalent to cutting his head off. Rather, sharing power is what it's all about.

Is it really, as classicist Martha Nussbaum has charged,[8] a wholesale "assault on reason" to suggest that Western notions of rationality have developed around the exclusion of qualities associated with the feminine or with "ways of knowing" developed by women in the domains allotted to them? Or is the elaboration and reconstruction of reason, engaged in by male philosophers from Aristotle and Hegel to James, Dewey, and Whitehead, off-limits to women? Perhaps the problem is that feminist philosophers, unlike these male reformers of "reason," have invoked a suppressed or unacknowledged *feminine* alterity as a way into criticism and reconstruction of dominant forms. So, for example, Iris Young's phenomenological study of pregnancy suggests that pregnancy may make uniquely available (although it does not guarantee) a very different experience of the relationship between mind and body, inner and outer, self and other than that presumed by Descartes, Hobbes, Locke, and other architects of the modernist subject.[9] Young's point, it should be emphasized, is not to glorify pregnancy but to interrogate the modernist model, to force it to confront its particularity and its limitations. Similarly, Sara Ruddick develops the notion of "maternal thinking"[10] not in celebration of a distinctively and exclusively female mode of rationality *or* in order to "assault" and abandon traditional concepts of reason but to diagnose and remedy what the latter lack.

There is no denying, however, that feminism has contributed to a generalized cultural skepticism about claims to knowledge and truth, particularly when they stake out applicability to the whole of human history and experience. This is not the place to sort out the insights and excesses of this skepticism, which takes many forms and is the product of many forces. Clearly, however, it was historically inevitable that centuries of universalizing talk about "human beings" and "human nature" would eventually become suspect and that new questions would begin to be asked. Just *who* is being described? Who does not fit in? What elements of human experience are emphasized? Which neglected? Set in motion by gender critique, the "subject" had in fact begun a shattering "great fall," and many now believe that it can never be put together again.

Some contemporary feminist philosophers, in the tradition of both Hume and various Eastern conceptions, question even the unity and stability of identity in the individual. In distinction to Humean and Eastern conceptions, however, recent feminist conceptions complicate the question of personal identity with a new understanding of the diverse and mutable elements that make up our *social* identity, as in Maria Lugones's influential piece on the "world-traveling" subject:

> I think that most of us who are outside the mainstream of, for example, the U.S. dominant construction or organization of life, are "world-travelers" as a matter of necessity and of survival. It seems to me that inhabiting more than one "world" at the same time and "traveling" between "worlds" is part and parcel of our experience and our situation. One can be at the same time in a "world" that constructs one as stereotypically Latin, for example, and in a "world" that constructs one as Latin. Being stereotypically Latin and being simply Latin are different simultaneous constructions of person that are part of different "worlds." . . .
>
> The shift from being one person to being a different person is what I call "travel." This shift may not be willful or even conscious . . . It is not a matter of acting. One does not pose as someone else, one does not pretend to be, for example, someone of a different personality or character or someone who uses space or language differently than the other person. Rather one is someone who has that personality or character or uses space and language in that particular way. The "one" here does not refer to some underlying "I." One does not *experience* any underlying "I."[11]

I will refer to these ideas again later in this essay. Now I only want to point out how rarely Lugones's and other feminist critiques of personhood and identity are represented as originary "postmodern" moments. No, it is Derrida who "deconstructs the 'I' "; Lugones represents the Other who stands outside the "I," the "difference" of the Latina living in Western culture. And when "the end of the regime of Man," "the death of the Subject," and so forth are described as constituting a turning point, crisis, or "postmodern moment" of general cultural significance, feminism is constructed—even by feminists such as Pamela McCallum—as a grateful little sister rather than generative mother of the transformation:

> There can be no doubt that the theorizing of those writers who have defined the postmodern movement—Jacques Derrida, Michel Foucault, Jean Baudrillard, Jean-Francois Lyotard, and Richard Rorty, among others—has produced a number of arguments which offer a substantial challenge to the assumptions of traditional Western philosophy . . . [e.g] that human reason is homogeneous and universal, unaffected by the specific experiences of the individual knower . . . that knowledge is generated from a free play of the intelligence and is not bound up with or implicated in forms of power and systems of domination.[12]

Concerning the relation of feminism to these challenges, McCallum suggests that feminists would surely "give assent" to them because they support a critique of male bias in philosophy; she then raises the question of whether feminists should "appropriate" postmodernism. Here we have yet another cultural reworking of the "Adam gave birth to Eve" fantasy, in which the questioning of the universality and neutrality of philosophical reason *precedes* rather than is *produced* by feminism. McCallum does not seem to recognize that feminist epistemologists such as Sandra Harding were questioning the presumptions of Western philosophy before Richard Rorty's *Philosophy and the Mirror of Nature* appeared, or that numerous feminists were exploring knowledge as "implicated in forms of power and systems of domination" at the same time as Foucault was developing his ideas. In McCallum's characterization the broad, general, theoretical challenges to culture originate with Rorty and Foucault; feminism "gives assent." The originary contribution of feminism is constructed as the more limited critique of exposing sexism and masculinism in philosophical traditions.

Sometimes this construction will involve serious misreadings of feminist work. My own book on Descartes, for example, discusses the "masculine" nature of seventeenth-century science only in the last of its six chapters and mentions Nancy Chodorow's ideas about gender difference just twice, once precisely in order to *distinguish* my use of developmental categories from Chodorow's. Yet the book is frequently read, by critics and sympathizers alike, as an application of Chodorow. It is worth quoting a description from the introduction to my book, then a recent characterization, in order to illuminate the kinds of misreadings feminist work is prey to:

> My use of developmental theory focuses, not on gender difference, but on very general categories—individuation, separation anxiety, object permanence—in an attempt to explore their relevance to existential and epistemological changes brought about by the dissolution of the organic, finite, maternal universe of the Middle Ages and Renaissance. In an important sense the separate self, conscious of itself and of its own distinctness from a world "outside" it, is born in the Cartesian era. It is a psychological birth—of "inwardness," of "subjectivity," of "locatedness" in time and space—generating new anxieties and, ultimately, new strategies for maintaining equilibrium in an utterly changed and alien world.[13]

The Flight to Objectivity, then, attempts to locate the work of Descartes and the Cartesian view of the self in the context of a general cultural transformation, the "birth of modernity." As to Chodorow's ideas about gender difference, I indicate in *Flight* that I consider her work suggestive and potentially applicable to understanding changes that took place during the Enlightenment. But I stress that such historical application has yet to be made and is certainly not attempted in the pages of my own book. Yet here is how my argument was recently described by Margaret Atherton:

"*The Flight to Objectivity* makes *heavy* use of categories of contemporary feminist theory, especially those provided by Evelyn Fox Keller and Nancy Chodorow, to illuminate Descartes theory, *as [Bordo] believes it affects women*" (emphasis mine).[14] Elsewhere Atherton repeats the idea; the point of my argument, she insists, is to show how Descartes's arguments have "given rise to a decline in the status of women."[15] Now to suggest, as I do, that the birth of modernity has a significant gender dimension—in separation of the self from the maternal universe of the Middle Ages and Renaissance —is hardly equivalent to an argument about the effects of Cartesianism "on women." To read the text in this way is, rather, to view it through the template of gender duality. Under that template the name "Chodorow" (whose work focuses on developmental differences between males and females and who has been charged with "essentializing" those differences) claims the imagination of the reader and simply won't let go. The result, unfortunately, is that "women's difference" becomes identified as a concern of the text, which becomes stamped as a work about the exclusion of women rather than about a transformation in the philosophical conception of self and world.

The feminist whose work has perhaps suffered most from such inscriptions is Carol Gilligan. On the face of it, among contemporary feminists, Gilligan appears to have most been given her due, to have achieved a *central* place on the intellectual landscape, even to have been recognized and celebrated outside the boundaries of academia. Any marking of her *In a Different Voice* as about "women's difference" might seem the fault (or intent) of the work itself, as the title alone suggests. This common reading of Gilligan, however, is only partially accurate. To be sure, the book's contrast between two modes of moral reasoning is articulated in terms of gender difference. Thus, according to Gilligan, the preference for abstract argument over assessments of particular, concrete situations is grounded in a blueprint of human interaction that is more characteristic of males than females. Because the "male" blueprint is atomistic, collisions between individuals are viewed as invitations to disaster and must be rigorously avoided—by abstract notions of "personhood" and "rights," which define clear boundaries around the individual and protect against collision. Women's blueprint, in contrast, is relational, as Gilligan argued. Here, the chief danger (what "disturbs the universe," if you will) is the fracturing of attachment, and the moral imperative is to restore human connection by a careful assessment of how to responsibly mend the fractures occurring in particular, concrete situations.

You will notice that I have not mentioned the word "care" in the foregoing description, a deliberate omission that will become clearer shortly. For now, I emphasize that while Gilligan's critique is articulated in terms of gender difference, it would be a serious mistake to see its implications as "only" involving gender. In the introduction to *In a Different Voice* she writes that the chief aim of the book is to "highlight a distinction between two modes of thought . . . rather than to represent a generalization about either sex." She stresses that the articulation of women's perspective is not an end in itself but propaedeutic to recognition of "a limitation in the conception of human condition."[16] For "once women are inserted into the picture," as Seyla Benhabib astutely points out, "be it as objects of social-scientific research or as subjects conducting the inquiry, established paradigms are unsettled. The definition of the *object domain* of a research paradigm, its units of measurement, its method of verification, the alleged neutrality of its theoretical terminology, and the claims to universality of its models and metaphors are all thrown into question."[17]

Gilligan's work has been extensively criticized by other feminists for "essentializing" a historically located, class- and race-biased construction of female "difference." And it is true that the book fails to raise questions about the generalizability of her findings, which were based on a limited and fairly homogeneous sample. The limits of her sample might have been taken, as Jane Martin points out, as calling for further research into the wider applicability of her hypothesis; instead, she was charged with racism and classism, and it was implied—without argument or demonstration—that the "different voice" was uniquely white and middle-class.[18] Arguably, the point here was not so much to challenge Gilligan's findings as to expose and protest (and not only in Gilligan's work, of course) the unselfconscious slippage from white feminist experiences to universalizing talk about "women's ways of knowing." But whatever their justice vis-à-vis Gilligan's empirical generalizations or white bias in feminist research, such criticisms miss an important dimension of her work.

What such criticisms overlook is Gilligan's heuristic use of gender alterity to expose the universalist pretensions of dominant norms and to envision alternatives. In terms of this aim, whether the proposed gender difference derives from biology or from socially constructed roles and whether it adequately reflects the situations of all women or an ethnically or class-specific construction of gender are not key issues. What gender difference here affords (as ethnic and other cultural differences can afford as well) is a "way into" cultural critique. In terms of this potential, it is not surprising that a number of important feminist theorists, Benhabib among them, have used Gilligan's insights to mount a critique of the possessive individualism of liberalism, the autonomous, "unencumbered self" presumed in the ontological blueprint identified by Gilligan as the dominant (rather than "different") mode.

These cultural applications of Gilligan's work may be well known to feminist philosophers. But when a recent article in the *Chronicle of Higher Education* surveyed academic work arguing for more relational, less "rights"-dominated models of the person and the state,[19] neither Gilligan herself nor Carole Pateman, Susan Moller Okin, Virginia Held, Iris Young, Nancy Fraser, Drucilla Cornell, or Seyla Benhabib were mentioned. This effacement of the general cultural critique implicit in Gilligan's work and explicitly carried out in the work of numerous feminist political theorists is manifest as well in philosophy textbooks. A revised, 1994 edition of *Philosophy: Contemporary Perspectives on Perennial Issues,*[20] for example, features a section called "State and Society." Feminist political theory is represented there by a piece by Alison Jaggar, "Political Philosophies of *Women's* Liberation" (emphasis added). "State and Society" could have included, in addition to Jaggar's very valuable piece, one of the many excellent feminist critiques of political liberalism. But the section was not conceptualized to allow for a feminist perspective on government or political theory. The presentation and argumentation regarding general political categories—"democracy," "libertarianism," "socialism," and "liberalism"—is reserved in the section for the "gender-neutral" (as it is presumed) scrutiny of four (male) nonfeminists; the role of the feminist philosopher is only to represent the "difference" of women's situation.

What Gilligan's work *has* been publicly associated with, not surprisingly, is precisely that "difference," the so-called "ethic of care." To some degree this association has been facilitated by Gilligan herself. She tries to make it clear that she is *not* arguing that women are moral angels while men are unconcerned with helping others; her argument (as I noted earlier) is rather that women and men have different ways of conceiving of "help," based on their different conceptions of what constitutes danger. But Gilligan's efforts to avoid promoting a new version of the nineteenth-century vision of woman-as-ministering-angel were hampered by her unfortunate choice of the term "ethic of care" to describe the female moral imperative. The suggestion that men do *not* "care" as much as women is immediately (and inaccurately) evoked. Moreover, the obvious and important connections to be made to the critique of the classical liberal model of the person become obscured. Unfortunately, the "ethic of care" swiftly became *the* category through which Gilligan's work was socially defined, reducing the transformative potential of women's "difference" to the familiar notion that we need more women to provide warmth and nurture in the workplace. (For this reason, I never use the term "care" when I teach Gilligan.)

The fault, however, is not entirely Gilligan's, as I hope this essay is helping to make clear. In a culture shaped by gender dualities, there is a powerful inclination to "read" feminist work as reinforcing those dualities. So, for example, Sara Ruddick's concept of "maternal thinking," despite Ruddick's strong and clear underscoring that she is describing an ideal suggested by a particular kind of parenting *practice* (it's thus not a contradiction in terms for a man to be a "maternal thinker"), continually gets read as "essentializing" a distinctively female perspective. More subtly and pervasively, and as I have been arguing throughout this paper, feminist theory swims upstream against powerful currents whenever it threatens to assume the mantle of *general* cultural critique rather than simply advocate for the greater inclusion or representation of women and their "differences."

WHO SPEAKS FOR PHILOSOPHY?

In *Fire with Fire* Naomi Wolf argues that in recent years a massive "genderquake" has occurred, sinking patriarchy into "deeper and deeper eclipse."[21] In the wake of this quake, she argues, it's time for women to stop complaining and start exercising our newly developed muscle. In the words of the Nike ad that she offers as a symbol of what she calls "power feminism," women need to stop whining and "Just Do It!"

But Wolf is mistaken if she believes that the ability of women to "just do it" is itself evidence that patriarchy is in eclipse. Feminist philosophy is a case in point, and it is a particularly powerful and troubling one. As critics of Western culture, feminist philosophers have been "just doing it" for some time. Yet, as I have argued, we remain the Other in the self-conception of our discipline, in intellectual history generally, and even in narratives about the very changes that we have brought about. To point this Otherness out is not to "whine" about how feminists have been "victimized" by their marginalization in cultural narratives or to make feminists into the heroines of a revised, "feminized" cultural history. Frequently nowadays feminist criticism is presented in such terms, by the popular media and by "power feminists" like Wolf, Roiphe, and Sommers. But the depiction of feminist criticism as "victim feminism" assumes, as Freud assumed in asking his famous question, that if women want something, it can only be for their sex, it can only be as the Other. This has been especially frustrating for those of us who have been drawn to feminist philosophy precisely for the vantage point it provides from which to analyze, evaluate, and participate in the transformation of *culture.*

Given this aim, it is imperative that we resist the ghettoization of feminist insight—at conferences, in anthologies, in the curriculum—and insist that feminist philosophy be read *as* cultural critique. More precisely, we need to insist that "gender theory" be read *for* the cultural critique that it offers. This is no easy task. It demands vigilance precisely because the struggle is not over *inclusion* (the liberal measure of female "power," assumed by Wolf, Sommers, and others) but over the cultural *meaning* of that inclusion. To make this distinction clear, let me provide an example. Several years ago I attended a national working conference entitled "The Responsibilities of Philosophers." The only feminist philosopher in my small group session, I had talked at length about the history of philosophy and about how inadequate was any understanding of the Western philosophical tradition which did not examine the racism and sexism that have been elements in many philosophical conceptions of human nature and reason. To make such an examination, I emphasized, does not mean trashing Western philosophical traditions but rather bringing the study of philosophy down from the timeless heavens and into the bodies of historical human beings. Later, at the plenary session, my participation was reported as consisting of the suggestion that "we need to pay much more attention to hiring women and minorities."

The salient point here is not that I wasn't listened to but that what was "heard" had been converted from cultural critique to simple advocacy for the "rights" of the Other. Constructed as advocacy for the rights of the Other, my remarks no longer impinged on the philosophical methods or identities of the men in my group. They could continue to exalt (and teach) the "Man of Reason" as the disembodied "subject" of philosophical history while presumably letting the women and minorities they would hire take care of "gender and race." Thus the insights of feminist philosophy are kept "in their place," where they make no claim on "philosophy proper." The voices of "difference" are permitted to speak, but business goes on as usual. So, for example, it becomes perfectly possible for a philosopher to assign Gilligan for a special class session on "women and morality" while continuing unselfconsciously and without remark to organize discussion around highly abstract and uncontextualized case studies.

In the case of more "postmodern" critiques, it has made an enormous philosophical difference that contemporary intellectuals have largely learned their lessons from the poststructuralist fathers rather than the feminist mothers. Freud's allegory of the primal tribe, which murders the patriarch only to nostalgically institutionalize and reproduce the conditions of his reign, is interesting to think about here. The "fathers" of postmodernism are, after all, also the *sons* of Enlightenment Man, the inheritors of both his privileges and his blind spots. They may be eager to prove their own manhood through rebellion against his rule. But do they know a different way of being?

Thus, while Man has been officially declared "dead," like Freddy Kruger, he just keeps popping up on Elm Street (and in the academy). His pretensions and fantasies—the transcendence of the body, the drive toward separation from and domination over nature, the ambition to create an authoritative scientific or philosophical discourse, all of which have been extensively critiqued by feminist theory—have simply been recycled. The modern, Cartesian erasure of the body ("the view from nowhere") has been traded, as I argue in *Unbearable Weight,* for a postmodern, Derridean version (the dream of being "everywhere"). The old model of man's mind as the pinnacle of God's creation has been replaced by the poststructuralist equivalent: human language as the ultimate architect and arbiter of reality. The analytic overseer of argument has been supplanted by the master of authoritative "theory." And old forms of dominating and excluding others through professional jargon and obscurantism have merely been replaced by new forms of discursive elitism.

Thus we see the unconscious reproduction of the "sins" of the (philosophical) fathers by poststructuralist sons not much closer than their fathers were to truly hearing the voice of woman's (or any other human) "difference." As Jane Flax has put it:

> Despite the rhetoric of "reading like a woman" or displacing "phallocentrism," postmodernists are unaware of the deeply gendered nature of their own recounting and interpretations of the Western Story and the strategies they oppose to its master narratives. Postmodernists still honor Man as the sole author and principal character in these stories, even if this Man is dying, his time running out. They retell the contemporary history of the West in and through the stories of the three deaths—of Man, (his) History, and (his) metaphysics. Whatever women have done with and in all this (becoming past) time is "outside" by definition and according to the conventions of (their) story line. . . . This absence or disappearance of concrete women and gender relations suggests the possibility that postmodernism is not only or simply opposed to phallocentrism but also may be "its latest ruse."[22]

Contemporary feminists have not been immune to the recyclings of phallocentrism. Many of us may want to prove *our* manhood too; this is, after all, where academic "power" (and, of course, not only *academic* power) resides. Ignoring, dismissing, or denouncing whole generations of ambitious and imaginative feminist work (while remaining remarkably tolerant of the mistakes and omissions of male philosophers),[23] some feminists have colluded in "the disappearance of women" of which Flax speaks.[24]

In response, other feminists participate in their *own* disappearance. Sensing that general cultural critique is too risky, fearing charges of "essentialism," racism, canon bashing, and white-male trashing, we may try to protect ourselves by keeping ourselves small, tidy, and specific (or by not saying much of anything at all).

For some feminists, too, it appears as though any identification with women's historical "differences" is equivalent to identification with victimhood and disempowerment.[25] For others, however, the "differences" of women's experiences, racial and ethnic as well as gendered, remain a wellspring from which to draw cultural and philosophical critique, to imagine alternatives that are unavailable or muted in the histories that men have told about their experience. Consider, for example, two distinctive approaches to the cultural deconstruction of the "subject" represented by Derrida and Lugones. Derrida's position is abstract and impersonal. "*I* do not select," he has written. "The interpretations select themselves." Here, while renouncing Cartesianism, Derrida perpetuates its controlling fiction that a person can negate the accidents of individual biography and speak with a purely philosophical voice.

In Maria Lugones's critique, by contrast, the personal (and cultural) aspects of identity remain fully present, even as the unity and permanence of the self is challenged. Like Minnie Bruce Pratt's "autobiography" of her constantly evolving identities of "skin, blood, heart," Lugones's account is vividly grounded in personal, often visceral experience. It stresses the concrete, social multiplicity rather than the abstract "disappearance" of the subject. The self is fractured because our social experience requires it of us—more from some than others; the experience of "unity" of identity is nothing more than the privilege of being at home in the dominant culture, of feeling integrated within in. Nonetheless, the fractured self, which has been *forced* to learn to be a shape shifter in foreign worlds, "as a matter of necessity and survival," can teach important lessons about how to be a subject in playful, adaptable, nonimperialist modes.

My point here is not to insist that every philosopher adopt a more personal or anecdotal style. Rather, it is to insist that there is a philosophical issue at stake in the difference between Derrida and Lugones, two competing views of "the death of the subject," if you will, reflecting the different "subjects" of history that each identifies with. This issue is effaced as long as Derrida alone is viewed as speaking for "philosophy" and "culture" while Lugones is taken to represent the voice of the Latina Other. If the rebellious sons had truly been listening to feminist voices—if they had been able to recognize feminist theory as representing not merely the "different" voice of Otherness but the authority of modes of being and knowing that are as historically pervasive, if not as culturally dominant, as their own—they might have been able to achieve a deeper understanding of phallocentrism and the subtle ways that it reproduces itself. If they had looked to a human history broader than their own, they might have been less ready to project the death of their own philosophical traditions onto all of culture. Within those traditions, the "self," "man," the author, subjectivity, took very particular forms by virtue of the experiences excluded from them. Those forms may indeed now be standing on rockier, less elevated ground than they once did. Nevertheless, other forms of being and knowing have been and continue to be available, waiting to be brought from the region of the Other, to join them on the central terrains of our culture.

MISSING

KITCHENS

with Binnie Klein

and Marilyn K. Silverman

Topoanalysis, then, would be the systematic psychological study of the sites of our intimate lives. In the theater of the past that is constituted by memory, the stage setting maintains the characters in their dominant roles. At times we think we know ourselves in time, when all we know is a sequence of fixations in the spaces of the being's stability—a being who does not want to melt away.

BACHELARD   *The Poetics of Space*

On a February night, three days before the unveiling of our father's stone in a cemetery on Long Island, we three sisters (Mickey, fifty-eight, a clinical psychologist; Susan, forty-nine, a university teacher and writer; Binnie, forty-five, a clinical social worker) assembled around Mickey's dining table to diagram the apartments we lived in when we were growing up. The chairs we sat upon were familiar, but that night, as we tilted toward each other, excitedly scrutinizing each other's memories, they seemed perches more than seats. Like neighboring monarchs mapping disputed territory, we prepared to do a gentle battle with the truth, that is, each of our "truths."

BINNIE KLEIN is a licensed clinical social worker in private practice in New Haven, Connecticut. She is on the staff of Yale University Health Services. She is a published poet and produces a music show for WPKN-FM radio. MARILYN SILVERMAN, Ph.D., is a clinical psychologist with a private practice in psychotherapy in Wilton, Connecticut. She is a consultant in Pediatrics and Psychiatry at Norwalk Hospital and holds academic appointments at Yale University and Vanderbilt University.

We had our assignment: to write something about bodies, place, and space. We shared the excitement of a first-time collaboration. Vying claims for the primacy and veracity of certain memories kept us laughing and crying as our diagrams of scattered blocks of furniture gave personal orientation to a room, an alcove, a hub of remembered activity. Mickey drew a "chair where I sat to do homework," outside her small Oldest Sister's Room. Susan and Binnie remembered a well-made, yellow leather chair with studded buttons, now given away to relatives; Mickey did not. We all recalled the one bedroom we at one time shared, with a crib nearly flush against a double bed. Our diagrams created open spaces with new angles and vectors onto which the sentiments and perversions of memory laid their claims. "Wasn't the bedroom bigger?" "I thought Daddy's chair was over there." "I didn't know you were still living there then."

Our different birth order in the history of our family and of our culture—Mickey was born before the Second World War, Susie during the first year of the postwar baby boom, Binnie at the dawn of the fifties—ensured that our geographical and familial memories would diverge as well as overlap. Mickey was born in Brooklyn and lived there until she was five, in the "old neighborhood" of Brownsville in an apartment with parents, grandparents, and uncles. Susan was born in Newark virtually nine months to the day after our father's return from the South Pacific, and she did all her growing-up in that city, in the two apartments where all of us lived at one point or another; the first apartment was tenementlike but spacious, in what we now would call the "inner city," the second was just behind the high school, in the racially mixed (Jewish/Black/Italian), lower- to middle-class neighborhood immortalized in Philip Roth's early novels. Binnie, who spent the first fifteen years of her life in Newark, was also the only one of us to experience life in the "suburbs" (a too-bourgeois term for the barrackslike complex adjacent to the New Jersey highway into which our family moved after Susan went away to college).

Once, sometime in the mid-fifties, a local radio show called to tell us that we would win some wonderful prize (probably two tickets to a downtown movie) if only we could identify the "Garden State." None of us could, although we were living in it. Perhaps it was hard for us to imagine New Jersey, which we knew via Newark, in such Eden-like terms. But, more deeply, we lacked the objective markers that give people a sense of place. During our childhood we were the most truly nuclear family we knew. We belonged to no community groups, no synagogue. Our mother, an émigré to this country at age thirteen and now uprooted from her family in Brooklyn, teetered on the edge of agoraphobia, suffering nervousness and various physical symptoms for most of her life. She died at the age of sixty-three from a series of strokes brought on by an intestinal illness that was never diagnosed, after a year of complaints that her doctors largely dismissed. Our father, a traveling salesman, was gone much of the time; when he returned, he seemed restless to "get out of the house" (to a movie, to New York City, even just for a drive on the highway to fill up the tank). They had both experienced the dislocations of the Depression, World War II, and the loss of their original community; first married to other people—a brother and sister—they had fallen in love at a family get-together and left Brooklyn.

Having come together in a passionate affair and then exodus, our parents seemed unable to ever really settle down. They were witty, warm, fearful, easily offended, superstitious, depressed, addicted to crisis. Our father had a fierce intelligence but was prone to brooding, angry moods over a life derailed by the Depression from its rightful course toward college and a career as a writer. Our mother worshipped, protected, and deeply resented him for their growing isolation and for his petty tyrannies. She loved her brothers and sisters and tried to extend our family to include them, but only rarely could she cajole my father into visiting relatives or going to neighborhood parties. Inside the nucleus of our immediate family, however, the intimacy—if not the communication—was intense. And in 1996, as we sisters sketched our maps to fill in the missing years, the missing rooms, we grew increasingly aware that being together was our real place.

In our talk, rooms and emotions surfaced and entwined. Memories of furniture gave way to discussions of how a particular armchair was transformed by whether daddy or mommy was sitting in it and how their presence and absence transformed the emotional climate of the spaces. We all remembered holding hands for reassurance and comfort at bedtime, Binnie reaching through the bars of her crib. In our train of associations we were now into dangerous and safe places. At this juncture we discovered, with an eerie jolt, that in sketching diagrams of the apartments we grew up in, none of us could place and describe the kitchens. We labeled the dilemma "The Missing Kitchens" and immediately realized that we had begun this process, this exploration of bodies, space, place, without acknowledging what, for want of a better term, might be described as our shared "spatial" difficulties, difficulties to which each of us might give different names and associate with different fears but which run through the family like physical resemblances, no two features exactly the same but unmistakably of our line.

Each of us has suffered, each in her own way, from a certain heightened consciousness of space and place and our body's relation to them: Spells of anxiety that could involve the feeling of losing one's place in space and time, events that profoundly affected how we existed in our respective worlds and how or whether we moved about in them. Bridges. Tunnels. Elevators. Open spaces. Closed spaces. In an effort to think about "places through the body" in an intimate and collaborative way, we decided to bracket theoretical and clinical questions and move in on these disturbances of self and place by following the associative trails we discovered: missing kitchens, disappearing bodies, presence and absence, safe and unsafe places.

Somewhat arbitrarily, but based on the topics we gravitated toward in our first attempts, we assigned each other one theme to explore more deeply. Binnie, the youngest of us, was still living at home as our mother's world became more and more limited and her body declined; she has written "Disappearing Kitchens and Other Non-Places." Susan, in the middle, had always experienced her life as a battle between the nesting and traveling sides of her self, and she has associated that conflict with the extremes of our parents' very different personalities; her piece is "The Agoraphobic and the Traveling Salesman." Mickey, who grew up before these parental modes had solidified, when our parents were simply trying to find a place to exist, describes the anxieties of space more existentially; the struggle to find location for oneself, to occupy a place, to know where one is and who one is in space: these are the themes of her piece, "Maps and Safe Places."

The missing kitchens, which set us on our exploration, led us to our parents' lives and the intimate imprints their absence and presence left on our psyches and bodies. But the missing kitchens also ultimately led us to consider larger disappearances and dislocations: cultural diaspora, the attenuation and for some—like us—the virtual disappearance of ethnic culture and religious community, postwar dislocations of gender, the fragmentation and increasing isolation of families. We had always thought of our own family as disconnected from the seemingly more communal and integrated lives around us. Writing this piece, we began to see how reflective our family's history was of a certain cultural trajectory of loss and disorientation. Writing this piece has set our little nuclear bubble down in time and place.

BINNIE: DISAPPEARING KITCHENS AND OTHER NON-PLACES

Is Home a Place?　　Home and place are concepts that are frequently idealized and imagined in terms that do not give credence to real life. Academic geographer Yi-Fu Tuan says that to know the world is to know one's place; he speaks of "visual pleasures; the sensual delight of physical contact; the fondness for place because it is familiar, because it is home and incarnates the past, because it provokes pride of ownership or creation."[1] I smile thinking of the word "place," since the Brooklyn candy factory where my father worked on the days not spent on the road was referred to by him as "the place," never anything else. He never said he was going to the office, or the factory, just "the place." Yet for my father this "place" bore no pleasure, mostly drudgery and defeat, at the hands of the more successful relatives who ran the company. Of course, many people do in fact experience their "place" in life negatively.

Philosopher Gaston Bachelard writes that "when we dream of the house we were born in, in the utmost depths of reverie, we participate in [an] original warmth, the well-tempered matter of the material paradise."[2] But a house is only truly safe and idealizable when the people who inhabit it live in a context of the outside world. The fire at the ski lodge feels the best after a day on the mountain. Even in paintings in caves (the earliest homes), the walls of the cave are dotted with depictions of what goes on outside, the hunt, interaction with the larger sphere. These symbolic totems refer to the outside as viewed from within the protected lair. For me, with a mother who was disconnected from the outside world, her kitchen was a place like an elevator, where you could get stuck, or like a great oceanic void, where you could get lost.

Yet even if cave/home/kitchen is a site of despair or fear, in the midst of a panic attack the idea "I must get home" becomes the only possibility for escaping the mind-numbing terror and confusion generated by a flood of chemicals in the brain. Then home is imaged as the safe harbor, where one will calm down, reconstitute, regain composure, remember and therefore potentially reexperience oneself as a competent entity traveling through space. Home becomes a floating anchor. Memories can soothe; the infant's thumb recalls the mother's breast. But is home a place? What if the sense of safety does not refer to a place at all but to a collection of objects, feelings, bodies? I stare at a certain clock and the familiar brightness of the hands recalls my mother's face, as if she, like an object seen every day for many years, ticks on through the object. Throughout my childhood I took daytime naps with my mother on one twin bed in my parents' bedroom. With one small part of my body in contact with one small part of hers, I could rest. My eldest sister recalls best being able to study on the living room couch, her two sisters on either side of her, leaning casually against her, keeping her anchored in place.

Simulations of the peace given by these moments of contact are projected onto the floating anchor of the home, the site of remembered juxtapositions. Yet the same sites of comfort may also recall places of pain where certain negative exchanges, heightened moments, and their emotional residues have resonated in time and space. These images shimmer with dread, the air charged with ions of anxiety. I remember living rooms in various apartments where we sat, my mother's eyes searching my father's face and gestures for evidence of the start of a dark mood. We were warned not to do anything to bother him. "Upsetting daddy" became a place, as agonized silences, meaningful glances, and tensed muscles imprinted themselves onto the scene. In our living room daddy occupied a certain chair when he was not traveling, and when he sat there the air was heavy with both his cigar smoke and the invisible but palpable tension of his unhappiness. If daddy is home, then mommy feels a certain way. Tense, maybe, but less lonely. If daddy is away and mommy is in the daddy chair, her cigarette smoke is less noxious than his cigar's, but her loneliness is a junior version of his despair. Many feeling states in me were encoded during moments like these while people were sitting in their places, doing very little. The atmosphere left a residue, and the imprint of these fossilized moments remains on my body. The pain of this inheritance becomes a place that is a bodily feeling; pain itself is a place.

Time can create a private space that becomes a place. At 4 A.M., in the living room, the chairs are empty of their people; my parents are asleep in their back bedroom. I am lying on the couch trying to reach sleep by watching a series of late movies until the screen goes blank the way it used to. It is 1968 and I have returned from the larger world called Boston, where I have dropped out of college, and I am home to rest my head upon the shore of my mother's lap. I have created a place for myself defined by time, in which the vectors link, as personal as a signature, the juxtapositions are sad and claustrophobic, but they are my creation and I am attached to them. My solitude is immense, it fills the room, it is a place of secret thoughts. If someone stirs in the back room, threatening to emerge to get a drink of water in the kitchen, I lose my place.

Entering a Missing Kitchen   We have mentioned that we couldn't locate the kitchens in our sketched diagrams. In one sense, perhaps, this absence is not surprising. Viewed as the province of our mother, whose powerlessness was often shown through her dependency and passivity, her inability to drive, her not working outside the home, the kitchen did not offer much comfort. Duncan Hines cakes might sit atop the refrigerator, with names like "Cherry Supreme," occasional interesting meals from the good recipes passed down from my orthodox grandmother might delight us, having my mother wash my long hair in the kitchen sink had a reassuring constancy, long talks at kitchen tables surely must have happened, although I cannot remember any. Perhaps the kitchens are lost because, as feminists have pointed out, such rooms have long served as mere background to the more important places men have traditionally occupied. Yet that background space is the place where family life often centers, where preparation and consumption of food and therefore life itself resides.

Through television we have been imprinted with ubiquitous images of the wife and mother of the 1950s, but they are drained of specificity and particularizing texture. The archetypal housewife/mother (pre-*Roseanne*) spins through our psyches with good-natured grace, in a cotton shirtwaist dress, giving lilting instructions to the rest of the family: "Come on now, dinner's ready!" "Sally, would you pass your brother some potatoes, please?"

"Not now, Hon, I've got to do the dishes." These images, bleached of ethnicity, do not reflect the reality of most people's lives.

The kitchen is where crucial aspects of culture and ethnicity are maintained, but it may also be the site where assimilation occurs. Among the features of the religious community of observant Jews are the potentially meaningful moments created by holiday gatherings and rituals. But our family was insulated, isolated from that community. My only contact with a kosher kitchen was through the orthodox practices of my one surviving grandparent, my maternal grandmother. In the kitchens of religious Jews the arrangement of dishes inside cabinets choreographs the "koshering" of that space: certain dishes for dairy, others for meat, used and washed separately, even the dishtowels. These practices were viewed as extreme in our family; as nonreligious Jews our kitchens were mostly stripped of ethnic lessons from the past. I would perform ordinary yet sacrilegious tasks (cutting with scissors, using electricity) on the Sabbath while my grandmother glared at me. I glared back, suspicious of her foreign tongue, her strange practices, her rigid notions of right and wrong. I shared a tendency that members of oppressed groups are vulnerable to, a view of our own identifying characteristics as unacceptable, "too much," because they mark us for curiosity, judgment, and exclusion by others.[3]

While the Jewish kitchen was "too much" for me, the missing kitchens of our diagrams, once we had discovered them, felt "not enough," hovering like sad balloons whose structure could not be grasped or appreciated. If mother is of the kitchen, and the kitchens are missing, then mother is missing. But our mother, although limited by her anxiety, was not missing for us. Simple absence causes wounds of neglect, a non-space, but ours are not exactly diagrams of neglect, they are diagrams of the pull toward accomplishment, movement, and embodiment and the simultaneous regressive pull backward to stasis, ill-health, fear, disorientation and isolation. On my first day of school I clutched my mother, the teacher pulling my arm while I screamed, "No, I don't want to!" In my mental picture both teacher and mother want a part of me. I didn't consciously know then that teacher represented the active, external world and mother a homebound passivity. I only knew that in the middle I was in agony, in no place at all.

The missing kitchens, as the rooms of confusion and loss, reflect such tension in spatial terms. When we sisters gazed at our diagrams, the kitchens were difficult to place. They were not completely gone, after all, but they were clouded by a mind-stopping rush of contrary images and emotions: too much, too little, oppressively there and not really anywhere. A space is not filled, something is missing. Is something wrong then? Perhaps what is wrong is that ambivalence makes it difficult to reconcile loss. Anger is a clarifying emotion, one that helps us differentiate and separate. If only the kitchens were . . . angry!! Instead they appear to be lost. "I don't know where I am," we say when we are lost. "I don't know if I am," I say in the boundaryless expanse of nature. I can't feel my borders—the rooms have all merged, there are no maps that apply.

And if the kitchen is the body/belly of the mother, I approach my relationship to my mother's body through the squinty protected vision of my fingers, as if I am watching a slow, plodding foreign film with disturbing images that occasionally poke through. I cannot take it all in at once. My mother's physical presence is a chunky, impenetrable block of tension. Standing, she looked like she was sitting. Sitting, she could be standing; you couldn't bend her. I have no image or memory of my mother assertively angry, and that leaves a hole inside me. The special block my mother's body inhabits in my psyche is how my head feels when I experience a preverbal sensation of my head being too heavy, too thick to bear, or perhaps simply to lift, as if I am an infant negotiating a new stage of physical mastery.

My mother's cooking was lazy. She opened cans, mostly peas, carrots. I didn't eat a mushroom until I was over twenty, and I didn't know what artichokes or avocados were until then either. I felt like I had spent my life eating in a fallout shelter. What was my mother's cooking about? It was partially about her mother, who was orthodox Jewish, born in Poland, and had lost her husband to a vague tale of the times; a solider, he had gone to America before her, to pave the way, but he was unfaithful and didn't send for her at first. When she did arrive in America, it was with her five children: Regina, Esther, Leon, Arthur, and Bobby. Many years later, widowed, depressed, pining, my grandmother was finally installed in the Brooklyn ghetto in her small apartment. She had never learned English out of that crazy defiance and passion for Yiddish, as if to say, "I refuse to engage with you, although I am here in my body in this country I am not really with you." Grandfather, dead the day after I was born, sat in a framed photograph atop a doily on her television console. In my grandmother's kitchen, meat purchased from the neighborhood kosher butcher and fashioned into elaborate recipes simmered on the stove for hours, fatty, impenetrable, inscrutable.

Tales are told by my sisters of special cooking done by my mother, but by my time she was getting tired and the simmering meat was just too much of an investment in an increasingly irrelevant process unnecessary to modern life. In general, my mother's kitchen efforts were seen as mundane daily events, neither special nor deficient, her cleaning of ashtrays an expected duty. I don't recall any words of thanks from my father. My father's relation to the values of the kitchen was both paradoxical and typical. Although he had been a chief baker aboard ship in the navy during World War II, he never made one meal, prepared one hot drink that I can remember, but always alluded proudly to the apple pie he had baked for 1,200 men. When he suffered in certain years from the discomfort of new teeth made to replace long-neglected ones, he would sullenly push away the plate of food my mother had prepared, muttering, "I can't eat this . . . it's too tough." "What can I make you instead?" she would plead, but by then he was in the rapturous arms of bitterness and martyrdom. Nothing would do now.

My mother's deep and growing fatigue was clearest to me after her death. We had gone to my parents' last apartment in New Jersey to go through her things and select those items we each wanted. When we examined mother's cabinets, the most heart-wrenching vision for me was of her inexpensive casserole dishes, which on inspection were dirty and stained with marks that suggested her distraction or preoccupations. I took some of the dishes, imagining her in her later years (she lived to be sixty-three) vaguely nauseated, headachy, and bloated. She was a hypochondriac for years, but like the boy who cried wolf, her last complaints were real—and not taken very seriously. She died of a mysterious illness whose only clues, found during exploratory surgery, were a foot's length of gangrenous intestine and a sigmoid adhered to a colon; my father forbade an autopsy. I am now left with the imprecise image of her body as a congested house.

In that last apartment in New Jersey the kitchen had just about disappeared. The last kitchen was a kitchenette without room for a table, without a door, spilling into a small dining "area" without a door, which spilled into a small living "area" without a door. So now from every direction my father could be seen, pushing his meat away at the dining area table or putting his head into his hands after work, while from every direction I could see my mother, seated temporarily in his club chair (she was in the living "area" while he ate because we hardly ever ate together as a family anymore), tensed, inhaling a shallow breath, watching him.

Now I find disquieting the realization that the small carriage house in which I have lived for many years has no distinct rooms on the first level; the open floor plan is like a loft: kitchen, dining, and living areas merge. If there are no accidents in life, as interpreters of behavior would say, then I have architected a repetition of the last setting in which I observed my parents together. I think there is another, more compelling source: I do not have to deal with a separate kitchen. I do not have to deal visually with the loss of my mother or the isolation of her life. And I do not cook, the man in my life does.

Panic   "Agoraphobia," I wrote in 1987, "which often develops shortly after marriage, clearly functions in many cases as a way to cement dependency and attachment in the face of unacceptable stirrings of dissatisfaction and restlessness."[4] What I did not write was that my own agoraphobia had developed shortly after my own marriage, into which I had drifted—at age twenty-one and a college dropout—like a sleepwalker, giving up bits and pieces of myself in such small increments (an ambition here, a fantasy there) that I was startled awake one day to discover that I was almost entirely gone. What woke me was my body, whose very being in the world suddenly shifted and changed everything. It was as though I had been in a fog, bobbing in a familiar sea between icebergs unknown to me, and then all at once I was stranded on an enormous one, rising high out of the sea, perched, precarious, desperate for walls to plant my hands against. The physical sensations of panic were so new and frightening—and so seemingly arbitrary—that my only anchoring thought was to get myself someplace where they would stop, where I would be safe. That place seemed to be the dreary, gray Hyde Park apartment in which I lived, without much pleasure, with my husband.

It happened on the Illinois Central, which had been taking me and my younger sister Binnie into the Loop. She was visiting me and we were planning to see a movie. I became faint, but instead of putting my head between my knees as a normal person would do, seeking to restore equilibrium through the trusted processes of one's own body, I responded like a drowning person, my only thought to find air. *I must get off this train. Get me off this train!* In the logic of the panic attack, it makes absolute, unanswerable sense, as places and bodies collude, become one: "If I don't get off this train, I'll faint." "This tunnel is suffocating me." "If I can only make it home, I won't die."

But what gives certain places the power to make panic? Freud theorized that his own train phobia was the result of having seen his mother naked during a train trip from the family village in Moravia to Vienna. But Freud was only one of many late Victorians who suffered from "train neurosis," a condition most physicians of the era attributed to traumas suffered in accidents, abrupt stops, loud noises. In the late sixties the psychiatrists and therapists that I went to, desperate for understanding and help for the baffling and seemingly inexorable thing that was happening to me, were uninterested in the places of my panic; true to their time, they were more interested in the "home" front, arguing that my agoraphobia was the result of my failure to accept my femininity and accommodate myself to marriage.

Only when I began to savor train trips—traveling to colleges later in my life, as a visiting speaker—did I understand the fine line that separates panic and excitement. The charge of leaving home, knowing that your body has been cut loose from the cycling habits of the domestic domain and is now moving unrooted across time and space, always to something new, alert to the defining gaze of strangers . . . What made this terrifying to me at one point in my life and invigorating at another? Victorians, utterly unused to the massive, indifferent, steel power that could bear them from the rural village of home to the noisy chaos of the city,[5] suffered from railroad anxieties and phobias virtually unheard of today. (Do we really need a naked mother to account for Freud's panic?) They had to learn to tolerate the stimulation, the "nervousness," as Freud put it, of modern life. Could it be that my numbed and muffled self, on that train in Chicago, had become a Victorian, allergic to excitement, experiencing any opening of limits, any fluttering of heart, any intimation that the world was far, far bigger than my home, as panic?

The Road   The father that Binnie and I knew was a traveling salesman. Everything changed when he came home. Fog would lift, the air became oxygenated as doors opened and the brisk outside rushed in, waking us up. We would have waited all day, wondering what our presents would be. There would be tiny hotel soaps, plastic dolls dressed in buckskin, pecan pralines, restaurant matchbooks to add to my collection. The thrill of suitcases opening. Whisking away for Chinese food, to an air-conditioned movie. The tenuous delight of the huge, good mood that he would be in for at least an evening as he recounted stories of the brokers who would deal only with him, the fabulous hotels and restaurants they ate in as they did their business, assorted oddballs he had run across. The drama was always high, no matter what the story. We often got giddy. And, as if to verify my parents' favorite superstitious warning—"If you laugh too hard, you're going to cry"—a crash was inevitable. Usually it began with a petty squabble between the kids. Always it escalated to something global, between our parents, and then metaphysical, between my father and God. "Why can't you ever . . . ?" "Why do I have to put up with . . . ?" "What did I do to deserve . . . ?" The downward spiral almost always happened on the way home.

Ever since I can remember, my father's comings and goings structured and colored my sense of time and place, masculinity and femininity, dream and reality. Other kids' fathers were always dependably but boringly around. To me, used to a father who descended only periodically, like Santa, they seemed almost extensions of the other kids' mothers, vaguely and unheroically domestic. They could stop faucets from dripping (which our father definitely could not), but only our father could do the *New York Times* Sunday Crossword—in ink—in a morning. I was proud that my father condescended to join the mundane world as a visitor rather than a regular inhabitant. He loved telling the story of how I, at some impossibly young age, still an infant, amazed everyone at Camp Whitelake by uttering a complete, perfectly grammatical sentence: "My daddy is coming home Saturday!" He would break up in laughter as he underscored what a "midget" I was and how agog the other bungalow dwellers were to see words coming out of my midget's mouth. (There was always a whiff of the freakshow even in my father's highest praise of us, as though our best talents were signs that we had dropped from another planet.)

What I cannot remember, however, is just how much time he spent "on the road." If I had to do it arithmetically, I'd say he was home one week out of every four. But then when did I get to see all those Broadway shows? Learn to play cutthroat scrabble? Memorize the meaning and portent of his every gesture? Perhaps he was home more than I remember. Or maybe real time only started when he walked through the door. My mother seemed always to be waiting, smoking or dozing in my father's armchair, putting canned goods away, feeding the cat, until called upon to spring into action on his return. She rarely left the house alone, except to buy groceries or occasionally to visit a nearby girlfriend; I have barely a memory of going anyplace with her without my father. School was real enough in its way, but anticipatory, preparatory—for summer, for the next term, for the transformation that would allow my life to really begin. But my father was undeniably present. And he made the external world present for me; he offered it as a bracing tonic against some domestic stupor into which I was continually being lured, a preventive measure against my own disappearance. The Midwest brokers, the hotels, the highway that led from Newark to Manhattan, trains and cars that took you from one state to another; it was as though they had a sign on them: "This way lies life."

And the other door? It's not that easy to say where that door leads. Unlike my sister Binnie, I love cooking, and my images of my mother's kitchen, snapped at an earlier, more communal time in her life, are warmer. In *Unbearable Weight* I wrote of

> the pride and pleasure that radiated from my mother when her famous stuffed cabbage was devoured enthusiastically and in huge quantities by all her family—husband, children, brothers, sister, and their children. As a little girl, I loved watching her roll each piece, enclosing just the right amount of filling, skillfully avoiding tearing the tender cabbage leaves as

she folded them around the meat. She was visibly pleased when I asked her to teach me exactly how to make the dish and thrilled when I even went so far as to write the quantities and instructions down as she tried to formulate them into a recipe (it had been passed through demonstration until then, and my mother considered that in writing it down I was conferring high status on it). Those periods in my life when I have found myself too busy writing, teaching, and traveling to find the time and energy to prepare special meals for people that I love have been periods when a deep aspect of my self has felt deprived, depressed.[6]

Yet for many years, in recovery from the debilitating agoraphobia that kept me housebound for the first part of my twenties, I had to go out for a while every morning before I could settle in to do my studying or writing. I needed that inoculation, that first contact with the outside world before I could feel safe at home. Before I could feel safe, that is, from the lure and illusion of safety, from my inclination to get stuck inside, habituated to a contracted world. Being outside, which when I was agoraphobic had left me feeling substanceless, a medium through which body, breath, and world would rush, squeezing my heart and dotting my vision, now gave me definition, body, focused my gaze. Armored, assured that I was vigorous, of the world, I could return home without fear of dissolving. For a while, my safest places were trains and hotel rooms; I love being en route, and its being someone else's professional business to care for me, bring me my coffee.

But for most of my life, whenever I strayed too far from that domestic world in which I like my mother was the professional caretaker, I would reel myself in, calling on my phobias to help. (Before my Ph.D. orals my panic disorder revisited me, and then again after a year unsuccessfully trying to become pregnant.) At those times it seemed that the most delicious thing in the world would be to be sitting again next to my mother, watching daytime soaps with her. But she was gone, and I had to console myself by reproducing her world, by bringing her body back through a more recessive invocation of my own. During one of those retreats, I wrote in my journal (only realizing later that I was writing about my mother as much as myself): "There is something touching to me about my diminished state. Puttering around, cooking soup, putting together packages for people I love, my mind gentle and nondemanding, the strict compulsive self gone, I feel a compassion and care for myself as I would for another person but never have before for myself. Who is this person? As I feel myself conquered, accepting my own diminished state and its requirements, the sweetness and dignity of the little tasks I do, desiring nothing more than simple renewal of contact with the world, are like those of a baby."

These cycling patterns led me to believe that I had learned how to move around in the big world from my father, while my mother taught me empathy and intimacy but left me prone to panic. Today I'm not so sure. When I was growing up, it was presented to me as the essence of their personalities that our father traveled and our mother stayed home, that he was bold where she was fearful, that he was autonomous while she was dependent. It was virtually impossible for me to put the indisputable accuracy of these definitions together with the much dimmer, historical facts that my mother had supposedly had a "wild" girlhood and also had worked in the office of a factory during the war—and apparently, had loved it. Vaguely I remember arguments about going back to work, which my father always won. "No wife of mine . . . Never!" (even though he had no life insurance and they couldn't save a penny from his salary toward a house of their own or funds for our education). But I cannot remember who was doing the arguing on the other side. Could it have been my older sister? It's hard for me to imagine it was ever my mother herself. But surely it must have been.

My mother, even when she was most anxious and depressed, would smile at strangers, strike up conversations, flirt with shopkeepers. Once, in a crowded supermarket, I felt a panic coming on and tried a technique my therapist had taught me. I imagined that everything that was frightening to me—the noise, the crying children, the pushing and shoving—was a warm, colorful blanket like the one my therapist had me imagine in his office, a kind of visual mantra of comfort. The blanket I had imagined was all green and gold and burnt sienna, colors that I recognized as those of a throw that my mother had knit me, rustic colors that still bring my mother to me unexpectedly as I pass by sunlit trees in autumn. In the supermarket I put that blanket around me with a great effort of imagination—and I amazed myself. I really did feel enveloped and calmed by the chattering people in the store who had seemed so alien to me just a moment ago. At the same moment I felt my mother's presence strongly, and I recognized that there was a terrible flaw in my picture of her. Her capacity for human connection, her warmth, was not some compensating factor, developed only to make a small and limited world bearable and less frightening. It was big, it was strong, it was powerful, and it was highly unusual, a remarkable gift. She wasn't afraid of people! She was an adventuress!

Today, looking through a folder of old letters, I found two postcards. Of all the cards and letters I received from my parents, somehow just these two survived. One, sent to me by my father while I was a freshman living in a dorm in Chicago, was from the "Fabulous White Way" of the "World Famous Las Vegas Strip." Inside, via a foldout display of casinos, hotels, and showgirls, it told the "story" of the Strip. My father had written, beside the photo of the Dunes, that he was staying there, and he sent "greetings from the land of lost wages, daughter!" Over the years I had received scores of cards like this from him, exuberant with the romance of travel. But the other postcard startled me. It was from my mother, written to me while I was living in Canada, struggling out of my agoraphobia and splitting up with my husband. It was from Florida, where she had apparently gone—on a plane!—with her best girlfriend at the time. My mother had not been afraid of planes, I now remembered, that was me and my sisters. But a vacation? Without my father? I couldn't remember it, couldn't imagine it, yet the evidence was in my hand.

The cartoon on the front showed a shapely, tanned woman on the beach, beside which my mother had written "Me," and, separated by a line, a little girl bundled up beside a snowman, beside which my mother had written "You." "I'll shovel sand for you in Florida . . . If you'll shovel snow for me up north," it read, with a space for the temperature, which my mother had filled in at 86 degrees. On the back was her more personal message to me: "Hiya Darling: The flight was smooth as silk. Got a little high and didn't feel anything but happy. Wish you were here. Love from Florence. Say hello to your roommates. Love you, Mom. P.S. Later Dad will come."

MICKEY: MAPS AND SAFE PLACES

Waking Up   In the middle of an obscure and heavy dialogue on "geography" as reflected in places, bodies, and madness, one of my sisters tactfully inserted a simplifying question: If they asked you where you were from, what would you say?

I would say: I am from the land of the three sisters—from Never-Never Land—from the near/far planet that sent out small bands of thin-skinned envoys to test their survival skills in the ghetto neighborhood of Newark. I was never, in fact, from anywhere that I actually lived.

I lived inside my family and even then in a private place far from its borders. I have since learned that family is often the conduit of the culture of a place, the specifier of the boundaries of its geography. When family *is* your place—encapsulated in its own climate—you gain a measure of independence from the arbitrariness of local places in exchange for the claustrophobic logic of a tenement apartment suspended above the stores and the street.

I had my maps:

- the map of lost treasures, like the house in Brooklyn that burned down with the Persian rugs, piano, and an immigrant family's newly acquired wealth . . .

- the map of the town and house we would have had if the depression hadn't come and my father's father hadn't been deceived by his nephew, and the war hadn't come . . .

- the map of the lost village in the Old Country where my mother was born, that no one could ever find or pronounce . . .

- the map of the peopled/storied neighborhood in Brooklyn from which my parents fled in exile to live out their "illicit" romance in New Jersey.

No wonder then that they never showed me the way to school, never warned me that Clinton Avenue was a dangerous place, never told me that New Jersey was the Garden State. The most important parts of my mother and father never existed in the places we were living.

I lived inside my mother's body, inside my father's dreams and nightmares. Lived on the shelf next to my books, lived in my books, and it never mattered that we had the best car on the block to take us to the Jersey shore. When I began the project of leaving, I took a bus to the downtown terminal, the Hudson Tubes to Port Authority. I walked across 42nd Street and took the Fifth Avenue bus to Washington Square. I did this five days a week for three years. I never knew that this was hard or unusual or impractical or risky. I calculated the trip as the distance between the bookshelves in my room and the bookshelves in the college library, the distance further foreshortened by the books I carried with me.

When I was attacked and tied to a tree, walking along Riverside Drive at midnight, the police told me I should have known that this was a dangerous place. I knew—frozen by sudden moments of discontinuity and

wordless dread—that I sometimes didn't know who I was. I never realized that I didn't know where I was and that this was something I should
have—could have—known: the cradled anchoring in the reality of place,
the grounding in the present, the topography of daily living in real/time
and real/space.

My books had come with their own maps of safe and dangerous places.
My parents, in an effort to protect me which proved to be both misguided
and inspired, had left me to my books, believing as I did that my immersion in my books gave me a special status, like a time-traveler in a forties
version of virtual reality. Unaware of real dangers but constantly on the
alert for the romantic and tragic possibilities of life as described in my books,
I navigated the blocks near our apartment with an odd combination of
courage and fear and trembling. What were the dangers of an occasional
mugging compared to the prospect of being snatched from the London
streets by Fagin? Why should I be afraid of the American Indian on the
street who was tormenting cats when I was dreaming of sharing a tent
with the last of the Mohicans? When I panicked at the sound of air-raid
sirens, I was thinking of tidal waves in Japan I had read about in a novel
that morning or a piercing call to arms against an alien invasion as
recounted in an H. G. Wells story. I traveled with "Lad, a dog" to protect
me and a book-inspired notion that if I meant no harm to anyone I would
not be harmed, and in fact I never was harmed during my childhood.

As part of the same effort to protect (and prevent me from ever leaving them?), my parents rarely explained or put into context or helped me
to anticipate anything contemporaneous with my own time and existence.
Mostly I was given, as a very special confidence and charge, the stories of
their past life, which I carried inside me like a great weighty epic novel
of the Brooklyn streets which had yet to be written. It was a novel about
exodus, success, catastrophic financial reversals, passion, scandal. The British
may have needed two hundred camels and as many servants to transport
the accoutrements of their culture and comfort to the colonies. My father's

family arrived from England with a suitcase and their wits, my mother's father, preceding his wife and children, with a knapsack and a sewing machine. I thought of them all as carrying within them invisible treasures, like a caravan of Russian nesting boxes filled with stories, Jewish lullabies, mandates for humanistic living that were thousands of years old.

I was proud to have European roots. This was a romantic image that tied me to cherished intellectual and cultural values and linked me to the authors of my books. I never really knew until I saw faces like my mother's in a pictorial history of Eastern Europe that in fact my mother had come from another place. She hadn't brought her memories with her or chose not to share them and I had never questioned her silence. When my grandmother tried to tell me about village life in a language I had forgotten, my mother did not translate. When uncles referred in passing to Grandpa's army service she never elaborated. It was in our kitchens that these aborted dialogues took place. It was the kitchen in which I felt my mother's silences most palpably. When I first began to lose the Yiddish in which the earliest experiences of my life were encoded, she never helped me to retrieve it, just as she had never spoken of the first twelve years of her own history in the Old Country. She stopped dressing me in lace blouses and flowered skirts. She stopped wrapping my braids around my head. She stopped baking apple cakes. She never laid claim to the mementos and photographs of her parents' early life. I wonder now if she thought that she had little of real value to contribute to the lives of her American daughters.

When I stepped out of my books and daydreams into real time, I understood finally the nature and scope of the real dangers and losses my parents and extended family had faced. I understood that the air-raid sirens had signaled a real war. I understood that my father, in his romantic naval uniform, had fought that real war in a very remote, very dangerous place in the world. I understood that my mother and other women left at home like a colony of the disenfranchised, negotiating dramas of reappearance and disappearance, were in fact dealing with real danger and real absence, listening to Gabriel Heater,[7] rationing food, diverting each other with stories of childbirth in their kitchens. When over the subsequent years my mother became increasingly withdrawn and her life constricted, I knew that part of what she had struggled with were actual losses, deaths, separations from family, and I wondered whether any of the psychiatrists whom she consulted had ever dealt with where she had come from, where she was going, and why she got stuck.

I have been tempted at times to see my parents' lives as a contemporary political parable: woman unfulfilled, housebound, man bitter and neglectful, daughters emancipated through education, psychotherapy, and the cultural endorsement of women's work. I had been tempted to think of my mother as a prisoner of her house, with my father, braver and more vital, able to escape into the wider world. Our mandate then seemed to be to get women out of their houses, out of their kitchens, winning for them the mobility that men enjoy. In my childhood I had been exempted from kitchen duties, given the status of a scholar who shouldn't have to be concerned about such things. In this view kitchens are demeaned the way some musicians relegate lyrics to a lesser place than melody and chords. I shared both biases. I saw home and hearth as a bird's nest with its fragments of stuff, used to support life but subordinated to the more important job of flying off and getting on with the real business of living. Now I understand that kitchens matter as the lyrics of melodies matter.

I realize now that both my parents were traumatized and diminished by the dislocations of their lives: immigration, the Depression, war and wartime, personal upheavals of the diaspora, uprootings from their families. My father, although working with persistence and success in the "outside world," traveled with his sample case of stories that were to him possessions salvaged from the destruction of a richer life. Our mother's tragedy was not confinement to her kitchen and women's work but her growing incapacity to occupy her house, to claim it as her own, to inhabit it fully. Her early years in Brooklyn—and mine—had been rooted in family and in neighborhoods.

Friendships were always a part of her life even in the worst period of depression and anxiety; the therapeutic group she joined became her friends. She had deep capacities for sympathetic, loving, nonjudgmental human attachment. But she could not hold onto her entitlement to her own history or the mandates of her own self-development in the face of cultural and emotional dislocations, a possessive husband, and, finally, the threats to the vitality and continuity of memory posed by aging. Our mother didn't disappear into her house, she disappeared within it.

Connections and Dislocations   Dramas of spatial meaning and safety from the perspective of self and identity are continuously played out around us. Like a play within a play, people move from point to point following the patterns and routines of apparently practical lives. But they carry with them maps of safe places and safe distances, maps of their internal landscapes, its topography built up of the history of past and present human relationships. These maps designate the way stations where one can be refueled, loved, reminded of one's identity.

Places have always been inseparable from people for me. Syracuse exists on my internal landscape because my sister Susie lived there and when she left, its continuing existence was guaranteed by my purchase of two paintings I loved from people I knew there. New Haven emerges in bold type on my map (Yale University noted in the legend) because my sister Binnie lives there now. Poland will always exist for me no matter who appropriates it because my mother was born there in a town I am still determined to locate on a pre–World War II map. England first came into being as the birthplace of Virginia Woolf, whom I admired. Though my childhood relationship to places was through my books and remote from the real places I lived in, it was still always personal. As a student I found only geography impossible to learn. I could not keep straight places that were not linked in some way to people with whom I had a connection.

Like the famous Steinberg cartoon of the New Yorker's view of the world, with New York City presiding huge and detailed over three-quarters of the map, the rest of the world misplaced and reduced, we all draw the places on our meaning-maps, large or small, depending on our emotional investments and worldview. But for me places hardly existed at all unless animated by memories of people. More intimate spaces take on the same dynamic. I am most aware of the different architectural features of the house my husband and I built as reflections of the preferences and biases of each person who contributed to the design. Objects in my house are links to specific relationships and are therefore always difficult to discard. In stark contrast, on a bureau inherited from my mother-in-law, arranged ever so artfully, visually compelling, sits a collection of shells from oceans all over the world which I discovered at a consignment shop. They seem to belong to no one and their anonymity never fails to be intrusive and disquieting.

I picture each individual's history of human connections as a flow of conscious, unconscious, and embodied memories that are the substrate of the continuity of mental life and the basis of the most fundamental sense of identity. Throughout life, concepts of home base and the safety of other places remain intimately linked to this sense of identity. Knowing where one is, knowing one's place, understanding the nature of real places in themselves requires first a centered self, grounded, embodied in deeply imprinted maps that record the memories of our history of human connections. Like tethers to a dock or a lifeline to shore, this living, internal history protects us from forgetting who we are, helps us to reconstitute when lost. Without that secure housing for self, places can be seen only as a threat to the stability and cohesiveness of the person. Places become metaphors for states of mind.

Spatial metaphors are well suited to capture the phenomenology of the particular form of panic that occurs when the most fundamental sense of existence and connection is at stake. You are on a well-lit stage. The scenery stands as background and support. You know your lines. Suddenly the stage disappears. The floor drops out. The players and set vanish or persist as unfamiliar figures in another script in which you have no part. You are in a stalled elevator, a traffic jam, on a becalmed sailboat, in confined or open spaces. Suddenly something inside stops. Is it that flow of images of past and present human connections that has been temporarily disrupted, eclipsed, leaving you in a freeze-frame moment of heightened awareness of discontinuity of self and the dread that there doesn't seem to be any way to get back to those way stations that remind you of who you are? Places, to the diminished, ahistorical self, may hardly seem to exist at all.

I try to imagine what my mother's map might have been like in the last decade of her life: a large, featureless area marked with an "x" and a "no reentry" zone and a faceless population, the Old Country; a small place in New Jersey disconnected from the rest of the states; an endless road needing repair leading to a handful of residents on a few named or numbered streets in Brooklyn. The most prominent feature would be the bridges to a few friends and friendly shopkeepers, bridges depicted as spanning hundreds of miles across uninhabited stretches. I can imagine arrows marking the directions her daughters would take in moving away and her husband would follow in his travels. During my visits to my mother that last decade, I always felt anxiety and tremendous sadness at her increasingly constricted life. The road there felt like limbo, an out-of-time and -place stretch of highway, forever foggy. But I never left without feeling oddly revived, reminded of who I was, what I wanted to do with my life, who and what I valued and loved.

Home, as a truly safe place, the container and springboard for integrated living, is the foundation of an ontologically secure existence. While my parents had not been able to provide that, they did give me some very special provisions for establishing roots in my own life in another place. Despite the dislocations, eclipse of tradition, loss of wealth in the Depression, upheavals of wartime, disillusionments of daily living, my parents' humanity, humor, intelligence, and idealism are after all what I invariably draw on to "place" myself in the universe and what fuels my capacity to survive and prevail, wherever I am. Where am I from? Through the process of writing this piece, I realized that I am from England, Poland, New York, Connecticut; I am from all the places I have lived in and that my relatives have lived in because I bring myself, my family, and my history with me. Periods of crisis in my life, spells of anxiety, have almost invariably been associated with a temporary eclipse of that connection.

Now we three are sitting in Binnie's real kitchen, surrounded by her totems and linking objects, grounded in the real work of our present, real lives. In tracking the missing kitchens together, we have also retrieved something vital that was passed down to us by our parents. Our father's continuing passion for words and stories, his mythic castings of everyday occurrences; our mother's deep perceptions into other people's feelings; fierce family arguments about the interpretation of past events—what really happened, who was to blame—imprinted on all of us a powerful desire to understand things, to give shape to them, to communicate them. Working together, we actualized these values once again as a family and so reconstructed another part of the missing kitchens. Momentary loss of boundaries, intensities of emotion, anxieties of "influence," all those dissolving and resolving challenges and redefining confrontations have not compromised the safety of the place we are for each other. We are holding hands again through the bars of cribs, leaning against each other on flowered couches, this time not to assure our existence but to celebrate it.

INTRODUCTION

1.   More about "anti-fashion" in "Never Just Pictures," in this volume.

2.   See especially "Material Girl" in my *Unbearable Weight: Feminism, Western Culture, and the Body* (Berkeley: University of California Press, 1993).

3.   See "Bringing Body to Theory," in this collection, for a more detailed discussion of my theoretical perspectives on body, nature, and culture.

4.   Susan Bordo, *My Father's Body and Other Unexplored Regions of Sex, Masculinity, and the Male Body* (New York: Farrar, Straus, and Giroux, forthcoming). See also Susan Bordo, "Reading the Male Body," in Laurence Goldstein, ed., *The Male Body* (Ann Arbor: University of Michigan Press, 1994), 265–306.

5.   The version of "Bringing Body to Theory" which will appear in Welton's collection contains some material not included in the version printed here, which was edited to avoid repetition of points made elsewhere in this volume and to eliminate some technical discussions.

BRAVEHEART, BABE, AND THE CONTEMPORARY BODY

1.   See Marcene Goodman, "Social, Psychological, and Developmental Factors in Women's Receptivity to Cosmetic Surgery," *Journal of Aging Studies* 8, no. 4 (1994): 375–396.

2.   Quoted in Sally Ogle Davis, "Knifestyles of the Rich and Famous," *Marie Claire,* May 1996, p. 46.

3.   Interview with Amanda de Cadenet, *Interview,* August 1995.

4.   Rush Limbaugh, in his tirades against feminists and the academic left, has apparently not noticed that among these groups too the "victim" is *not* politically correct

but passé. In the 1990s postmodern academics look around and see not "oppressive" systems (which would be old-fashioned and "totalizing," so very "sixties") but "resistance," "subversion," and "creative negotiation" of the culture. (These academics may balk at being lined up on the side of *Braveheart* and Nike; they might be surprised at how often the trope of cultural "resistance" appears in automobile ads.) In exalting the creative power and efficacy of the individual, the right and left—polarized around so many other issues—seem to be revelers at the same party.

5. Naomi Wolf, *Fire with Fire* (New York: Random House, 1993), 45.

6. Friedan quote and "Tell them to get some therapy" in Debra Rosenberg, Stanley Holmes, Martha Brant, Donna Foote, and Nina Biddle, "Sexual Correctness," *Newsweek,* October 25, 1993, p. 56.

7. Kathy Davis, *Reshaping the Female Body: The Dilemma of Cosmetic Surgery* (New York: Routledge, 1995), 60–62.

8. See "Material Girl: The Effacements of Postmodern Culture," in my *Unbearable Weight* (Berkeley: University of California Press, 1993).

9. In 1994 there were nearly 400,000 aesthetic cosmetic surgeries performed in the United States, of which 65 percent were done on people with family incomes under $50,000 a year, even though health insurance does not cover cosmetic surgery. At the same time the number of people who say they approve of aesthetic surgery has increased 50 percent in the last decade. See Charles Siebert, "The Cuts That Go Deeper," *New York Times Magazine,* July 7, 1996, pp. 20–26, 40–44.

10. Diana Dull and Candace West's research suggests that while "limited economic resources may *hinder* the pursuit of cosmetic surgery, they do not necessarily *prevent* that pursuit." They cite cases of people who have taken out loans for breast augmentations or who have scrimped and saved for years for their operations. See their "Accounting for Cosmetic Surgery: The Accomplishment of Gender," *Social Problems* 18, no. 1 (February 1991): 54–70.

11. In S. O. Davis, "Knifestyles," *Marie Claire,* May 1996, p. 46.

12. Amy Spindler, "It's a Face-Lifted, Tummy-Tucked Jungle Out There," *New York Times,* Sunday, June 9, 1996, pp. 6–10.

13. Quoted in Patricia Morrisroe, "Forever Young," *New York,* June 9, 1986, p. 47.

14. Letty Cottin Pogrebin, *Getting Over Getting Older* (New York: Little Brown, 1996), 132.

15. Lily Burana, "Bend Me, Shape Me," *New York,* July 15, 1996, pp. 30–34.

16. Holly Brubach, "The Athletic Esthetic," *New York Times Magazine,* June 23, 1996, pp. 48–51.

1.   See Katha Pollitt, "Pomolotov Cocktail," *The Nation,* November 22, 1996.

2.   Moran and Parker quoted in Vincent Bugliosi, *Outrage* (New York: Norton, 1966), 57.

3.   Alan Bloom, *The Closing of the American Mind* (New York: Simon and Schuster, 1987).

4.   Dinesh D'Souza, *Illiberal Education: The Politics of Race and Sex on Campus* (New York: Free Press, 1991).

5.   Katie Roiphe, *The Morning After: Sex, Fear, and Feminism* (Boston: Little, Brown, 1993).

6.   The *epistemological* theater of the culture wars—present but not especially prominent in the Bloom/D'Souza construction of things—has recently moved from a background skirmish of philosophers and theorists to a center-stage conflagration over the nature of truth and objectivity. Scholarly debates over the contributions of Egypt to Greek culture have been frequent on the pages of the *Chronicle of Higher Education,* and the disclosure of Sokol's hoax generated weeks of letters, Op-Ed pieces, and articles about the status of scientific objectivity in the *New York Times,* the *Nation, Lingua Franca,* and the *Chronicle of Higher Education.* Competing political agendas figure into these debates, certainly. But who's "policing" whom is not the focus in these debates; the question is, rather, whose version of reality should be trusted.

7.   Stephen Burd, "Cultural Crossfire," *The Chronicle of Higher Education,* February 3, 1995, p. A22.

8.   "Feel-Good History Bad for the Nation," *Daily News,* Monday, July 15, 1991.

9.   C. Vann Woodward, "Freedom and the Universities," *New York Review of Books,* July 18, 1991, p. 32.

10.   Georg Wilhelm Friedrich Hegel, *Introduction: Reason in History,* in *Lectures on the Philosophy of World History,* trans. H. B. Nisbet (Cambridge: Cambridge University Press, 1975), 173–174, 176–177, 190.

11.   Catharine Stimpson, "On Differences," in Burd, "Cultural Crossfire," A45.

12.   Reported in Carolyn Mooney, "Sweeping Curricular Change Is Under Way at Stanford," *The Chronicle of Higher Education,* December 14, 1988, p. A12.

13.   Stanley Fish quoted in Richard Bernstein, "Academia's Liberals Defend Their Carnival of Canons against Bloom's 'Killer B's,'" *New York Times,* September 25, 1988.

14.   Frank Lentricchia quoted in Scott Heller, "A Constellation of Recently Hired

Professors Illuminates the English Department at Duke," *The Chronicle of Higher Education,* May 27, 1987, p. 13.

15.   Stanley Fish quoted in Elizabeth Greene, "Under Siege, Advocates of a More Diverse Curriculum Prepare for Continued Struggle in the Coming Year," *The Chronicle of Higher Education,* September 28, 1988, p. A13. Arguments such as Lentricchia's and Fish's have a region of validity, of course. Often they are based on some very important insights of French theorist Michel Foucault (who himself owes quite a bit to Marx here). Foucault held that all truth, no matter how seemingly "scientific" or impartial—and including the belief in truth itself—is the product of the prevailing "regime" of "knowledge/power." For many of us, such insights offered a welcome corrective to the hubris of imagining that any discipline, paradigm, or individual has a disinterested view of reality. Some academics, however, went on to convert what to my mind was an edifying *critique* of epistemological arrogance into a rather arrogant dogma of its own. According to this dogma, any argument that dares to speak the language of "truth" (however conceived: adequacy, accuracy, comprehensiveness, coherence, correspondence, etc) is suspect and should not be challenged on its own terms but rather politically "deconstructed" to reveal the ideological commitments that underlie it. Postmodern literary theorists Donald Morton and Mas'ud Zavardzadeh explain: "We are not writing to reveal the Truth and then use that Truth to expose the Untruth of [those we criticize.] We find such a pursuit of Truth philosophically and politically uninteresting, historically obsolete, and more of an amusement for liberal humanists than a serious endeavor for committed intellectuals." Morton and Zavardzadeh find it more important to "indicate why [a certain position] is attractive ('truthful') and to indicate, when a reader nods in agreement with [that position], what ideological series lies behind that nod." What has happened here is that the edifying recognition that notions of "truth" are never neutral or disinterested but always mediated by ideological commitments has been converted to the notion that "truth" is *mere* ideology, with nothing "left over." See Morton and Zavardzadeh, "The Nostalgia for Law and Order and the Policing of Knowledge: The Politics of Contemporary Literary Theory," *Syracuse Scholar,* Spring 1987, pp. 28–29.

16.   Houston Baker quoted in Joseph Berger, "U.S. Literature: Canon under Siege," *New York Times,* January 6, 1988, p. B6.

17.   Irving Howe, "The Value of the Canon," in *Debating P.C.,* ed. Paul Berman (New York: Dell, 1992), 166.

18.   Richard Rorty, *Rorty and Pragmatism* (Nashville: Vanderbilt University Press, 1995), 70–71.

19.   Saul Bellow quoted in Richard Bernstein, "In Dispute on Bias, Stanford Is Likely to Alter Western Civilization Program," *New York Times,* Tuesday, January 19, 1988, p. A12.

20.   Charles Hagen, "The Power of a Video Image Depends on the Caption," *The New York Times,* Sunday, May 10, 1992, p. 32.

21.   Pretrial studies done by jury consultants for both the defense and the prosecution concluded that of all groups, African-American females (who wound up constituting the majority of the jury) had the most sympathy for Simpson. But racial and gender identifications and biases have frequently played a powerful role in jurors' interpretations and evaluations. In this regard, the Simpson trial was unusual only in the fact that a jury composed largely of black women was calling the verdict and that in such circumstances suddenly white America was "noticing"—news flash!—that racial identification and experience can shape perception.

22.   M. L. Rantala, *O.J. Unmasked* (Chicago: Catfeet Press, 1996), 205.

23.   Lawrence Schiller and James Willwerth, *American Tragedy* (New York: Random House, 1996), 329–331.

24.   In a short essay such as this, I cannot take the time and space to defend this judgment. Moreover, my focus here is not on arguing that the jurors were wrong but rather on exploring the *way* in which they went wrong. In defense of my claim, I refer readers to M. L. Rantala's recent book (see note 22), which argues quite brilliantly and decisively on this issue. Unlike the other Simpson books, Rantala's is not written by a participant or media celebrity or high-profile journalist. It is not constructed around a sensationalizing "story" or definite theory, and the author seems to have no particular animus against any of the players in the case; rather, she undertakes a logical, scholarly, painstaking dissection of the evidence.

25.   Believing the defense's narrative was necessary if the jurors were to believe there was any doubt about Simpson's guilt. For even if other factors in the prosecution's case may not have been seamlessly convincing (for example, the prosecution may have had the time of the murders wrong), such weaknesses could not make the enormous amount of decisive blood evidence (in many different locations) disappear. One could have reasonable doubt about Simpson's guilt only if one doubted that *he* himself had left blood in those locations. But there was never any *evidence* that anyone other than Simpson had left that trail of blood; in fact, there was much to suggest that it would have been virtually impossible for such a frame-up to have taken place.

26.   Some of these examples of media concoctions are taken from Vincent Bugliosi, *Outrage* (New York: Norton, 1996).

27.   See also Jan Pieterse, *White on Black: Images of Africa and Blacks in Western Popular Culture* (New Haven: Yale University Press, 1995).

28.   Peter Jackson, "Black Male: Advertising and the Cultural Politics of Masculinity," *Gender, Place, and Culture* 1, no. 1 (1994): 49–59.

29.   Henry Louis Gates, "Thirteen Ways of Looking at a Black Man," *The New Yorker,* October 23, 1995, p. 63.

30.   Schiller and Willwerth, *American Tragedy,* 374.

31.   Bell hooks is quoted in Gates, "Thirteen Ways of Looking at a Black Man," 63.

32.   A side note on the relation between murder and domestic violence: Alan Dershowitz, on national television, misleadingly presented statistics to show that only about one-tenth of batterers murder their wives. But, of course, the relevant statistics for this case would compute the likelihood not of whether a batterer might murder but—given that a woman was both battered by her husband and also murdered by someone—of the murderer being her husband. Professor Jack Good, a statistician at Virginia Tech, computed this statistic and found that the probability was over 50 percent that a woman battered by her husband and then found murdered was killed by her husband (M. L. Rantala, *O.J. Unmasked,* 21).

33.   Bell hooks, *Yearning* (Boston: South End Press, 1990), 59.

NEVER JUST PICTURES

1.   I give great credit to Alicia Silverstone for her response to these taunts. In *Vanity Fair* she says "I do my best. But it's much more important to me that my brain be working in the morning than getting up early and doing exercise . . . The most important thing for me is that I eat and that I sleep and that I get the work done, but unfortunately . . . it's the perception that women in film should look a certain way" ("Hollywood Princess," September 1996, pp. 292–294). One wonders how long she will manage to retain such a sane attitude!

2.   Holly Brubach, "The Athletic Esthetic," *The New York Times Magazine,* June 23, 1996, p. 51.

3.   In early 1996 the Swiss watch manufacturer Omega threatened to stop advertising in British *Vogue* because of *Vogue*'s use of such hyperthin models, but it later reversed this decision. The furor was reminiscent of boycotts that were threatened in 1994 when Calvin Klein and Coca-Cola first began to use photos of Kate Moss in their ads. In neither case has the fashion industry acknowledged any validity to the

charge that their imagery encourages eating disorders. Instead, they have responded with defensive "rebuttals," whose arguments I will be considering later in this piece.

4.   Despite media attention to eating disorders, an air of scornful impatience with "victim feminism" has infected attitudes toward women's body issues. Christina Hoff-Sommers charges Naomi Wolf (*The Beauty Myth*) with grossly inflating statistics on eating disorders and she poo-poos the notion that women are dying from dieting. Even if some particular set of statistics is inaccurate, why would Sommers want to deny the reality of the problem, which as a teacher she can surely see right before her eyes? See *"Braveheart, Babe,* and the Contemporary Body," in this volume, for more on charges against so-called victim feminists.

5.   For the spread of eating disorders in minority groups, see, for example, "The Art of Integrating Diversity: Addressing Treatment Issues of Minority Women in the 90's," in *The Renfrew Perspective,* Winter 1994; see also Becky Thompson, *A Hunger So Wide and So Deep* (Minneapolis: University of Minnesota Press, 1994).

6.   See my *Unbearable Weight* (Berkeley: University of California Press, 1993).

7.   Stephanie Grant, *The Passion of Alice* (New York: Houghton Mifflin, 1995), 58.

8.   Zoe Fleischauer quoted in "Rockers, Models, and the New Allure of Heroin," *Newsweek,* August 26, 1996.

9.   Hilton Als, "Buying the Fantasy," *The New Yorker,* October 10, 1996, p. 70.

10.   On the boycott see Stuart Elliott's "Advertising" column in *The New York Times,* April 26, 1994, p. D18.

11.   See "Whose Body Is This? Feminism, Medicine, and the Conceptualization of Eating Disorders," in my *Unbearable Weight,* for a discussion of the long-standing neglect of cultural factors in the medical literature on eating disorders.

12.   Susie Ohrbach, Susan and Wayne Wooley, Marlene Boskind White, Susan Gutwill, Andrea Gitter, and Kim Chernin stand out here as pioneers in the relation of cultural images to eating disorders. See *Eating Problems: A Feminist Psychoanalytic Treatment Model,* coauthored by Carol Bloom, Andrea Gitter, Susan Gutwill, Laura Kogel, and Lela Zaphiropoulos (New York: Basic Books, 1994), for the most rigorous, penetrating analysis to date of how cultural images shape our emotional lives.

13.   Michael Strober in "How Thin Is Too Thin," *People,* September 20, 1993, p. 80.

14.   John Mead in ibid.

15.   Rhoda Lee Fisher on parents' messages, in *Syracuse Herald Journal,* September 14, 1993, p. C3.

16.   See my *Unbearable Weight* for elaboration. See also "Mission Impossible," *People,* June 3, 1996.

17.   "Mission Impossible," *People,* June 3, 1996, p. 66.

18.   For Northrop quote see Stuart Elliott's "Advertising" column, *The New York Times,* Tuesday, April 26, 1994.

19.   Josie Natori in "Beauty's New Debate: Anorexic versus Waif," *Harper's Bazaar,* July 1993, p. 78.

20.   David Bonnouvrier, who is Annie Morton's agent, comments: "She drinks beer. We go to dinner and I can tell you, she's not a cheap date" ("Skeletal Models Create Furor over British Vogue," *The New York Times,* Monday, June 3, 1996). Moss, we were continually told when she first became popular, "eats like a horse." Even if this were true—which I doubt—it is of course irrelevant to the question of what sorts of eating habits her images encourage in teenage consumers.

21.   Scott MacDonald, "Confessions of a Feminist Porn Watcher," in Michael Kimmel, ed., *Men Confront Pornography* (New York: Meridian), 41.

22.   Of course, not all women find compliant poses demeaning. Women have different reactions to such depictions. Many find them erotic and have no problem with them. The meanings of certain poses may change too in the context of lesbian pornography. For the purposes of this piece I cannot go into the complex and diverse "readings" that pornographic motifs would require if their interpretation were my main point, which it is not here. Here I am presenting two different (and heterosexualized) "readings" as an example of a point about the representation of bodies; I am not attempting a definitive (or even near-definitive) analysis of soft-core porn. See also, in this collection, "Can a Woman Harass a Man?" for more on the cultural meaning of sexual gestures.

23.   Grant, *The Passion of Alice,* 2.

24.   Quoted in Marcia Millman, *Such a Pretty Face* (New York: Berkeley Books, 1980), 174.

25.   Even in the world of professional female bodybuilding, as Leslie Heywood points out in *Bodymakers: A Cultural Anthropology of Women's Bodybuilding* (New Brunswick, N.J.: Rutgers University Press, 1997), notions of appropriately deferential, male-pleasing feminine behavior and appearance continue to influence standards for judging, competitors' dress and presentation (breast implants are now *de rigueur*), photographs, and advertisements for products.

26.   Alice Walker, "Giving the Party," *Ms.,* May/June 1994, pp. 22–25.

27.   Adrienne Rich, "Resisting Amnesia: History and Personal Life," in *Blood, Bread and Poetry* (New York: Norton, 1986), 142.

28.   See also Becky Thompson, *A Hunger So Wide and So Deep.*

29.   David Gilmore, *Manhood in the Making* (New Haven: Yale University Press, 1990), 127.

30.   Arl Spencer Nadel, "My Dinner with Fat Jewish Dykes," *Bridges* 4, no. 2 (Winter 1994/1995): 79.

CAN A WOMAN HARASS A MAN?

1.   As I explore and criticize these constructions, I will *not* be interested in the legal or policy dimensions of sexual harassment, not because I do not consider those important but because I believe that the inadequacy of current discussions of issues of sexual politics is partially a result of our lack of practice at and/or unwillingness to linger very long over the exploration of meaning. The popular media seems obsessed with the (narrowly conceived) "morality" of issues. Discussions of breast implants invariably focus on questions of consumer "choice" and medical malpractice; they rarely interrogate the cultural significance of plastic body parts—particularly breasts—setting our norms of physical attractiveness. *Newsweek* and *Time* rushed to raise questions about Calvin Klein's use of underage models in a recent (now yanked) "CK" perfume ad campaign but seemed unconcerned with the constructions of sexuality and power depicted in the ads themselves. In contrast, my emphasis in this essay is analytical and interpretive—an emphasis that may leave the issue of sexual harassment in a less resolved state than an ethical "fix" but that will have the virtue, I hope, of redirecting conversation back to the subject of gender.

2.   Bernard Weintraub, "A Man. A Woman. Just a Movie. Not a Polemic," *The New York Times,* December 6, 1994, p. C15.

3.   Michael Crichton, *Disclosure* (New York: Ballantine, 1993).

4.   Evan Thomas and Thomas Rosensteil, "Decline and Fall," *Newsweek,* September 18, 1995, p. 32.

5.   Jill Mayer and Jill Abramson, *Strange Justice* (New York: Houghton Mifflin, 1994), 96.

6.   Ibid., 136.

7.   Ellen Willis, "Villains and Victims," *Salmagundi* 101/102 (1994): 74.

8.   Lorenzo Middleton, "Sexual Harassment by Professors: An 'Increasingly Visible' Problem," *The Chronicle of Higher Education,* September 15, 1980, p. 4.

9.   See my "Reading the Male Body," *Michigan Quarterly Review* 32, no. 4 (1993): 696–737, for an exploration of issues of male vulnerability and power as embodied

in the distinction between the phallus—the impenetrable and masterful presence and authority that men are supposed to embody (at least, in certain constructions of masculinity)—and the penis, as representing the often less-than-powerful reality of actual men in their historical specificity and fleshly vulnerability.

10.   Michel Foucault, *The Use of Pleasure* (New York: Random House, 1985).

11.   Tomas Almaguer, "Chicano Men: A Cartography of Homosexual Identity and Behavior," *Differences* 3, no. 2 (1991): 78.

12.   Jean-Paul Sartre, *Being and Nothingness* (New York: Washington Square Press, 1966), 448.

13.   Simone de Beauvoir, *The Second Sex* (New York: Vintage, 1952), 729; Sartre, ibid., 445.

14.   David Gilmore, *Manhood in the Making* (New Haven: Yale University Press, 1995).

15.   The sources of such a territorial stance as definitive of masculinity are, of course, by no means transparent or uncontested. While biologists may look to continuities with primate behavior, Gilmore consults object-relations theory, with its insights into the necessities and costs of decisive male separation from an early maternal symbiosis. Gilmore also stresses the cross-cultural prevalence of such associations; in contrast, historian Anthony Rotundo argues that these constructions of manliness develop, within a Western context at any rate, only with the modern emergence of competitive individualism and a new model of self-assertive, contestational manhood (*American Manhood* [New York: Basic Books, 1993]). Luckily, for the purposes of this essay, it is not necessary to take a position on such debates, only to note the contours of the subjectivity in question.

16.   Harry Stein, "The Post-Sensitive Man Is Coming," *Esquire,* May 1994, p. 56.

17.   Ibid., 58.

18.   Richard Majors and Janet Billson, *Cool Pose: The Dilemmas of Black Manhood in America* (New York: Lexington Books, 1992).

19.   As bell hooks points out, it is a mistake to ignore the degree to which dominant phallocentric norms have shaped black as well as white conceptions of masculinity, allowing "white and black men [to] share a common sensibility about sex roles and the importance of male domination" and encouraging some black men to equate racial liberation with claiming or redeeming their "manhood" *as* phallocentrism (*Yearning* [Boston: South End Press, 1990], 59). Certainly such equations, continually evoked and invoked by Louis Farrakhan (for example, as one of the guiding metaphors of the "Million Man March" of November 1995) have contributed to his appeal and that of the patriarchal Nation of Islam.

1.   Susan Hekman, "Material Bodies," in Donn Welton, ed., *Body and Flesh* (Oxford: Blackwell, 1997).

2.   I take issue with some of those critiques of theory in "Feminism, Postmodernism, and Gender-Skepticism" in *Unbearable Weight* (Berkeley: University of California Press, 1993). I think general theories can play a crucial role in breaking apart sedimented ways of thinking and helping people to see things in radically new ways. Where would feminist theory, for example, be without the bold strokes of those who first looked around and saw *gender* where it had previously been invisible? That those theories needed to be complicated (by race, for example) should not be seen as their "fatal flaw" but as part of the necessary elaboration of the theory.

3.   In Carolyn Romanzanoglu, ed., *Up Against Foucault* (New York: Routledge, 1993).

4.   "Material Girl: The Effacements of Postmodern Culture," *Michigan Quarterly Review* (Fall 1990), later reprinted in *Unbearable Weight*.

5.   Maxine Sheets-Johnstone, *The Roots of Thinking* (Philadelphia: Temple University Press, 1990), 8–9.

6.   Susan Bordo, *The Flight to Objectivity: Essays on Cartesianism and Culture* (New York: SUNY Press, 1987).

7.   "The Cultural Overseer and the Tragic Hero," *Soundings* 65, no. 2 (Summer 1982): 181–205.

8.   "Feminism, Postmodernism, and Gender Skepticism," in Linda Nicholson, ed., *Feminism/Postmodernism* (New York: Routledge, 1989). Later reprinted in my *Unbearable Weight*.

9.   "Feminist Skepticism and the 'Maleness' of Philosophy," abridged version in the *Journal of Philosophy* 75, no. 11 (November 1988); full version in E. Harvey and K. O'Kruhlik, eds., *Women and Reason* (Ann Arbor: University of Michigan Press, 1992).

10.   "Postmodern Subjects, Postmodern Bodies," *Feminist Studies* 18, no. 1 (Spring 1992): 159–176; later reprinted in my *Unbearable Weight*.

11.   Susan Bordo and Mario Moussa, "Rehabilitating the 'I,'" in Hugh Silverman, ed., *Questioning Foundations* (New York: Routledge, 1993).

12.   Foucault in "On the Genealogy of Ethics," an interview with H. Dreyfus and P. Rabinow, in *Michel Foucault: Beyond Structuralism and Hermeneutics* (Chicago: University of Chicago Press, 1982), 251–252.

13.   Foucault in "Clarifications on the Question of Power," an interview with Pasquale Pasquino, in *Foucault Live* (New York: Semiotext[e], 1989), 191.

1.   Edward Said, *Musical Elaborations* (New York: Columbia University Press, 1991), xiv,xv.

2.   Anna Antonopoulos, "Simone de Beauvoir and the Differance of Translation," *Institut Simone de Beauvoir Bulletin* 14 (1994): 99–101.

3.   See Susan Bordo, *Unbearable Weight* (Berkeley: University of California Press, 1993), especially pp. 15–42.

4.   Linda Zerilli, "Rememoration or War? French Feminist Narrative and the Politics of Self-Representation," *Differences* 3, no. 1 (1991): 2–3.

5.   Susan Bordo, "Organized Sex," *Cross Currents* 30, no. 3 (1980): 194–198.

6.   Andrea Dworkin, *Woman-Hating* (New York: Dutton, 1974), 113–114. Emphasis Dworkin's.

7.   I thank Leslie Heywood for this last point, made to me in personal communication.

8.   Martha Nussbaum, "Feminists and Philosophy," *The New York Review of Books,* October 20, 1994, pp. 59–63.

9.   Iris Young, "Pregnant Embodiment: Subjectivity and Alienation," *Journal of Medicine and Philosophy* (January 1984), pp. 45–62.

10.   Sara Ruddick, *Maternal Thinking* (Boston: Beacon Press, 1989).

11.   Maria Lugones, "Playfulness, 'World'-Traveling, and Loving Perception," *Hypatia* 2, no. 2 (Summer 1987): 11–12.

12.   Pamela McCallum, "The Construction of Knowledge and Epistemologies of Marked Subjectivities," *University of Toronto Quarterly* 61, no. 4 (Summer 1992): 431.

13.   Susan Bordo, *The Flight to Objectivity: Essays on Cartesianism and Culture* (New York: SUNY Press, 1987), 6–7.

14.   Margaret Atherton in *APA Newsletter on Feminism and Philosophy* 92, no. 2 (Fall 1993): 45 (emphasis added).

15.   Margaret Atherton, "Cartesian Reason and Gendered Reason," in Louise Antony and Carlotte Witt, eds., *A Mind of One's Own* (Boulder: Westview, 1993), 20.

16.   Carol Gilligan, *In a Different Voice* (Cambridge: Harvard University Press, 1982), 2.

17.   Seyla Benhabib, *The Situated Self: Gender, Community , and Postmodernism in Contemporary Ethics* (New York: Routledge, 1992), 178.

18.   Jane Roland Martin, "Methodological Essentialism, False Difference, and Other Dangerous Traps," *Signs* 19, no. 3 (Spring 1994): 652.

19.   "Point of View: Clinton and the Promise of Communitarianism," *The Chronicle of Higher Education,* December 2, 1992, p. A52.

20.   E. D. Klemke, A. David Kline, and Robert Holinger, eds., *Philosophy: Contemporary Perspectives on Perennial Issues* (New York: St. Martin's Press, 1994).

21.   Naomi Wolf, *Fire with Fire: The New Female Power and How It Will Change the Twenty-First Century* (New York: Random House, 1993), 11.

22.   Jane Flax, *Thinking Fragments: Psychoanalysis, Feminism, and Postmodernism in the Contemporary West* (Berkeley: University of California Press, 1990), 214, 216.

23.   See Jane Martin, "Methodological Essentialism," 651, for an insightful discussion of this "discrepancy between our cordial treatment of the men's theories and our punitive approach to the women's."

24.   See, for example, Martha Nussbaum, "Feminists and Philosophy," as well as the many discrediting attacks on feminist "essentialism" (see Martin, "Methodological Essentialism," for an excellent critical discussion of such attacks). On the more popular front, Naomi Wolf gushes ecstatically about "the drama of women's capturing male authority and power," symbolized for her by the depiction in commercial advertisements of phallic objects "emerging . . . from *women's* groins" (Wolf, *Fire with Fire,* 29). Yet at the same time as she celebrates the cultural sprouting of the female phallus, she has no qualms about dismissing—without attending concretely to any of it—several decades of feminist writing.

25.   See my "Feminism, Postmodernism, and Gender Skepticism" in *Unbearable Weight* for discussion of feminism's ambivalence toward female "difference."

MISSING KITCHENS

1.   Y.-F. Tuan, *Topophilia: A Study of Environment, Perception, Attitudes, and Values* (Englewood Cliffs, N.J.: Prentice-Hall, 1974), 247.

2.   Gaston Bachelard, *The Poetics of Space* (Boston: Beacon Press, 1969), 7.

3.   For Henry Louis Gates Jr. the kitchen was not only for cooking and bathing but was the place where his mother would "do" people's heads—shampooing, curling, straightening. The kitchen was transformed into a hair salon via the presence of one important object, the shears. This place created by an object became then a larger community of people and a site of conversation and the dissemination of values. The word *kitchen* thus acquired another meaning: . . . it was used quite literally to describe "the very kinky bit of hair at the back of the head, where the neck meets the shirt collar . . . which you trimmed off as best you could" (*Colored People: A Memoir* [New York: Vintage Books, 1995], 42). That bodily marker of black identity signaled what was desirable and what was not, arguably defined by white aesthetics. It was "too much," and that unwanted piece was cut off in the kitchen.

4.   Susan Bordo, *Unbearable Weight: Feminism, Western Culture, and the Body* (Berkeley: University of California Press, 1993), 176.

5.   In *The Birth of Neurosis* (New York: Simon and Schuster, 1984) George Drinka describes one aspect of the changes in life and landscape in the Victorian era: "Between 1850 and 1910 the railway systems of America and Europe became webs binding together the landscapes into skeins that could be traversed in hours rather than days. Between 1850 and 1860 the French railways system expanded from 3,000 to more than 9,000 kilometers of track. By 1880 the French railways had almost tripled in size again, and by 1910 redoubled, so that many of the provincial sections of France could be reached from Paris in hours. Similar statistics and comparable mobility were also the case in Germany, Britain, Italy, especially America, and even Russia. The railway—like the telegraph and later the telephone—stands out as a technological wonder tying the national landscapes together and telescoping time and distance in a manner unimaginable to earlier generations" (p. 110).

6.   Quote from my *Unbearable Weight*, 123–124.

7.   Gabriel Heater was a radio commentator, known for his deep and ominous voice, reporting nightly on the war abroad.

"Abs." *See* Stomach

Absolute: being, 77; truth, 12, 17

Abuse: child, 90; domestic, 71, 101; psychology of, 101–102; sexual, 131; spouse, 36, 99–100, 146; and Simpson trial, 99–101, 104, 146, 248n.32. *See also* Power

Academic: academia, 73, 180, 210; academics, 13, 15, 18, 23, 24, 74, 87, 181, 184, 185, 187, 189; bias, 24; campus politics, 170; culture, 19–20, 72, 178; discourse, 20, 175, 246n.15; elite, 73; harassment in, 148, 166–67; left, 67, 72, 74, 82, 243n.4; power, 211; scholarship, 25, 136, 175, 182; theories, 19, 21, 23, 24, 36, 58, 142, 175; would-be academics, 83. *See also* Education

Academy Awards, 27, 44, 60, 107

Achebe, Chinua, 83

Action, 27, 28, 29–30, 35, 40, 44; active, 37, 40; effectiveness of, 191; free versus determined acts, 187–88; and gender, 151; individual versus collective, 191; political, 189; and theory, 189

Advertisements, 30, 38, 39, 42, 52, 55, 60, 62, 104, 108, 110, 112, 115, 123, 135, 150, 151, 158, 160, 161, 243n.4, 248n.3; ad campaigns, 32, 91, 108, 113; advertisers, 15, 30, 32–33, 51, 130; athletic imagery in, 5, 35, 46; cosmetic surgery, 46, 48, 51; fashion, 113–14; gender reversal in, 151; perfume, 114; personals, 5, 138; underwear, 154–57, 159, 163, 164. *See also* Advertising

Advertising: 2(x)ist, 157, 164; Armani, 162; AT&T, 30; Calvin Klein, 5–7, 114, 161; CitriLean, 108, 110; Coca-Cola, 151, 154; Crunch Fitness, 40; Dior, 3–4, 157; Fruit of the Loom, 155–56, 159; Gap, 33; Gerber, 62; Guess, 101–02, 105; Hero, 152; Lucky, 149, 161, 162, 164; Marlboro, 161, 162; Matchabelli, 154, 159; Murad, 47, 48; Nike, 29, 60–61, 172, 208; Omega, 122; Pond's, 33; Revlon, 12, 33, 45; Jil Sander, 108, 111, 114; Sector, 30, 31; O. J. Simpson in, 98; Starter, 163; Versace, 163; Versus, 165; Woodbury's Facial Soap, 41. *See also* Bally; Nike; Reebok; Revlon

Aesthetic: of advertisements, 112; aesthetization, 3, 175; anorexic, 58, 108; and the body, 44, 125, 185; ideals, 35; images, 2; inventions, 113; of limitation, 133; of perfection, 28; preferences, 124

Affection: gestures of, 147; reactions to, 147–48

Affirmative action, 141, 142

Africa, 76–80; Africans, 76, 77, 82, 135; Afrocentricism, 66–67, 79; appearance, 49; as savage, 79

African American, 100, 103–105, 166, 172, 215; and animality, 90, 135; athletes, 98–99; authors, 194; black/white dualism, 185; black or white, 5, 69, 87, 101, 133, 134, 136; body, 49–50, 135; caricatures of, 98, 134, 136, 137; females, 109, 135, 172; and history of philosophy, 80; and juries, 89; males, 89, 98, 104, 105, 169, 171, 172; as other, 194; as savage, 101, 105; studies, 72. *See also* Race; Simpson trial; White

Age, 45, 69, 148; age-defying, 33, 45; ageless, 3; aging, 14, 44, 54, 238; aging process, 47; attitudes towards, 16, 32; correction of, 44–45, 47, 187; markers of, 49; old age, 5

Agency, 15, 21, 38, 57–58, 61, 62, 187; agents, 39–40, 42, 188, 191; female, 35, 122; and feminism, 37; power as, 33; rhetoric of, 36, 52

Agoraphobia, 26, 216, 218, 226–27, 230, 321

AIDS, 79, 113

Almaguer, Thomas, 158

Als, Hilton, 112–13

Analytical thinking. *See* Critical: thinking

Ancient Greece, 155, 157, 160

Animal House, 150

Animality: animal imagery, 79, 98; animal man, 78–79; blacks and, 90, 97–98, 135; Jews and, 135; males and, 104, 149–150, 165. *See also* Savage; Stereotypes

Aniston, Jennifer, 8

Ann-Margret, 131

Anorexia, 112, 116–17, 120, 130–31;

aesthetics of, 58; anorexic thinking, 130; glamour of, 108, 111; males and, 108

Appearance, 26, 38, 91; alien appearance, 134; contentment with, 42, 55–56; equating behavior, 95–96, 101–02; importance of, 50, 118–19, 151; manipulation of, 12; physical appearance, 49, 64, 115, 123–24; vs. reality, 2, 91, 95

Appetite, 128; connection of food and sex, 131–34; voraciousness of, 131. *See also* Desire

Aristophanes, 19

Aristotle, 81, 199

Arnold, Roseanne, 42, 221

Art, 151, 158, 159; interpretation of, 193; values of, 199

Asian: and eating disorders, 134

Assimilation, 49, 62, 134, 136, 138, 222, 236. *See also* Culture

Atherton, Margeret, 203–04

Athletes, 29; advertising and, 30; African-American, 98–99; athletic body, 5, 58, 115, 138; athletic culture, 104; athletic perfection, 28; athletic training, 31; female, 63, 109. *See also* Olympics; Sports

Augustine, 187

Aunt Jemima. *See* African American: caricatures of

Authenticity, 32

Autonomy, 57, 187, 231; and actions, 186–87; autonomous self, 206; autonomous spirits, 123; and choices, 50, 187; metaphysical, 187

Baartman, Saartje, 135

Babe, 21, 27, 57, 60–65, 107

Baby-boom, 13, 88, 215

Bachelard, Gaston, 26, 214, 219

Baker, Houston, 83

Bally Fitness, 35

BAM (Boycott Anorexic Marketing), 115, 121, 122, 123, 130
Barbarism, 76–79
"Barbie" doll, 73
Barthes, Roland, 193
Baudrillard, Jean, 91, 202
Beardsly, 122
Beauty, 8, 37, 40, 55, 95, 113; adoration of, 127; of athlete, 5; attitudes toward, 16, 23, 34, 133; beautification, 5; the beautiful, 5, 75, 84; beautiful people, 28, 103, 121, 122; changes in, 184; construction of, 196; decline of, 45; and depression, 113, 132; and ethnicity, 9, 23, 32, 49, 133–34; and fragility, 47; feature, 42; of human body, 5; ideals of, 8, 9, 23, 32, 56, 107–08, 115, 134; preservation of, 49, 42; regime, 39, 112; slenderness as, 127; standards of, 196; system, 34, 39, 47; tips, 39; unchained, 5. *See also* Appearance; Body
Beauty and the Beast, 149–50
The Beauty Myth (Wolf), 34
Beauvoir, Simone de, 159, 192, 194–95, 198–99
Behavior: context of, 147; equated with appearance, 95–96, 101–02; feminine, 124, 139, 144; harassing, 143–45, 147, 168; improper, 144–45; of individuals, 43, 120, 170; interpretation of, 225; justification of, 12; as reinforcement, 50; of society, 120. *See also* Eating disorders
Bellah, Robert, 72
Bellow, Saul, 84
Beneke, Timothy, 132
Benhabib, Seyla, 205, 206
Bennet, William, 74–75, 82, 105
Berger, John, 151, 154
Bernstein, Richard, 72, 79
Bias: class, 182; gender, 24, 85, 101, 182, 202; intellectual, 176; of juries, 94; racial, 24, 85, 182, 206; of scholars, 237. *See also* Stereotypes
Bingeing, 15, 59, 111, 120. *See also* Eating disorders
Biology, 80, 180, 182; biological determinism, 196; biological norm, 17; biological paradigms, 178; biological traits, 80, 117; zoologist, 195, 197. *See also* Genetics; Science
Birth: childbirth, 237; defects, 42; order, 26, 215
Bishop, Elizabeth, 83
Blacks. *See* African American
Blond: as ideal 8, 105. *See also* Hair
Bloom, Alan, 21, 68, 72–73, 85, 105
Bobbit, Lorena, 199
Bodies That Matter (Butler), 186, 188
Body, 9, 15, 17, 21, 24, 26, 34, 173, 179, 224, 243n.3; acceptance of, 43, 55, 58, 112, 121, 134; alteration of, 30, 39, 42, 47, 112, 182, 196; anxiety over, 11, 13; appearance of, 3, 5, 29, 33, 38, 107, 116, 118, 138; athletic, 5; attraction to, 5, 124, 132, 144; bodily aspects, 2, 226; bodily practices, 21, 134; Cartesian, 210; computer generated, 3, 15, 91; and connection with world, 192, 226; containment of, 134; control of, 38, 62, 112, 197; cultural construction of, 182, 188, 195–96; cultural influence upon/as site of culture, 17, 26, 151, 183; detachment from, 29; disappearing, 217; doubles, 3, 125; as escape from, 182; evolution of, 182; as excessive, 134, 135; female, 104, 124, 132, 133, 149, 183, 192, 196–98; fetishization of, 125; flawed, 8; as flesh, 182, 183, 184, 198; as force of nature, 150; gender-coded, 28; gestures, 148, 157, 196; as hindrance, 192; history of, 183;

Body (*continued*)
human, 8, 17; ideal, 17, 38, 108,
112, 135; image, 13, 42, 43–44, 58,
108, 109, 116, 118, 120, 133–34,
159; imperfections, 40, 108; as
imprinted upon, 218, 20; improvement of, 38, 42, 107, 196; as
machine, 113; male, 23, 42, 149,
151, 154, 158–159, 161, 184, 192,
198, 243n.4; malleability of, 9, 43;
materiality of, 24, 124, 174, 177–78,
181, 183, 185, 195–97; as mindless,
180; of mother, 223, 231, 234; natural, 17, 121, 124, 178, 188, 190,
196–97; as object, 198; parodic, 185;
parts, 107, 124–25, 135, 146, 161,
184; peculiarities of, 198; physical
perfection of, 3, 55, 107, 121; and
pleasure, 158; politics and, 177, 196;
and post-modernism, 175, 185;
racialized, 23, 135; reduction of
women to, 124–26; relationship to,
43, 196, 198; relationship of to place
and space, 215, 217, 226–27, 229;
resistance of, 191; shame about,
42–43, 121, 134–35, 144; in shape,
35, 38, 58, 107, 114, 123; and soul,
46; as speaking, 124; as status symbol, 8; as text, 128, 185; theory
about, 175; thinness and, 108, 130–
31; transcendence of, 60, 210; transformation of, 9, 63, 124, 134; use
of, 123, 197; view of, 147; writing
of, 185. *See also* Aesthetic; Appearance; Beauty; Fat; Muscularity; Self
Body and Flesh (Welton), 24
Body Image Disturbance Syndrome,
108, 116, 119. *See also* Eating disorders
Braveheart, 21, 26, 29–30, 32, 60, 61,
62, 150, 165, 243n.4
Breasts, 8, 38, 44, 64, 125, 135, 143;
binding, 44; enlargements, 3, 32, 36,

43–44, 121; micromastia ("too
small"), 39, 42, 44; mother's, 219.
See also Implants
Brownmiller, Susan, 133
Brubach, Holly, 58
Bulimia, 35, 115, 116, 127, 130–31.
See also Eating disorders
Bundy, Ted, 96
Burana, Lily, 55
Butler, Judith, 24–25, 173–74, 179,
185–86, 188–90, 191
Buttocks, 8, 38, 125, 135, 146, 155

Calvin Klein, 5–7, 19, 63, 114, 251n.1.
See also Advertising
Canon, 21, 68, 71, 79, 83–84; bashing,
199, 212
Cartoons, 136, 154–56; children's,
149–50; political, 19; racist, 135
Censorship, 68, 73, 76, 161
Chapman, Shawn, 100
Cheney, Lynne, 74–76, 81, 84, 96, 105
Cher, 9, 11, 50
Chodorow, Nancy, 203–04
Choice, 15, 16, 36, 37, 57, 123; of
clothing, 186–187; context of, 35, 50;
and cosmetic surgery, 49; "Healthy
Choice," 59; individual, 43, 44, 50;
lack of, 83, 130; as own, 187
Christianity, 134, 187
Cixous, Helene, 193
Clark, Marcia, 96. *See also* Simpson
trial
Clark, Mary Ellen, 29
Class, 96; ability to afford cosmetic
procedures, 15, 44, 45; accident of,
82; and beauty industry, 8, 45; bias,
205; classist, 83, 206; consideration
of, 149, 150, 160, 172, 182, 193;
construction of gender, 206; and
eating disorders, 109, 120, 134; middle, 215; and purchasing power, 70
Cleaver, Eldridge, 104

Clinton, Bill, 151

The Closing of the American Mind (Bloom), 21, 72

Clothing, as choice, 186, 187; as symbolic, 15, 33, 132, 134, 138

Clueless, 106

Cochran, Johnnie, 96, 99–100

Coding, 28, 101; and age, 45, 47; decoding, 127; gender coding, 144, 151, 154, 156, 158–59, 160, 175; racial coding 23, 135, 160, 175; sleep and, 158–59

Colonization, 195; European, 80

Commercial, 21, 29–30, 60; commercialism, 21, 29–30, 60; rhetoric, 33; war, 114. *See also* Advertising

Community, 147, 216, 222

Competition, 34, 35

Compulsion, 57, 108; compulsive eating, 118. *See also* Exercise

Computer images. *See* Body: image

Conformity, 63, 150, 187

Conrad, Joseph, 79

Consciousness: lack of, 77, 79

Conservativism, 9, 12

Consumer, 38, 42, 50, 55, 91, 96; consumer capitalism, 55, 86; consumer groups, 115, 121; consumerism, 14, 35, 38, 51, 105; material consumption, 30, 35

Control: of body, 35, 38, 42, 197; illusion of, 51; lack of, 104; of life, 61, 112, 184; taking, 58, 59

Cool, 127–29; coolness, 128, 171; lack of, 114; wastedness as, 113

Cool Pose (Majors), 171

Cornell, Drucilla, 206

Correction. *See* Age; Defect

Cosmetic dentistry. *See* Dentistry

Cosmetic surgery, 8, 32, 45, 55, 244n. 9, 244n.10; advertisements for, 46, 48, 51; affordability of, 47, 49; criticisms of, 16; cultural/social aspects

of, 43–44, 49; as empowerment, 21, 35, 42; and men, 45, 154; normalization of, 3, 43, 47, 54, 184, 187; surgeons, 52, 54–55. *See also* Plastic surgery

Cosmetics. *See* Makeup

Crawford, Cindy, 131

Crichton, Michael, 140, 141–143, 172. See also *Disclosure*

Critical: attitude, 190; thinking, 81, 84, 86, 88, 95, 97, 103, 105, 181

Cultural: accouterments, 235; affirmation, 75, 150; analysis, 42; anxiety, 113, 117, 160, 199; application, 206; associations, 79, 81, 117, 124, 131, 158, 164, 167, 185; bias, 181; construction, 182, 188, 190, 212; context, 22, 35, 36, 43, 50, 66, 116, 158, 181, 183, 185; criticism, 13–14, 16, 52, 99, 101, 105, 115, 174, 178, 183, 192–93, 195, 206, 208–09, 212; determinism, 188; diagnosis, 174, 187; diaspora, 218, 237; difference, 206; discourse, 183; diversity, 21, 23, 73; "dope," 36–37, 51; exclusion, 190; expose, 26; fantasies, 21, 60, 202; fetishes, 125; forms, 17, 18, 81, 149, 177, 179, 194; heritage, 8, 133; history, 126, 133, 208; identity, 212; ideology, 196; ignorance, 84; images 1, 2, 9, 13, 20, 22, 23, 24, 25, 36–37, 64, 69, 79, 86, 93, 95, 97–98, 113, 114, 116–18, 121, 123, 127, 134–35, 140, 145, 160, 221; invisibility, 16, 34, 58; meanings, 209; messages, 50, 117, 119, 121, 134; mystification, 18, 51; narratives, 93, 198, 208; nostalgia, 14; observer, 55; overseer, 177, 182; perceptions, 82, 107–08, 122, 126, 139; period, 39; pleasures, 14; practices, 16, 43, 59, 83, 103, 174, 181, 184, 222; psyche, 113, 127, 147; relativism, 104; studies,

Cultural (*continued*)
66, 193; time, 26, 117, 119, 154;
traditions, 37, 97; transformation,
62, 64, 202, 209; treadmill, 64;
trends, 43, 113, 118, 124–25, 146
Culture: common, 12, 17, 75–76; construction of, 15, 16; consumer culture, 35, 38, 50, 91, 111; counter-
culture, 118, 133; "culture wars,"
21, 22, 23, 66–69, 71–74, 80, 82,
86, 106, 245n.6; dominant, 134,
212, 213; futuristic, 9, 15, 188; lack
of, 77; makers, 15, 50; operation of,
193, 194; participation in, 13, 15,
118, 122, 187; popular, 14, 19–20,
24, 103, 118, 147, 150, 160, 184;
postmodern, 91; racial dynamics in,
69–60; relationship to, 13; subcul-
ture, 133; trickle-down effect, 45;
victim, 33–34. *See also* Academic;
Cultural; Politics; Public; Social;
Sports

Davis, Kathy, 35–38, 42–43, 51, 55,
244n.7
De la Beckwith, Byron, 89
Dead White Males, 21, 66, 80
Death, 61; avoidance of, 47, 49; deathlike appearance, 108, 112; fashion
as, 113; of the subject, 201, 210–11
Deconstruction, 36, 246n.15; of the
body, 43; and fashion, 113; of gender, 183; of the 'I', 201
Defect: correction of, 39, 43; imagined, 115; pedegogy of, 37; physical,
21, 38–39, 42–43, 45, 55, 57; self as
defective, 51–52, 63; sites of, 42
Dentistry: cosmetic, 52, 54, 55–56;
family, 57
Depression, 62, 113, 118, 120, 132,
216, 231, 238; clinical depression,
52; the Depression (historical era),
216, 237

Dermatologist, 54
Derrida, Jacques, 193, 201, 202, 210,
212–13
Descartes, Rene, 92, 94–95, 124, 177,
200; and the body, 210; Cartesian
view of self, 203–04; Cartesianism,
177, 180, 182, 212
Desire: for acceptance, 126; to achieve
ideals, 38; beyond desire, 112–13,
128; human, 51; manipulation of,
38, 56, 111, 122; as negative 128,
130; for normalcy, 55; romantic, 145;
sexual, 125, 133, 145; uncontrollable, 131
Detachment, 1, 15, 18, 64, 127–28; as
fashion/body ideal, 112; of models,
112
Determinism, 186, 187; biological, 196
Devers, Gail, 29
Dewey, John, 182, 184, 199
Dieting, 15, 59, 108, 110, 115–16, 119,
121, 128, 130; compulsive dieting,
58; diet product, 52, 107; diet program, 30, 107; diet syndrome, 59;
normalization of, 197; pressure to
diet, 109; and starvation, 109, 134.
See also Eating disorders
Difference: voices of, 206, 210. *See
also* Class; Culture; Ethnic; Gender;
Race
Disabilities: physical, 107–08
Discipline: of self and body, 193, 196,
198
Disclosure, 23–24, 140, 145, 147, 170,
172
Discourse, 180; academic, 20; critical,
195; cultural, 183; discursivity, 38,
146, 189, 211; outside of, 178; philosophical, 210; political, 15; resistance
to, 190
Discrimination, 82, 95, 148, 180;
reverse discrimination, 148. *See also*
Gender; Race; Sex

Disorder, 57. *See also* Eating disorders; Panic: disorder

Diversity, 30, 68, 70–71, 81, 114; beyond, 80; cultural, 7, 21, 73; historical, 184; model, 69, 82, 96

DNA, 93–94, 97

Dogma, 12, 21, 23, 36, 66, 88, 246n.15

Domestic violence. *See* Abuse

Dopes. *See* Cultural: "dope"

Doubt: Cartesian, 92; in Rodney King trial, 90; reasonable doubt, 91–93

Douglas, Michael, 140–41

Drag, 186; as parody, 185

D'Souza, Dinesh, 68, 73–75, 81, 82, 96, 105

Dualism, 185; dualistic thinking, 18; duality, 51, 112, 124, 175; gendered, 197, 208; transcendence of, 185. *See also* Mind: mind/body dualism; Polarization

Dunaway, Faye, 9–10

Dworkin, Andrea, 196–98

Dyson, Michael, 99

Eating disorders, 8, 13, 35, 58, 108–09, 111–18, 120, 122, 130–31, 136, 248n.3, 249n.4; and athletes, 109; cultural dimensions of, 22–23, 109, 111, 113–14, 118, 122, 136, 249n.12; males and, 109; profiles, 109, 120, 134. *See also* Anorexia; Bulimia; Psychology; Sex

Economic, 82; and beauty industry, 197, 244n.10; economic context, 50; economic security, 117; economics, 83, 91; profit motive, 113–14. *See also* Class; Cosmetic surgery

Education: college, 12, 21, 66, 72, 81–82, 105–06; curriculum, 66, 73, 74–75, 78, 81–82, 84, 209; emancipation through, 237; general, 195; goals of, 84; jury members and, 70; multiculturalism and, 71–75; as

symbol, 27–28; reform, 80–81. *See also* Academic

Egypt, 66–67; reform, 81

Ejaculation, 126

Emasculation, 199

Embodiment, 149, 222; embodied beings, 178, 180, 199; of fantasies, 130; of ideals, 105, 127; of images, 125–26; of theory, 197; visual, 112

Empowerment, 36, 43, 58, 61–62; context of, 51; disempowerment, 39, 80, 148, 169, 212; personal empowerment, 21, 34, 35, 36, 42–43, 50, 80; of women, 36, 127

Enlightenment, 25, 203, 210; new, 73; personal, 2; and Plato, 14

Epistemology, 69, 71, 78, 84–85, 87, 92, 181, 245n.6; change in, 203; feminist, 202

Erotica, 161, 163

Esquivel, Laura, 133

Essentialism: 25, 175, 183, 197, 255n.24; as critique, 66, 177, 205, 212; essential notions of gender, 104, 143; essential subject, 182; essentialist view of body, 196; and gender differences, 204; male as essential, 194

Ethics, 12, 15, 49, 91, 156, 181, 185; of care, 207; Senate Ethics Committee, 140, 171

Ethnic: art, 133; carnival, 81–82; cheerleading, 75; cleansing, 50; communities, 147, 218; construction of gender, 206; difference, 109, 212; ethnicity, 142, 148, 222; experience, 212; lessons, 222; shame, 133, 135–36; tradition, 133. *See also* Beauty: ideals of; Race

"Ethnic notions," 97

Ethnocentrism, 66

Eurocentrism, 67, 76, 195

Evers, Medgar, 89

Evidence, 88–93, 95–96, 103, 172

Ewen, Stewart, 3

Exercise, 15, 35, 38, 52, 59, 64, 116,
118, 120, 122; exercise compulsion,
58, 109, 120. *See also* Fitness

Existentialism, 12, 49, 61, 181, 203;
and space, 218

Eyes, 38, 44, 46, 95, 131, 143, 161;
color, 32, 105, 124; need for correction, 50, 54, 49, 55; gaze and, 159,
160; and Japanese professionals, 49;
mind's eye, 2

Face, 9, 17, 43, 46, 47, 114; alteration
of, 197; face-lift, 16, 44–46, 60, 187;
facial deformity, 42, 43, 52. *See also*
Cosmetic surgery

Family: and eating disorders, 109, 117–
19; and ethnicity, 136; in memoir,
215–40; and socialization, 147

Fantasy, 60, 92, 107, 112, 122–23, 166;
of acceptance, 63; cultural, 14, 18,
21, 172, 202; of detachment, 18;
embodiment of, 130; of empowerment, 62; as fiction, 179; of gender
reversal, 147, 155; male, 141, 144;
nightmare, 147; of perpetual youth,
61; personal, 17, 226; vs. reality, 3, 9;
of self, 51; site of, 114; of view from
nowhere, 182; world, 158. *See also*
Desire; Reality

Fashion, 38–39, 113–14, 116, 124; as
anti-fashion, 5, 243n.1; connection
with fitness, 35; deconstruction of,
113; icons of, 8, 128; ideal, 112;
industry, 22, 108, 113, 115, 121–23,
130; vs. reality, 122. *See also* Models;
Waif

Fat, 52, 71, 138; as defect, 39, 107–08,
131; as devil, 107; fear of, 22, 118,
119; hatred of, 138; low body fat, 5,
30, 108–09; name-calling and, 107,
118; self-perception as, 108, 120,
130; as symbol, 111, 130, 131, 135–36

Fatal Attraction, 147

Father, 50, 64, 117, 124, 139–40; ghost
in *Braveheart,* 27; as memoir, 215–
16, 219–20, 224–25, 227–28, 231–
37; Pilgrims as, 134; rejection by,
131. *See also* Family; Parent-child
relationship

Femininity, 23, 105, 133, 228; acceptance of, 227; as aesthetic of limitation, 133; appearance as, 134, 135–
36, 138, 161; association with
appearing, 151–53; art of, 198;
and behavior, 124, 139, 144; category of feminine, 192; challenges
to, 150, 172; constructs of, 14, 39,
133, 136, 137, 138, 148, 153, 160,
164, 168, 171–72, 196; course in,
96; and morality, 207; representations of, 125, 156, 158, 159, 164;
strength and, 58; vanity and, 46. *See
also* Behavior; Body; Feminism;
Feminist; Norms; Women

Feminism: academic, 37, 85, 196, 199;
and advocacy, 209; agency, 37–38;
analytic, 143; bad vs. good feminist,
99, 36, 142; and beauty industry, 36;
as challenge, 202, 208; and concept
of self-identity, 25, 200–02; constructions of, 19, 142, 183, 201–03,
208–09; contemporary, 178, 195–
96, 211; as criticism, 124–25, 182–
83, 201–02, 205, 207, 208–09; and
cultural history, 208–09; and disappearance of women, 211–12; equity,
142, 172; feminazis, 21, 25; gender,
142; generation gap and, 138; and
harassment, 142, 145, 146, 155;
marginalization and, 195; misreadings of, 203; and multiculturalism,
66, 68, 73–74, 106; as negative force,
21, 37, 74, 100, 243n.4; "new," 2,
36; "old," 35–36, 37, 51; as Other,
194–95; postmodern, 183, 202;

power, 28, 34, 35, 37, 58, 63, 122, 133, 137, 151, 172, 208–09; as puritanical, 74; role of, 196; victim, 34, 35–37, 39, 58, 208–09; and views of sex/gender, 183, 208. *See also* Femininity; Gender; Marginalization; Women

Feminist: agenda, 74; analysis, 142; classrooms, 71; criticism, 193–94, 199; epistemology, 72, 202; experience, 206; feminists, 24, 33, 39, 96, 122, 125, 133; literature, 196, 197; as Other, 25–26, 194; philosophy, 85, 177, 195, 198, 200, 206–07, 208–10; politics, 29,139, 206–07; postfeminist age, 58, 133; research, 206; scholarship, 25, 178, 208, 211; skepticism, 182, 199–200; theory, 30, 174, 178, 192–93, 199, 204, 206, 208, 210–11, 213, 253n.2; voice, 211, 213; writers, 121, 176. *See also* Femininity; Feminist; Women

Fiddler on the Roof, 194

Fight Fire with Fire (Wolf), 34, 208

Fish, Stanley, 81, 83, 193

Fishburne, Laurence, 79

Fisher, Rhoda Lee, 117

Fitness, 38, 52, 59; fitness craze, 35; as sign of competence. *See also* Exercise

Flashdance, 62

Flaws, 114; flawed body, 8

Flax, Jane, 211

Fleischauer, Zoe, 112

Flesh: abhorrence of, 107; admiration of, 23, 133; as excessive, 118, 131; exposure of, 155; fleshy bodies, 182, 183, 184, 198

Fleiss, Heidi, 146

Flight to Objectivity (Bordo), 182, 203

Folklore, 97–98

Food, 120, 128, 133; connections with sex, 131, 133–34; cultural associations with, 117–18; eating, 184; as

problematic, 58, 116, 134; relationship to, 221, 223–24

Foucault, Michel, 30, 146, 157, 175, 177–78, 188, 189, 191, 193, 196, 202, 246n.15

Foundationalism, 175; discourse and, 179; privilege of, 177

Fragility, 125

France, 77

Fraser, Nancy, 206

Freedom, 27, 57, 113, 177, 190; "fighters," 71; free choice, 50; from longing, 113; and manhood, 104; personal, 187; rhetoric of, 15

Friedan, Betty, 34, 244n.6

"Friends," 8, 14, 121

Freud, Sigmund, 113, 209, 210, 226–27

Frye, Marilyn, 191

Fuhrman, Mark, 70, 89. *See also* Simpson trial

Garafalo, Janeane, 121

Gates Jr., Henry Louis, 98, 105, 255n.3

Gay. *See* Homosexual

Gaze (the Look), 55, 154, 159–60, 230; authority of, 160; definition by, 159, 227; female, 154, 168; male, 171; medical, 55; as sexual, 169; as test of manhood, 160

Gender, 51, 71, 81,101, 139, 150, 160, 166, 177, 182, 210; accident of, 82; alterity, 206; asymmetry, 147, 158; avoidance of, 193–94; bias, 85, 182; as choice, 185; constructs of, 158, 168, 177, 206; core, 182; critique, 196, 200; deconstruction of, 183; difference, 180, 197, 203–06, 212; dimension, 204; dislocation of, 218; duality, 204, 208; engendered being, 199; as essential, 182; gap, 45, 109, 169; gendered experiences, 148, 155, 212; gendered images, 75; gendering, 26, 186; genderless, 194;

Gender (*continued*)

"genderquake," 208; generalizations about, 205; fictions of, 183; history, 126; ideals, 128, 150; identity, 186; ideology, 104, 172; inequities, 184; interplay with race, 96–97, 100; as invisible, 100–01; morality and, 205; as mute, 5, 69, 193; neutrality, 142, 159, 160, 172, 198, 207; norms, 30; politics, 140, 141; post-gender age, 150; relations, 192, 211; representations, 149, 151–54; reversal, 141, 147, 148, 151, 170; roles, 158, 164, 168, 195; as specialized critique, 193; stereotypes, 24, 166–67; theory, 209. *See also* Bias; Femininity; Male; Masculinity; Women

Gender Trouble (Butler), 185–86

Generation Gap, 88

"Generation X," 88, 127

Genetics: genetic disorders, 30; genetic predisposition, 8, 179–80, 187

The German Ideology (Marx), 176, 188

Get Shorty, 160

Ghetto, 224

Ghettoization. *See* Marginalization

Gibson, Mel, 61, 150. See also *Braveheart*

Gilbert, Sandra, 193

Gilligan, Carol, 204–07, 210

Gilmore, David, 136, 160

Glamour, 8, 9, 145; anorexia and, 110, 112; death and, 113; detachment and, 128; veneer of, 114

"Glass ceilings," 133

Goddess: female body as, 131; imagery of, 134

Goff, Trish, 108, 122

Goldman, Ron, 95, 97. *See also* Simpson trial

Gorovitz, Samuel, 72

Goya, 146

Grant, Stephanie, 112, 130

Greer, Germaine, 193

Griffith, Melanie, 45

Gubar, Susan, 193

Guilt, 125, 126

Gurly-Brown, Helen, 131

Gymnastics, 29; female gymnasts, 109

Hair, 112, 123, 124, 131–32, 138, 143, 144, 161; blond, 8, 32, 105; coloring, 35, 134; gray, 45; straightness of, 14, 134

Hall, Stuart, 193

Harassment, 74, 169, 170, 172, 251n. 1; gender harassment, 169; racial harassment, 169; sexual harassment, 23, 139–49, 155, 164, 166–67. *See also* Affection; Gender; Power; Sex

Harding, Sandra, 202

Hatch, Orrin, 145. *See also* Ethics; Thomas/Hill hearings

Hayden, Barbara, 32

Health, 52, 120; health care professionals, 13, 55; health consciousness, 51; healthy appearance, 108; "Healthy Choice," 59; physical, 15, 108

Heater, Gabriel, 237, 256n.7

Hegel, Georg W. F., 68, 76–80, 82, 177, 199

Height, 13

Hekman, Susan, 24, 173–74, 181, 183, 188

Held, Virginia, 206

Hero(ine), 29, 62, 63, 87, 96, 154; feminist, 208; heroic representation, 159, 161; heroism, 51, 62, 99; of movies, 27, 149, 165; and parents, 228; O. J. Simpson as, 86, 87, 95–96; tragic, 182

"Heroin chic," 112–14, 128

Hill, Anita, 103, 139, 145, 168, 171, 172. *See also* Thomas/Hill hearings

Hippies, 72

Hips, 124, 135, 138, 143

History, 27, 81, 86, 88–89, 96–97, 200; education, 12, 95; of Egypt, 76–78; gender, 126; as gendered, 211; historical accuracy, 195; historical analysis, 175; historical context, 18, 95, 183, 186; historical critique, 197; historical forms, 174; historical location, 179, 181, 185; historical narratives, 193; historical realities, 95, 97, 170; historical suffering, 194; historical time, 2; historicism, 177; of ideas/thought, 20, 25, 67, 76, 82, 177, 180, 208, 211, 213; and ideology, 27, 80; military, 194; outside of, 189; personal, 96; proper, 194; versions of, 14; women's, 25, 194. *See also* Culture

History of Sexuality, volume I (Foucault), 196

Hitchens, Christopher, 74

Hobbes, Thomas, 75, 200

Holocaust, 86, 103; denial of, 86

Homosexuality, 5, 154, 157; appearance and, 154; biology and, 180; in *Braveheart,* 28; categorization in, 158; heterosexism, 195; homoerotica, 161; marketing and, 161; queer theory, 195. *See also* Lesbian; Sex: sexual orientation

Hooks, bell, 101, 104

Howe, Irving, 83

Human: activity, 177; connections, 239, 240; experience, 200; humanness, 79; interaction, 204; as man, 192; nature, 66, 192, 200. *See also* Culture; History

Humanities, 180

Hume, David, 200

Hypochondria, 225

Hysteria, 116

Ideals, 17, 94; aesthetic, 35; beauty, 8, 9, 23, 32, 56, 107–08, 115, 134; body, 17, 38, 108, 112, 135; gender, 128, 250; idealism, 74, 184; surface, 114

Identity: accidents of biology, 212; critiques of theories of, 201; nomadic identity, 18; personal, 201, 212; perspective of, 238; and place, 239–40; sense of, 239; social, 201, 212; unified, 199–200, 212. *See also* Personhood

Ideology, 33, 176, 179; cultural, 196; gender, 104, 149, 172; and history, 27, 80; political, 84, 86, 106

Illiberal Education (D'Souza), 73

Illusion, 92, 190; of control, 51, 61; creation of, 91; culture of, 21; as mask, 5; as mystification, 13; as reality, 1, 15; veil of, 20

Images, 38, 50, 55, 90, 94, 95, 113, 114, 121, 125, 185, 223, 240; alternative, 134; bedazzlement of, 9; body, 13, 23, 46, 58, 112, 115–16, 127, 154, 225; consciousness of, 9; construction of, 2, 3, 15, 86, 91, 96; cultural, 20, 22, 36, 69, 113, 121; of detachment, 130; falsity of, 20; fashion, 122; influence of, 32, 36, 90, 93, 109, 113, 115–16, 123, 154, 221; makers of, 184; masters of, 12; media, 32; and normalization, 44, 109, 222; pathological, 140; photographic, 87; popular, 23, 24, 184; resistance to, 130; self, 55; value-laden, 127. *See also* Body; Cultural; Media

Implants 3, 52, 55. *See also* Breasts

In a Different Voice (Gilligan), 204–05

Independence Day, 165

Individualism, 15, 30, 33, 36, 50, 51, 56, 122, 206

Infomercials, 107; culture of, 9, 12

Intellectuals. *See* Academic

Intimacy, 2, 62, 170, 216; intimate spaces, 239

Jackson, Peter, 98
Jaggar, Alison, 207
James, WIlliam, 199
Jameson, Fredric, 193
Japan: and beauty ideals, 49
Jenny Craig, 64
Jewell, Richard, 94
Jewish, 136, 138, 194, 222, 224, 236; appearance, 49; associations of, 133, 138; attributes, 132, 134; body 23, 50, 135, 187; Jewish-American culture, 136, 215; kosher, 222; mother, 136, 138; typing as, 99; Yiddish, 222, 236
Jourdain, Rose, 146
"Just Do It," 8, 12, 21, 26, 29, 33–34, 45, 51, 58, 61, 63, 208

Kant, Immanuel, 179
Keller, Evelyn Fox, 204
Kempainen, Bob, 29
Kennedy, Carolyn Bisset, 8
Kennedy, John F.: assassination, 9
King, Rodney: trial, 9, 69, 87, 88–90, 97–98
Kierkegaard, Soren, 61
Kitchen, 26, 133, 223–24, 237, 255n.3; as female space, 237; images of, 229; as inferior place, 221, 237; kosher, 222; missing, 214, 217, 221–23, 241; as site of assimilation, 222; as site of fear, 219
Klein, Binnie, 214, 217–225, 240
Knowledge, 72–74, 197; certain, 191; generation of, 202; individual knower, 202; limits of, 191; maleness, 193; as perspectival, 85; racial knowledge, 89; and responsibility, 170; right to, 12; of science, 179; specialized, 38; ways of knowing, 199, 206, 213. See also Epistemology

Kourany, Janet, 25
Kramer, Hilton, 75, 79
Kramer, Peter, 44
Krantz, Judith, 83
Kuhn, Thomas, 85, 193

Lack, 30, 39, 51
Language, 179, 236, 246n.15; arbiter of reality, 210; of disciplines, 19, 180; foreign, 222, 224, 236; linguistic arena, 189; outside of, 178
Latino: culture and homosexuality, 158; Latina, 134, 141, 201, 213
Law: laws of nature, 30–31, 105; legal reform, 51; moral laws, 78
Lee, Henry, 93, 96. See also Simpson trial
Left (politically), 9, 33, 66, 67, 68–69, 71, 73, 82, 86–87
Legs, 125, 135; hind, 149; piano, 147
Legends of the Fall, 165
Lentricchia, Frank, 82
Lesbian, 133, 134, 138, 153. See also Homosexuality; Sex: sexual orientation
Levinson, Barry, 140, 141. See also Disclosure
Liberal, 33, 73
Like Water for Chocolate (Esquivel), 133
Limbaugh, Rush, 9, 25, 33, 243n.4
Limits, 30–31, 187; of feminist critique, 193; of knowledge, 191; of materiality, 181; of modernist subject, 200; limitedness of world, 218
Liposuction, 32, 42, 45, 55, 60. See also Cosmetic surgery; Plastic surgery
Lips: augmentation of, 52, 55; and cosmetic surgery 9; fullness of, 45, 134
Lipsyte, Robert, 99
Locatedness: of body, 182, 185; determining, 218; dislocatedness, 238;

historical, 205; in time and space, 191, 203
Locke, John, 200
Locklear, Heather, 9
Look: experience of looking, 123
Lorde, Audre, 133
Loren, Sophia, 131
Love, Courtney, 33
Lugones, Maria, 81, 201, 212–13
Lunden, Joan, 107
Lyotard, Jean-Francois, 202

MacDonald, Scott, 126
Madonna, 50, 64
Majors, Richard, 171
Makeup, 33, 34, 38–39, 114, 123; and man, 197
Male: anxiety, 141, 146, 147, 148; as atomistic, 204; cultural, 142; male/female dualism, 185; as positive and neutral, 192
Mamet, David, 170
Mammy figure. See African American: caricatures of
Manhood, 104, 171, 176; the gaze and, 160; men's movement, 28; proving, 210–11. See also Gender; Homosexuality; Masculinity
Manhood in the Making (Gilmore), 136
Mansfield, Jayne, 131
Mapplethorpe, Robert, 5
Maps, 218, 233–34, 238, 239
Marcuse, Herbert, 196
Marginalization, 82, 195; ghettoization of female writers/scholars, 26, 193–95, 198–99, 209, 211; marginalized perspective, 74–75. See also Feminist
Marketing, 35, 115, 130. See also Advertisements; Selling
Marking, 165–166, 195
Martin, Jane, 205
Marty, Martin, 72

Marx, Karl, 176–77, 188
Masculinity, 23, 28, 105, 124, 147, 171, 182, 184, 228; in ancient Greece, 156–57; association with activity, 151–54; black, 105; challenges to, 150, 158, 166; and competition, 45; constructs of, 104, 149–51, 153, 155, 160, 161, 164–65, 168, 171–72, 252n.15; course in, 96; and domination, 105, 125–26, 155, 156, 163; as essential, 104; "*faux* male" ideal, 166; and hardness, 151; images of, 125; independence and, 165; and machismo, 28, 149; masculine civility, 149; masculine confrontation, 160; masculine forms, 177; masculinism, 202; and morality, 207; and privilige, 171; science, 203; stereotypes of, 28. *See also* Gender; Homosexuality; Manhood
Material: arena, 189; body, 198; materiality, 61, 124, 175, 177, 181, 182, 195–96; paradise, 219; realism, 27; realm, 177; rewards, 150
Materialism, 35, 175. *See also* Consumer
Matter: versus form, 181. *See also* Body
McCallum, Pamela, 202
McCarthyism, 73
Mead, John, 117, 120, 121
Media, 18, 69–71, 95, 97, 106, 109, 121–23; as children, 144; and entertainment, 70; media analysis, 69, 94, 100; media images, 20, 23, 32, 95, 121, 123, 195; and name-calling, 151; nightly news, 96; popular, 208; sensationalizing, 146; Simpson trial and, 22, 88, 95, 99–100; tabloids, 107
Melrose Place, 121
Melting Pot, 49–50
Menendez trial, 9, 90
Menstruation, 109

Michelle, Shelley, 3
Middle Ages, 203
Militia movement, 30
Mind: mind/body dualism, 51, 112, 124, 185, 197; mind/body relationship, 200; pure mind, 175, 180, 198
Minorities, 21, 75, 209
Miss Universe, 22
Models (fashion), 8, 33, 44, 108, 114, 116, 123, 128, 184; eating habits of, 122, 128, 250n.20; hyper thinness of, 22, 108, 112, 115–16, 121, 248n.3; masculinity in, 155–58, 160, 161–63; sexualization of, 131
Modernity, 200; birth of, 204; philosophical, 198
Mona Lisa, 17, 122
Moore, Demi, 140–41
Moore, Mary Tyler, 14
Morality: gendered approach, 28, 207, 210; moral content, 87; moral critique, 86; moral reason, 204. See also Ethics; Values
Moran, Brenda, 70–71. See also Simpson trial
Morrison, Toni, 83
Morton, Annie, 108, 122. See also Models
Moss, Kate, 58, 108, 115, 117, 121, 127–30, 133, 248n.3
Mother, 50, 62, 64, 110, 136, 228; as housewife, 221; as memoir, 215–16, 219–24, 229–37; mother-daughter relationship, 138, 236; as powerless, 221; surrogate, 62
Moussa, Mario, 189
Movies, 3, 27, 104, 121, 141, 160; movie culture, 147
Movie stars, 2, 3, 8, 9, 15, 32, 44, 96, 108, 131, 138, 151
Multiculturalism, 66, 68, 71, 74–75, 81–82, 83, 86, 106
Multidimensionalism, 22, 70, 103, 117

Muscularity, 5, 28, 33, 58, 108; female, 150, 208, 250n.25; male, 154, 155, 160, 161; social, 150, 177. See also Body
Mystic Pizza, 124
Myth/mythology: clinical, 23, 66, 76

Narcissism: coded as female, 144, 154; sleep and, 158. See also Vanity
Nast, Heidi, 26
Native Americans, 109
Natori, Josie, 122
Nazi, 86
NBC, 5
Need, 130; needy, 127–28, 130; triumph over, 130. See also Desire
NEH (National Endowment for the Humanities), 74
Nietzsche, Friedrich, 18, 20, 177, 182
Nike, 12, 29–30, 34, 35, 36, 51, 60, 133, 172, 208, 243n.4. See also "Just Do It"
Norms, 8, 15, 17, 120; academic, 192; biological, 17; body parts, 53, 114; challenges to, 171; cultural and social norms, 16, 30, 32, 36, 43, 44, 49, 52, 64, 69, 108, 109, 113, 120, 135, 171, 187, 197; deviations from, 52; dominant, 206; gender, 30; as gendered, 198; notions of normality, 107, 140, 144, 184; perfected nature of, 47–49, 55; racial, 30, 32, 49–50, 194; resistance of, 186; sexual, 134, 144, 188, 194. See also Cultural; Images; Stereotypes
Northrop, Peggy, 122, 123
Nose, 32, 53, 55; ethnicity and, 9, 32, 49–50, 187; nose pores, 39–41, 47; ring, 184
Nussbaum, Martha, 199

Obesity, 71
Objectification: of bodies, 151, 159;

objects of sight, 151, 163; of women, 34, 124, 125

Objectivity, 55, 66, 76, 77, 82; male, 192; scientific, 181, 245n.6

Obsession, 58; with appearance, 64, 107; with fitness, 52; with sex, 145; with youthfulness, 32

An Officer and a Gentleman, 160

Okin, Susan Moller, 206

Oleanna, 170

Olympics, 62; advertisements during, 30; athletes in, 28–29, 58, 109; Centennial Park bomb, 94; 1996 games, 3, 21, 28, 34, 108; Leni Riefenstahl films of, 5, 28; Special Olympics, 63

One-Dimensional Man (Marcuse), 196

Oppression: oppressed groups, 75; oppressive history, 89

Oral sex. *See* Sex

Orlan, 17

"Other," 24, 26, 77, 134, 195; cultural form of, 194; dark other, 136; definition by, 159; as deviant, 144; dominated, 155; look/gaze of, 159–60; rights of, 209; self and, 200; specter of, 194; voice of, 213; woman as, 194–95, 198, 208–09

Packwood, Bob, 23, 140, 143–44, 148, 168, 169

Paglia, Camille, 74, 166

Panic, 226–27, 239; disorder, 227, 230

Pain, 57; rising above, 28, 29

Paradigms, 72, 79, 85, 96, 108, 116, 178, 179; of method, 199; objects of, 205; of truth, 199; as universal, 205

Paranoia, 59, 74, 147

Parent-child relationship, 62, 117, 219. *See also* Father; Mother

Parker, Kathleen, 71

The Passion of Alice (Grant), 112, 130

Passivity, 122, 127, 158, 163, 221;

homebound, 223; passive consumer, 96, 130; women and, 36–37, 126, 127, 156, 158

Pateman, Carole, 206

Pathological, 17, 108, 119; images, 140; social pathology, 116

Penis, 163, 251n.9; erection, 126, 161; penile enhancement, 46, 52; size of, 135, 145, 158, 161

Perception, 2, 95; of harassment, 148

Perfectionism, 5, 16, 119; of body, 2, 3, 8, 55, 118

Performance art, 17

Personhood, 205, 206. *See also* Identity

Pfeiffer, Michelle, 57

Phallus, 101, 184, 251n.9; phallic armor, 155; phallic authority, 171, 184; phallic power, 154, 158; phallic splendor, 149; phallic subject, 154, 161; phallocentrism, 104, 171, 199, 211, 213, 252n.19. *See also* Penis

Phenomenology, 14, 174, 195, 200, 239

Philosopher-kings, 12, 19

Philosophy: as abstract, 209; challenges to, 202; contributions to, 195; critics of, 190, 193, 202; critique, 212; discourse, 210; Eastern, 200; fantasies of, 182, 212; feminist, 85, 177, 195, 198, 200, 206–07, 208–10; maleness of, 182, 202, 211; method of, 85, 209; norms of, 193, 198; philosophers, 166, 168, 174–75, 184, 189, 208, 213; political, 207; presumptions of, 202; reason, 193, 199; textbooks, 106; traditional views of, 177, 182, 202, 209–10, 213; as unbiased, 202. *See also* History; Western

Philosophy: Contemporary Perspectives on Perennial Issues, 206

Philosophy and the Mirror of Nature (Rorty), 202

Philosophy in a Feminist Voice (Kourany), 25

Philosophy of History (Hegel), 76–78

Physical perfection, 8,13; as symbol, 151. *See also* Body; Beauty

Physicality, 124, 138; physical located-ness, 181

Physics, 66

Pile, Steve, 26

Place, 26, 133, 215, 217–19, 221, 240; bodily feeling as, 220; connection with persons, 238; creation of, 221, 228; dislocation from, 234; home as, 218, 233; non-places, 217, 218, 220, 241; pain as, 220; and panic, 226; private, 233; reality of, 235; safe, 217, 219, 230, 233, 238, 240, 241; as state of mind, 239. *See also* Space

Places through the Body (Nast and Pile), 26

Plastic surgery, 8, 15, 35, 44–45, 55–56; and age of patients, 46; look-alike syndrome, 9–11; and men 45–46; plastic surgeons, 18, 44, 45–46, 52, 54–55. *See also* Cosmetic surgery

Plato, 1, 5, 12–14, 16–19, 81, 94–95, 177; cave analogy, 1–2, 12, 14–16, 18

Pogrebin, Letty Cottin, 54

Polarization, 21, 22, 66, 88, 103, 125, 174; of science and humanities, 180. *See also* Dualism

Political, 2, 12, 35, 82, 93, 138, 179; affiliation, 192; agenda, 75, 140, 141, 144; analysis, 175; cartoons, 19, 135, 136; categories, 207; commentators, 91; context, 37, 185; correctness, 21, 22, 66, 68, 71–74, 80, 96, 105, 140, 141, 243n.4; currents, 146; discourse, 15; inequalities, 69; inter-est, 84; messages, 30; movements, 189; parable, 237; personal as, 74, 196; philosophy, 207; realities, 97; reform, 51; resistance, 33; theory,

206; transformation, 74; tyranny, 27. *See also* Politics

Politics, 9, 18, 19, 67, 72, 81–82, 141, 146, 177; of experience, 191; politi-cos, 29, 36, 72; racial, 71. *See also* Conservativism; Feminist; Left; Lib-eral; Political; Race; Right

Popular culture, 14, 19–20, 24, 103, 118, 147, 160, 184. *See also* Culture; Images

Pornography, 86, 250n21; heterosex-ual, 125–26

Postmodernism, 12, 17–18, 19, 66–67, 88, 91, 173, 181–83, 198, 210, 244n. 4; appropriation of by feminism, 202; authors, 186; critique of, 174; dream of being everywhere, 182, 210; identity, 201; moment, 201; questions, 189; and text, 190; view of the subject, 211

Poststructuralism, 194, 210–11

Poverty, 8, 117

Power, 28, 69, 81,104, 113, 139, 154, 172, 180; abuse of, 141, 144, 155, 170; academic, 211; action, 189; and agency, 33, 62; balance of, 168; conceptions of, 143; conquest, 146; cultural, 170; destabilization of, 185; economic, 30; features of, 172; female, 133, 141, 168, 209; forms of, 202; harassment and, 141; of images, 13, 23; male, 141, 184; opposition to, 191; personal, 36; phallic, 154, 158, 184; powerlessness, 39, 134, 221; promotion of, 191; purchasing power, 70; sharing, 199. *See also* Empowerment; Feminism

Practice, 190; criticism of, 191; practi-cal arena, 189; of resistance, 190

Pratt, Minnie Bruce, 212

Pregnancy, 33, 200

Pretty Woman, 3, 125

Privilege: of author, 173; of dominant

culture, 212; language as privileged shrine, 179; male, 170, 171; of meta-theory, 175; of ownership, 171; underprivileged, 62

Professional world: and appearance, 45, 47, 115

Proust, Marcel, 159

Prozac, 52

Psyche, 113, 173, 218, 221, 223; female, 133. *See also* Cultural psyche

Psychology: and abuse, 101–02; and development, 197, 203; and eating disorders, 108; psychotherapy, 116, 227, 237; psychological, 117; psychological advisors, 91; psychological currents, 146; psychological realities, 97, 197; psychological well-being, 15, 117; psychologists, 117

Public, 82; activities, 16; dialogue, 88, 139–40; perception, 68, 99; responsibilities, 16, 170. *See also* Social; Space

Purge, 15, 107, 119, 120

Pygmalions, 52

Race, 45, 51, 95, 103–04, 109, 194, 210; accident of, 82; and beauty ideals, 23, 32; and biology, 80; consideration of, 148, 149, 150, 160, 182, 193; cosmetic surgery and, 49; discourse on, 195; and eating disorders, 109, 134; and Egypt, 79–80; and gender, 103; issues of, 69, 81; mixed, 215; as mute, 51, 69; notions of, 23; racial bias, 85, 205; racial coding, 23; racial difference, 49–50, 109, 180, 194; racial diversity, 5; racial dynamics, 69–70, 104; racial epithets, 170; racial experience, 212; racial fictions, 183; racial identification, 103, 136, 172; racial images, 127, 133, 135; racial inequities, 184; racial knowledge, 89; racial perspec-

tive, 94; racial polarization, 88; racial politics, 71, 93; racial solidarity, 172; racial stereotypes, 24, 100, 104, 134, 135, 137, 138; racial theory, 79–80; racism, 34, 49, 66, 70, 79–80, 82, 84–86, 88–90, 98–101, 103, 135, 172, 205, 209, 212; and Simpson trial, 70, 87–89, 95, 97, 99–100; white racism, 70. *See also* Norm; Simpson trial; Stereotypes

Radicalism, 191

Rantala, M. L., 88

Rape, 74; date rape, 37, 150

Reagan, Nancy, 33

Reaganite, 73

Realism, 63

Reality, 2, 18, 57, 85, 95, 96, 122, 184; alternative reality, 9, 58; appearance and, 2, 18, 91, 95; computer-generated, 4; as constructed, 2, 12, 69, 91; cultural, 36, 116; falsification of, 60, 91, 122; history as, 89; and illusion 1, 12, 91, 93, 228; and language, 210–11; masking of, 33; mirroring of, 185; as neutral state, 199; perception of, 96; and race, 89; real world, 2, 62, 93, 105, 142; realities, 2, 15, 86, 91, 96; as text, 19, 87; unreal, 15, 91, 93; versions of, 13, 171, 245n.6; virtual, 2, 91, 96, 235; as whole, 70

Reason: critique of, 193–94; as male, 199–200; man of, 210; moral, 204; notions of, 199; reconstruction of, 199; standards of, 199; as universal, 177, 202; and women, 200

Rebellion: rebellious wives, 29

Reebok, 35. *See also* Advertising

Reece, Gabriel, 58

Reductionism, 70, 180

Reformation, 94

Relativism, 12, 21, 69, 72–73, 94–95, 175

Renaissance, 94, 203
Repression, 184
The Republic (Plato), 1–2
Resistance, 15, 174, 186, 190; in
   Braveheart, 28, 33; as constructed,
   188; costs of, 49; encouragement of,
   190; to norms, 49, 64; origination
   of, 190; participation in, 191; politi-
   cal, 33; possibility of, 180, 189; from
   within, 188
Responsibility, 37–38, 50, 74, 86, 90,
   94
Revlon, 12, 33, 45
Reynolds, Mel, 146
Rhinoplasty, 55
Rich, Adrienne, 134
Riefenstahl, Leni, 5, 28
Riggs, Marlon, 97
Right (political right-wing), 33, 66,
   67, 68, 71, 82–83, 86, 106. *See also*
   Conservativism
Rights: advocacy of, 209; to existence,
   65; to information, 12; lack of, 88;
   to look good, 33, 34; of men, 104;
   of minorities, 75; rights-based mod-
   els, 206; notions of, 205
Roberts, Julia, 3, 124–25, 130, 133, 138
Rocky, 60, 62–63
Roiphe, Katie, 37, 74, 142, 209
Rorty, Richard, 83, 193, 202
Rosaldo, Renato, 81
Rossetti, 122
Roth, Philip, 215
Rubens, 133
Ruddick, Sara, 200, 208
Ryan, Meg, 138

Said, Edward, 193–194, 195
Sambo. *See* African American: carica-
   tures of
Sartre, Jean-Paul, 159–60
Savage, 101; savagery, 76–78. *See also*
   Animality

Scheck, Barry, 90. *See also* Simpson
   trial
Schiller, Lawrence, 90, 100
Schlesinger, Arthur, 75, 81, 82
Scholarship. *See* Academic; Feminist
Science: critics of, 193, 199; discourse,
   210; fiction, 179; of image making,
   91; masculine nature of, 203; norms
   of, 193, 198; racial difference and,
   135; scientific laws, 83; scientific
   theory, 97; scientism, 179; scientists,
   181, 183; Western, 66. *See also*
   Biology
The Second Sex (de Beauvoir), 159,
   192, 195, 197
Self, 25, 36, 57, 213; centered, 239;
   conception of, 204, 208; conflict in,
   218; construction of, 25; deconstruction of, 18, 113, 212; essential
   self, 130; as finite, 181–82; "for me"/
   "for oneself," 32, 36, 38, 43, 50,
   54; fractured, 212; historical, 240;
   mutating selves, 18; numbed, 227;
   and other, 200; and place, 217;
   "real," 47; self-awareness, 79; self-
   consciousness, 79; self-contained,
   64, 81, 128, 212; self-control, 38,
   42, 131; self-deception, 19, 21, 33,
   182; self-definition, 36, 43, 154–
   55, 159, 168; self-determination,
   34; self-development, 238; self-
   discipline, 111; self-doubt, 57, 117,
   120; self-esteem, 58, 64, 75, 117,
   120; self-image, 55, 117, 120; self-
   improvement, 18, 36, 61, 154; self-
   interest, 75, 130; self-justifying,
   81; self-knowledge, 134, 159, 239;
   self-perception, 46–48, 55, 58,
   108, 115, 148, 184, 187, 238; self-
   preservation, 20, 21; self-scrutiny,
   58; self-subordination, 171; self-
   transformation, 52, 60; self-worth,
   159; separate, 203–04; unity of, 212

Selling, 12, 29–30, 39, 113, 123. *See also* Marketing

Semitic, 9; anti-Semitism, 79, 195. *See also* Jewish

Sensuousness, 133

Sex: act, 126, 131–32, 141, 143, 144, 145, 158; "sex fiend," 139, 140, 145, 146; roles, 149, 161; sexism, 34, 80, 82–83, 85, 86, 88, 99, 148, 167, 195, 202, 209; sexlessness, 134, 136, 143; sexual, 82; sexual abuse, 131; sexual advance, 167, 170; sexual analogy, 147; sexual anatomy, 192; sexual associations, 131, 134–35, 138, 148; sexual codes, 160; sexual coming of age, 134; sexual conduct, 74, 147, 161, 168; sexual consent, 144; sexual desire, 133, 150; sexual difference, 154, 194; sexual dimensions in eating disorders, 130–31, 134; sexual epithets, 170; sexual excess, 131, 135, 161; sexual games, 171; sexual gestures, 147–48, 167, 168, 169; sexual inequality, 140; sexual liberation, 72; sexual misconduct, 140, 144, 146–47, 168; sexual monstrosity, 135; sexual mores, 168; sexual object, 163; sexual orientation, 148, 154; sexual promiscuity, 101; sexual references, 147; sexual representations, 158; sexual shame, 144; sexual taunting, 131; the workplace and, 139, 147–48

Sexual harassment. *See* Harassment

Sexuality, 2, 23, 131, 133, 145, 149, 168; and body parts, 38, 40, 124, 135, 167; constructs of, 101, 104, 105, 124, 126, 131, 133; deconstruction of, 183; female, 196; sexualization, 149, 154, 169; and relationship to voluptuousness, 131

Shakespeare, William, 83

Shame, 130, 133, 157, 159, 168; of body, 43, 126; of defect, 55, 63. *See also* Ethnic: shame

Sheets-Johnstone, Maxine, 179

Sheldon, Sidney, 83

Showalter, Elaine, 193

Silber, John, 12

Silverman, Marilyn, 214–25, 218, 233–241

Silverstone, Alicia, 107, 248n.1

Simpson, Nicole Brown, 95, 97, 99–101, 103, 104–05. *See also* Simpson trial

Simpson, O. J., 22, 66, 69–71, 84, 86–90, 93, 95–101, 103, 104–05, 146. *See also* Simpson trial

Simpson trial, 14, 20, 22, 68–71, 86–90, 93–97, 99–101, 247n.25; conspiracy and, 89–90, 99, 103; jurors and, 87–89, 90, 93–94, 101, 103, 146, 247n.21; lawyers and, 9, 90; media and, 70; public perception of, 247n.21; verdict, 86–89, 91, 247n.24. *See also* Race; Simpson, O. J.

Sischy, Ingrid, 5, 184

Situation comedies, 136

Skepticism, 1, 94, 101, 105, 182, 199–200

Skin: cancer of, 54; elasticity of, 46; skin color, 39; wrinkled, 3, 45, 46–48, 64

Slavery, 103; emancipation from, 98; slaves, 76, 98

Sleep: as symbol, 156–57, 158–59

Slenderness, 23, 114, 118, 127; appeal of, 127; ideal of, 127; images of, 50, 123; as symbol, 136; tyranny of, 131

Smith, Dorothy, 38–39

Snitow, Ann, 183

Social: acceptability, 64; agenda, 72; analysis, 175; change, 190; construction, 116, 179, 181, 182, 206; context, 35, 36, 37, 61, 150, 175, 185–86; conventions, 20, 30, 111, 150,

Social (*continued*)
164; criticism, 179, 190; despair, 33;
disembodiment, 123; experience,
212; forces, 36; inequalities, 69, 126;
issues, 49; justice, 87; movements, 51;
myths, 177; pathology, 116; preference, 32; privilege, 62; production,
155; realities, 95; rewards, 150; roles,
28, 61, 126, 140, 171, 206; standards,
44; transformation, 74, 191; world,
194. *See also* Culture; Norms

Social theory, 175
Socrates, 19, 20, 24
Sokol, Alan, 66–67, 83, 105
Sommers, Christina Hoff, 142, 209
Soul, 46–48, 106
Soul on Ice (Cleaver), 104
Space, 215, 217–18; anxiety over, 217;
cultural, 14, 117, 118; emotional
climate of, 217, 220; experience of
self in, 219; inner, 32; intimate, 239;
locatedness in time and, 181; non-
space, 222; personal, 74, 168, 235;
private, 220; public, 138, 170, 171
Spain, 76
Spatial, 26, 124, 217, 223, 238;
metaphor, 239
Spectacle, 151
Spectator, 160; imagined, 151
Spiegelman, Art, 154, 156
Spirituality, 193
Spivak, Gayatri, 193
Sports, 5, 87, 96; sports culture as
male, 104, 150, 166
StairMaster, 8, 59, 184
Standards: beauty, 196; ethical, 12,
199; lack of, 83–85; unreal, 116
Starvation, 34, 122, 134, 151, 184. *See
also* Eating disorders; Dieting
Steinberg, Art, 239
Stereotypes, 20, 81; cultural, 97, 133,
141; and "culture wars," 21, 22, 23;
in *Disclosure,* 24; gender, 24, 28, 141;

and harassment, 140; participation
in, 19; racial, 24, 100, 134–38. *See
also* Bias; Culture; Gender; Norms;
Race
Stimpson, Catharine, 72, 80, 81
Stomach, 38–40, 107, 120
Stone, Oliver, 9, 12
Strength, 29
Strober, Michael, 117, 120, 121, 123
Structure of Scientific Revolutions (Kuhn),
85
Strug, Kerri, 29
Subject, 39, 168; death of, 201, 210–
11, 213; deconstruction of, 212;
disembodied, 210; essential female,
182; Man as, 210–11; modernist,
200; as neutral, 199; subject posi-
tions, 148; "world-traveling," 201,
212
Subjective, 76, 166; dominating sub-
jectivities, 147, 160, 169; self, 192;
subjectivity, 39, 125, 126, 155, 157,
169, 203, 213; transcendental subjectivity, 177
Subservience, 134
Subversion, 186
Surgeons, 32; as savior, 52, 55. *See also*
Cosmetic surgery; Plastic surgery
Surgery. *See* Cosmetic Surgery; Plastic
surgery
The Symposium (Plato), 5

Talk shows, 12, 32, 43, 69, 86
Taylor, Charles, 193
Taylor, Liz, 42
Technology, 2, 15, 42, 52; and the
body, 8, 182; and images, 15, 91
Text, 173–74; as authoritative, 230;
construction of, 94; examination of,
193; instability of, 185; as instruction, 38–39; as infinitely interpret-
able, 12, 68, 88; manipulation of, 86;
postmodernism and, 190; reality as,

19, 87; studies of, 193; textuality, 177

Theory: academic, 19, 21, 24; accessories of, 24; of action, 189; as abstract, 184, 197–98; adherence to, 191; "antitheory," 175; art, 17; authority of, 211; and body, 173; of the body, 175, 198, 243n.2; critique of, 174, 182, 253n.2; embodiment of, 197; fashionable, 141–42, 177, 183; feminist, 30, 36, 174, 178, 192–93, 199, 204, 206, 208, 210–11, 213, 253n.2; of interpretation, 12; as male, 176, 197–98; metatheory, 175, 180; as neutral, 205; performative, 179; political, 36, 206; postmodern, 174–75; vs. practice, 175, 179; as privileged, 175, 184; queer, 186; race, 79–80; and resistance, 174, 188–90; theoretical platform, 86; theoreticians, 175; theorist, 174; theorizing, 13, 25, 70, 174–75; use of, 174; work as theoretical, 174–76, 195. *See also* Philosophy; Postmodernism

Therapy, 80; college courses as form of, 75, 105; regarding eating disorders, 35; therapeutic community, 121; therapists, 13, 22, 115, 121

Thighs: cysts upon, 54; size of, 52, 64, 107

Thinness: as attractive, 128, 131; cultural obsession with/veneration of, 22, 107, 115, 127, 138; self-perception and, 108, 120; as visual code, 128, 134, 138

Thomas, Clarence, 103–04, 139, 168, 171. *See also* Thomas/Hill hearings

Thomas/Hill hearings, 103, 139, 140, 144, 171. *See also* Ethics; Hill; Thomas

Thurman, Uma, 121

Tolstoy, Leo, 84

"Too much": anxiety over being, 130,

133, 135; ethnic association as, 222; mother as, 138; women as, 127, 130. *See also* Fat; Self; Sex

Topoanalysis, 214; topography, 235, 238

Torrence, Gwen, 29

Touch, 147, 167; as requirement for sexual harassment, 147

Transcendence, 177, 182, 183, 185

Transvestites, 197

Truth, 22, 66, 68, 72, 75, 76, 82–85, 130, 173, 246n.15; abandonment of, 67, 68, 71; absolute/eternal truths, 12, 17, 71, 83–84, 88, 92, 175; concealment of, 68, 76; emotional truth, 61; as fiction, 18; geometric truths, 92; guardians of, 9, 68; and illusion, 71, 94; interpretations of, 87–88; multiple, 22, 88; paradigms of, 199; personal nature of, 12, 17, 69, 85, 214; and politics, 74, 81; rehabilitation of, 22; relativistic, 69; truth seeking, 18, 21, 69, 71, 80, 8, 96

The Truth about Cats and Dogs, 121

Tuan, Yi-Fu, 218

Tummy. *See* Stomach

Twiggy, 116

Twilight Zone, 9, 20

Unbearable Weight (Bordo), 9, 19, 22, 23, 26, 37, 49, 109, 127, 185, 190, 210, 229

Uncle Tom. *See* African American: caricatures of

Universal: culture, 117, 159; experience, 206; forms, 149; heritage, 75; male as, 194, 198–9; norms, 206; paradigms, 205; reason, 177, 202; spirit, 77; subject, 199, 200; universalizing, 175; Western philosophy as, 76

Vaginas: morphology of, 135

Values: actualization of, 241; alternative, 63, 118; artistic, 199; of character, 27; conference of, 154; cultural, 30, 32, 118, 127, 130, 170; dominant, 63; enduring, 72; external, 32; individualized, 81, 123; transformation of, 62; value of persons, 58, 65, 159. *See also* Cultural; Morality

Van Dyken, Amy, 29

Vanity: as desirable in women, 153; and men

Vannatter, Philip, 93. *See also* Simpson trial

Vanos, Lucky, 151. *See also* Advertisements

Venus (Botticelli), 17

Victim, 34, 35–36, 37, 103, 104, 117, 122, 123, 141, 172, 243n.4; victim culture, 33–34; victimhood, 212; victim's revolution, 73, 75

Victory. *See* Winning

Voluptuousness: constructs of beauty and, 131; as dated ideal, 108; as excessive, 130–131; as symbol of sexual animality, 135

Vomit, 64; as used in art, 34–35; in eating disorders, 109 ; in Nike advertisement, 39. *See also* Eating disorders

Vulnerability, 61, 91, 168, 184, 222; to cultural images, 23, 115, 121; eating disorders and, 117, 120; harassment and, 146, 166; invulnerable, 127; to the Other, 159; physical, 47, 111, 113; representations of, 124–25, 138

Waif: look, 22, 108, 115–16, 122, 151

Walker, Alice, 134

Weight: anxiety about, 13, 58, 118, 120; distribution of, 135; loss, 8, 59, 63, 107; obsession over, 120–21; specifications for, 5; training, 58

Welton, Donn, 24

West, Mae, 131

Western: beauty ideals, 49; civilization, 82; history of philosophy, 80; traditions, 76. *See also* History; Science

White: bias, 206; as norm, 49, 98, 134–35, 206; whiteness 5, 8, 69–70; whites, 79, 87–89, 97, 99, 100, 102, 137, 141, 166, 172

White, Hayden, 193

Whitehead, Albert, 199–200

Will, George, 75, 82

Williams, Gordon, 72

Williams, Raymond, 193

Williams, Sue, 34–35

Willis, Ellen, 146

Winfrey, Oprah, 34, 43

Winning: constructs of, 34

Wolf, 165–166

Wolf, Naomi, 34, 208–09, 255n.24

Wollenstonecraft, Mary, 25

Women: advancement of, 28; caricatures of, 23; as child, 36; and difference, 205, 207–08, 211–12; empowerment of, 36; erasure of, 211, evaluation of, 54–55, 76; exclusion of, 204; expectations of, 111; experience of being, 197; ideal, 17; natural role, 195; as negative, 192; as oppressed, 36; as passive sponge, 36–37, 115, 122; perspective, 205; real, 15, 35, 183; as receptacle, 125; as relational, 205; representations of, 151; as reward, 147; situation of, 175, 207; status of, 58, 204; unnatural, 135–36; as victim, 34, 35–37; virgin/whore dichotomy, 101; womanliness, 124; women's lib, 33; women's studies, 72; on workplace, 237. *See also* Feminity; Feminism

Woodward, C.Vann, 75

World War II, 215, 216, 224, 238; women during, 236

Wright, Angela, 145, 146. *See also* Thomas/Hill hearings
Wrinkles. *See* Skin

Young, Iris, 200, 206
Youth, 5, 69; appearance as, 44, 46, 49, 56, 134; as desirable, 16, 61, 184; obsession with, 32; and professional world, 43–44; as sign of competence, 45; as social requirement, 43–45. *See also* Age
Yuppie, 33

Zami (Lorde), 133
Zeno: paradox, 189

Designer:	Steve Renick
Compositor:	Integrated Composition Systems
Text:	11/15 Bembo
Display:	Gill Sans & Bembo
Printer:	Edwards Bros.
Binder:	Edwards Bros.